Lean Management Principles for Information Technology

Lean Management Principles
for Information Technology

Gerhard J. Plenert

CRC Press
Taylor & Francis Group
Boca Raton London New York

CRC Press is an imprint of the
Taylor & Francis Group, an **informa** business

The views expressed in this book are those of the author and Wipro does not subscribe to the substance, veracity or truthfulness of the said opinion.

Artwork for Chapter 1 is provided by Gerick (Rick) Johannes Plenert.

CRC Press
Taylor & Francis Group
6000 Broken Sound Parkway NW, Suite 300
Boca Raton, FL 33487-2742

© 2012 by Taylor & Francis Group, LLC
CRC Press is an imprint of Taylor & Francis Group, an Informa business

No claim to original U.S. Government works

Version Date: 20110831

International Standard Book Number: 978-1-4200-7860-2 (Hardback)

Library of Congress Cataloging-in-Publication Data

Plenert, Gerhard Johannes.
   Lean management principles for information technology / Gerhard J. Plenert.
     p. cm. -- (Series on Resource management)
   Includes bibliographical references and index.
   ISBN 978-1-4200-7860-2 (hardback)
   1. Information technology--Management. 2. Business enterprises--Computer network resources. 3. Information resources management--Economic aspects. 4. Industrial efficiency. I. Title. II. Series.

HD30.2.P597 2011
004.068′4--dc22   2011012048

Visit the Taylor & Francis Web site at
http://www.taylorandfrancis.com

and the CRC Press Web site at
http://www.crcpress.com

To the Love of My Life —

Renee Sangray Plenert

Who makes my life better!!!

And to my Kids, their Spouses, & of course the Grandkids —

Heidi, Dawn, Gregory, & Debbie, Gerick, Joshua, & Amy, Natasha &

Mark, Zackary, Chelsey, Lucas, Boston, Evan, Lincoln, & Livy Jay

Who keep life interesting!!!!!

They are the source of lots of data but information is often lacking.

Contents

SECTION III Lean Information
Technology (IT) on into the Future

Preface

The June 2010 issue of *Discover* magazine ran a feature article titled "The Power Plan" (pp. 47–51). A quote from that article reads, "A stunning 57 percent of our energy ends up wasted. . . . Investing in energy efficiency would be equivalent to tapping an entirely new source of energy." In other words, we could more than double our energy availability, without increasing pollution, without increased risk of oil spills, without worrying about additional global warming, and without additional cost, simply by eliminating "waste."

So why am I talking about energy in a book about information technology? Because never yet, in my 30 years of working with, installing, and sometimes even pulling out IT systems, have I found an IT environment that I would consider to be 100% efficient. Most are not even 43% efficient as in the energy example. There are usually one or more of the following IT plagues:

- Systems overconstruction
- Systems forced upon a user that do not fit
- Work-arounds
- Systems that miss the boat and part of the process has to be done by hand
- Duplicate data entry
- In extreme cases, systems where the process is done by hand and then input into the computer so that the data can be maintained on a database

The purpose of this book is to give the reader a methodology for eliminating "waste" in the IT environment. Much like energy generation, a good 50% to 60+% of the IT effort is "waste." Waste because of a lack of understanding of expectations. Waste because of the "prima donna" effect, where IT "knows best." Waste because of the rework. Waste because of poor planning. And the list goes on.

The goal of this book is to give the reader the tools to make improved decisions that will result in increased efficiencies. In this book the reader will learn Toyota Production System principles applied to IT, focused on Leaning out IT and eliminating waste. The tools in this book could improve IT efficiency by doubling, if not tripling, its output. The tools are tried and proven principles of success.

The reader needs to break the IT functional silo. And this book offers him or her tools to accomplish this demolition. The reader needs to join the information revolution which is focused on the Value of Information, looking for those nuggets that are value-added, and rejecting the non-value-added waste that nearly all systems now generate. We exist in an environment that is data rich and information starved. Often, we are not only plagued with too much data, but the data we have is the wrong data and does not supply us with the information we need to make accurate decisions. And that brings us back to the goal of this book: "to help the reader make improved decisions," both in the IT development process, and in the data and information utilization process.

If every organization in the world worked in exactly the same way, this book would have been very easy to write. Unfortunately, no two work alike. Therefore, it is impossible to come up with one book that can claim to be the perfect way to run all IT organizations. This reminds me of Newton's law for organizations: For Every Manager with a Perfect Solution There is an Equal and Opposite Manager with a Perfect Solution.

This book contains simplistic IT and Lean ideas that have proven to be enormously effective. Most of them will fit to any organizational environment from commercial sector to government, but they are not all intended to fit perfectly in every environment. This brings us to the purpose of this book. This book is designed to be a starting point in discovering the power of Leaning out your IT environment. With that as our goal, we can now move forward in improving our IT performance.

> Too much data is worse than no data—because we wasted time collecting useless input to generate meaningless or incorrect output.
>
> **Gerhard Plenert**

Acknowledgments

In order to give credit where credit is due I would need to create a long list of individuals, companies, universities, and countries with whom I have worked. In my most recent academic past I have had the pleasure of working with universities like:

- the University of San Diego in their Supply Chain Management Institute
- Brigham Young University
- California State University, Chico
- numerous international universities

Professionally I have had the pleasure of working with organizations like:

- Wipro Consulting as a practice partner
- MainStream Management as a Senior Strategy and Lean Consultant
- Infosys as a senior principal heading the Lean/Six Sigma/Change Management Practice
- American Management Systems (AMS) as a senior principal in their Corporate Technology Group
- Precision Printers as executive director of quality, engineering, R&D, customer service, production scheduling and planning, and facilities management

Other organizations that I have worked for include (but are not limited to):

- the US Air Force and Department of Defense
- the State of California
- the State of Texas
- the United Nations

As you can imagine, it is challenging to "Lean" out any office, especially an office full of lawyers or accountants. But we have achieved impressive results. For example, I successfully tripled the throughput of a legal office operation in two weeks' time using the same number of employees, without increasing the IT footprint.

I have lived and worked in factories in Latin America, Asia, and Europe. I have coauthored articles and books and have worked with academics and professionals from as far away as Europe, Japan, and Australia. My broad exposure to a variety of manufacturing and service facilities all over the world has given me the background I needed to write this book.

I specifically want to recognize and thank Romit Dey, Arindam Banerji, USAF Captain Brian Abrigo, and William T. Walker, CFPIM, CIRM, CSCP, resource management series editor for CRC Press/Taylor & Francis, each of whom shared ideas with me as I worked on this book.

Gerhard Plenert
President, Institute of World Class Management
Gerhard.Plenert@wipro.com

Introduction

We want to adopt proven and successful business practices that have been used in the commercial marketplace. We want to do business like business does business.

David Falvey
Business Systems Modernization program manager
Defense Logistics Agency

A young, bright naval officer was called into his commander's office. His commander wanted to know how many "local" Hawaiians were on ship. Quickly receiving his tasking, off went the officer who was determined to impress his "boss" with his research prowess and task oriented character. The academy taught this young officer how to "get things done." His religious upbringing instilled in him that "with all that you do, do it with all your might." With willing eagerness, the officer scanned through a myriad of resources, various references, comparable data, and manning documents for the ship. After a long week of collecting information, analyzing and confirming the data, formatting the document, and finally encasing his work in a shiny document cover, he was ready to present the information to the commander. Hoping to impress his commander, the young officer reviewed his work, wondering if he missed anything in his report. He had not.

Time came for the presentation, and the commander quickly scanned the table of contents, turned to page 14 of the report, and declared, "Hmmm, seven Hawaiians—that's great!" Returning the graph filled report with its tables of data and analytical demographic forecasts he excused the young officer.

The discouraged young officer was disappointed by this empty dismissal which did not include as much as a "thanks for all the hard work" or "thanks for all the data" or "I needed it to make my decision." Obviously he had missed something on this report. What was missing?

The Page 14 lesson delivered a blow to the officer's ego, catapulting in him a sense of urgency to find a better, cheaper, and faster way of successfully completing an information task without wasting time and energy.

The officer incorrectly assumed the boss wanted all the information provided. The hope was that the boss will take into consideration all the focus and effort exerted. And that was the mistake!

Page 14 taught the officer that excessive effort is not required for all information tasks. Not all tasks require full access to resources. Not all information tasks require quality packaging. However, all information tasks require an understanding of the required form, fit, function, quality, cost, and speed of comprehension and completion. The officer needed to learn the "real" reason why he chose to waste time.

This book will discuss information production processes, information technology (IT) systems, and change management through the lens of Lean principles. The book will discuss how to integrate Lean tools together with information production and IT systems to form an integrated, world-class learning environment.

The author went into a government attorney general's office of about 30 employees, many of them lawyers. Initially he interviewed the office manager and the managing attorney. Then he performed a scan of the office personnel where he went around the office and spent about 15 to 30 minutes with each of the employees. He asked questions about workflow, volume, and capacities. He was looking for the non-value-added content of their work and for bottlenecks, concepts that will be discussed in more detail later in this book. He spent most of the day performing these interviews. At the end of the day he met with the office manager and the managing attorney. He made specific recommendations about work assignments and workflow. He made suggestions about work buildups and backlogs. The managers took these suggestions seriously (which is critical to any success) and implemented them immediately. Less than two weeks later the author received a call that informed him that this office had tripled their daily output of work. This was accomplished without any hiring or layoffs. It was accomplished without the need to crack a whip on the employees. It was accomplished without any IT transformations or upgrades. It was accomplished by "Leaning" out both the paperwork and the information flow process within the organization. Similar results can be achieved in any "information generating" organization. And it results from effectively applying Lean tools and principles to IT systems—the same tools and principles that you will learn about in this book.

This book will discuss Lean tools and techniques like:

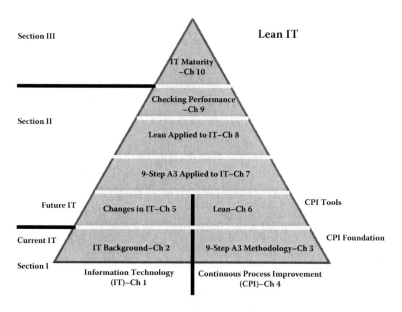

FIGURE 1
Lean IT

- Lean management
- Six Sigma
- Cycle time
- Value stream mapping
- Spaghetti charting
- Value-added vs. non-value-added activities
- Bottlenecks

This book will also discuss information technology (IT) tools and environments. The book will then discuss how to integrate Lean tools together with IT environments to form an integrated, world-class IT organization.

This book is broken into three sections, as follows (see Figure 1).

SECTION I—WHY A BOOK ON LEAN INFORMATION TECHNOLOGY (IT)?

This first section discusses the need for IT to become "Leaner." It discusses how we are data rich but information starved, and what lessons Lean teaches us about improving the information we work with. The section goes on to give an overview of change management and how it works.

Chapters 1 and 2 explore IT and the need for IT improvements.

Chapter 3 explores a structured methodology that has proven itself extremely effective in analyzing and dissecting problems and processes.

Chapter 4 gives an overview of continuous process improvement (CPI) alternatives. The CPI methodology that will then become the focus of this book is Lean.

SECTION II—BRINGING LEAN INTO INFORMATION TECHNOLOGY

This section delves into the details of how Lean can be utilized to eliminate waste in IT. It discusses the cultural acceptance tools that are required to build acceptance for Lean in IT. It discusses the technical tools that are available to generate the desired improvements. It discusses how these technical tools are used to identify non-value-added opportunities for improvement. It then discusses the improvement process. It discusses the operational details behind running a Lean event. This section also explores the process of developing meaningful information metrics.

Chapter 5 explores some of the future changes that are anticipated in IT. Being ready for these changes requires a CPI strategy.

Chapter 6 goes through a detailed discussion of Lean tools that are applicable to IT.

Chapter 7 integrates IT changes with the use of the 9-step A3 tool discussed in Chapter 3 and the Lean tools discussed in Chapter 6.

Chapter 8 discusses the use of the Lean Rapid Improvement Event (RIE) to execute improvement processes within an IT organization.

Chapter 9 discusses the importance of metrics for defining whether success and improvement are actually achieved.

SECTION III—LEAN INFORMATION TECHNOLOGY ON INTO THE FUTURE

This section recommends a methodology for assessing an organization's IT maturity. This section focuses on the next generation of Lean and its application to IT, and it ends by discussing how Lean can drive the success of IT environments of the future. The objective is to create world-class information processing organizations.

Chapter 10 focuses on defining maturing within your IT organization.

Section I

Why a Book on Lean Information Technology (IT)?

1

Why Look at IT? What Is the Problem?

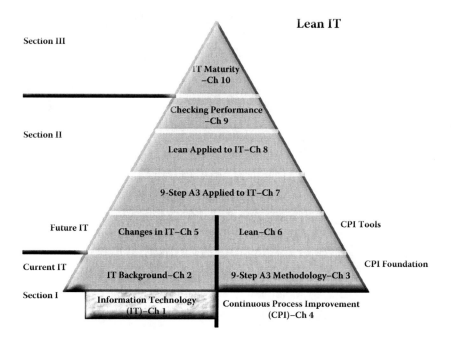

Lean IT

Section III — IT Maturity –Ch 10

Section II — Checking Performance –Ch 9 — Lean Applied to IT–Ch 8 — 9-Step A3 Applied to IT–Ch 7

Future IT — Changes in IT–Ch 5 — Lean–Ch 6 — CPI Tools

Current IT — IT Background–Ch 2 — 9-Step A3 Methodology–Ch 3 — CPI Foundation

Section I — Information Technology (IT)–Ch 1 — Continuous Process Improvement (CPI)–Ch 4

If not well considered, and sometimes even when they are—today's solutions become tomorrow's problems.

Col. George E. Reed, USAF

SOME EXAMPLES

In a large, corporate-based, IT organization, patches and software updates are sent out on a regular basis. The expectation is that the local units would implement and apply these updates quickly and efficiently. The following is an actual Lean process improvement event that took place, focused on improving the implementation of software patches.

Problem statement: There is a lack of guidance and understanding of the network patching tools, process, and responsibility, causing inefficiency and delays in securing the network and accurately reporting.

Performance gaps:
- Data indicate there is inaccuracy in reporting the number of systems which are compliant versus those systems that are noncompliant.
- System patches take weeks or months to get pushed out and implemented.

Improvement targets:
1. Reduce package delivery time
2. Reduction of "out-of-compliance" systems
3. 100% compliant in all updates

Improvement results:
1. Immediate reduction of package delivery from 18 days to 12 days
2. Reduction of "out-of-compliance" systems by:
   - 50% in 2 months
   - 100% compliant in 4 months
   - Monthly scans thereafter = 100%
3. 100% compliant in 4 months

The tool used to accomplish this compliance is Lean, which is the primary change management mechanism that will be discussed in this book. Here is a second, similar example where a completely different organization utilized Lean to streamline their system updating process:

Problem statement: There is an inability to accomplish regularly required system updates within the allotted time (5 days).

Performance gaps:
- Inadequate network infrastructure leads to manual updates.
- Data indicate inaccuracy in reporting number of systems compliant versus systems non-compliant.
- System patches take weeks or months to get pushed to systems.

Improvement targets:
1. Reduce manual update time
2. Decrease downtime of laptop inventory
3. Increase auto-update rate

Improvement results:
1. Manual update time reduced from 45 minutes to 10 minutes
2. 75+% decrease of laptops "in repair" inventory
3. 100% compliant with auto-updates in 4 months

One more, slightly different "real-life" example of Lean applied to IT looks at data input and the processes used for data input.

Problem statement: The current medical in-processing procedure for setting up new subscribers within a hospital does not provide for timely completion of critical path tasks and significantly delays analysis and treatment of patients.

Performance gaps:
- Data indicated that only 40% of in-processing requirements are completed on time.
- Average overdue time is 45 days past due, with a best-case completion of 7 days and a worst-case completion of over 240 days.

Improvement targets:
1. Optimize current process to reflect critical path.
2. Eliminate non-value-added tasks to ensure completion of critical path activities.
3. Reduce overdue products and subsequent follow-up actions.

Improvement results:
1. 90% completion of all tasks within 3 days of arrival

2. 90% patient completion rate to be achieved within 2 months of the Lean event

I can continue to list examples like this. However, as you can see, Lean can provide significant improvement opportunities in the IT world.

SO WHAT DOES LEAN BRING TO THE TABLE?

Lean is a methodology that is focused on the elimination of "waste." Introducing Lean into an organization that likes to think of themselves as leading-edge innovators and as the masters of efficiency and improvement, like information technology (IT), is often considered to be offensive and demeaning. There is often resentment by the implication that there may be "waste" in their IT process. That is why IT has become one of the last frontiers for the introduction of Lean tools.

Lean is a tool that facilitates the elimination of waste. And waste can be identified in a multitude of resource areas, including organizations, processes, and systems. Lean is not focused on making anyone work harder. Rather, Lean is focused on reducing the amount of time spent on "non-value-added" activities that add nothing to the timing or the quality of the output. For example, filling out redundant paperwork, whether it is electronic or on actual paper, is a plague that everyone deals with, including IT professionals. And it does not make the end product any better, nor is the customer any happier.

Any, and probably all, of the resource areas identified as part of the IT world contain waste. Lean is the methodology that identifies the waste and then utilizes a bag of tools to attempt to eliminate this waste. The more waste is eliminated, the greater the value-added time, resulting in greater throughput, lower costs, increased capacity, and reduced cycle times. In the end, utilizing Lean principles provides an IT environment that is more efficient and more responsive to the customer and, therefore, more competitive overall.

Let us take a quick look at a graphic example of how Lean works. In Figure 1.1 we see an example of a typical process that we all experience at one time or another, a visit to the doctor. In this process we encounter both value-added and non-value-added activities. Value-added and non-value-added will be defined in detail in Chapter 6 and beyond. For now,

Lean is a standardized method and mindset for *reducing waste and non–value-added work* in all of the processes we use to execute our mission…based on the view of the customer

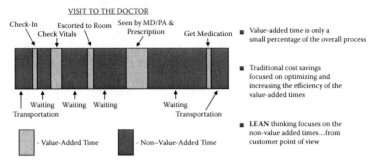

■ Value-added time is only a small percentage of the overall process

■ Traditional cost savings focused on optimizing and increasing the efficiency of the value-added times

■ LEAN thinking focuses on the non-value added times…from customer point of view

FIGURE 1.1
The Lean focus.

think of value-added as something that has an impact on you the patient, and non-value-added as the time you spend sitting around waiting for something to happen. Lean looks for these non-value-added opportunities, referred to as waste. Rarely do we find less than 90% of a process is non-value-added. Therefore, most of the time we spend in a process or working on a process adds no value to the outcome of the process.

Moving on to Figure 1.2, we see an example of the effect of Lean on the typical process. If we assume a process to be 95% non-value-added, and 5% value-added, then Lean searches for and identifies opportunities for improvement in the 95% and does not necessarily focus on driving increased performance in the 5%. In our example, if we reduce the

Rarely is there a process where the value-added content is greater than 10%. Typically the non–value-added content is around 95%.

Lean attacks the 95% non–value-added and reduces its impact.

Reducing the 95% to 90% has the following impact:
  Double the output/throughput/capacity
  No increase in actual value-added work per unit produced

FIGURE 1.2
The Lean effect.

non-value-added content of this process from 95% to 90% and increase the value-added content from 5% to 10%, we really have not had very much of an effect on the overall non-value-added pieces of the process. However, the impact on the over-all performance of the process is enormous. The impact includes:

- Double the throughput—twice as much time is now applied to value-added activities.
- Double the capacity—twice as much time is spent on throughput-generating activities.
- No one has to work harder at production activities; they just spend more time doing productive activities and less time on waste activities

Applying these principles to IT is easy. IT includes numerous functional processes, which will be explored in the next few chapters. These include activities like software development, software implementation, software upgrades, hardware upgrades, user training, quality control, piloting, etc. Each of these needs to be looked at as an IT process. And each of these processes is repeated regularly during the lifetime of an IT organization, which makes them prime targets of Lean waste elimination.

Taking this thought process to a higher level, IT finds itself in a world that is saturated with data and starved for information. This book will explore the IT shortcomings that have evolved us into an environment where we are not balanced in the utilization of data from a systems, process, and organizational perspective. Each of these three seems to have their own agenda when it comes to what is value-added and what is waste. This book explores the integrated, optimized balance of these three so that, if achieved, this balance will increase the value of information for the entire enterprise. The synergy of balancing these can bring about the elimination of waste, which is the fundamental goal of Lean systems.

WHAT DOES AN IT SYSTEM LOOK LIKE?

You have seen these "trees of confusion" before. Unfortunately they are extremely relevant when we lay out an IT system. For example, if the process we are tasked with is to design and implement a new IT environment, let us take a look at how this shapes up: A customer comes to the store of an enterprise resource planning (ERP) vendor and defines their needs and expectations. Their goal is maximum utility at minimum cost. They draw a picture similar to Figure 1.3.

The project leader at the customer's site writes up a definition of how he sees the project and brings in some of his or her own personal expectations, making sure all their needs are met. The goal for the project leader is to create a definition that satisfies all customer requirements from all future users. The result is something similar to Figure 1.4.

The analysts at the vendor's shop listens closely to the customer and their project leader. The analysts have some confusion between what the customer is saying and what the project leader is saying, so they introduce some of their own preconceptions of what is best for the customer. The goal of the analyst is to make sure all the customer's expectations are clearly defined and that the programmer's work is minimized. Based on their understanding, the analysts write up their version of the project, and the result is something similar to Figure 1.5.

Then we turn the project over to the programmers, and they wear an entirely different set of glasses. Their goal is to create a software product

FIGURE 1.3
IT project as defined by the customer.

FIGURE 1.4
IT project as defined by the project leader.

FIGURE 1.5
IT project definitions written by the analyst.

that does everything and is architecturally beautiful. They end up with something similar to Figure 1.6.

Next on the scene are the documentation writers. They read the project manager's and analysts' material, interview the programmers, and create their version of what the IT project is intended to accomplish. Their goal is to create a useful, easy-to-read product, but they do not always understand the use and functionality of the product. They end up with something similar to Figure 1.7.

IT operations receives the software product and looks at what it takes to execute the software, from a technology point of view. Their goal is to give the users the accessibility they need at minimum cost. They create something similar to Figure 1.8.

Once programmed and documented, the IT installation team takes the software and implements it at the user location. These individuals work closely with the users and are somewhat in tune with customer expectations. But they also need to work within the limitations of the software that was handed to them. Their goal is to create a satisfied user in the minimum amount of time. They end up with something similar to Figure 1.9.

FIGURE 1.6
IT project software written by programmer.

FIGURE 1.7
IT project documentation.

FIGURE 1.8
IT project executed by operations.

Next comes the need for IT support, both from the vendor and internal to the customer. The goal of the support team is to minimize their workload and to not get any unanswerable questions. They end up with something similar to Figure 1.10.

Of course, when it comes time for billing, the vendor feels that they achieved above and beyond the customer's expectations. The goal of billing is to maximize revenue. They end up with something like Figure 1.11.

Unfortunately, after installation, the vendor has moved on to their next sales opportunity, and the customer is left wondering what happened to their "best friend." The vendor's goal is to increase market share. The result is Figure 1.12.

In the end, we need to ask the question; "What was it that the customer really wanted? Did they get anything close to what they were after?" Rarely can this question be answered with a resounding "Yes!" Far too often we end up with the customer having to "make due" with the product that they ended up with. It is either overbuilt, making it hard to use, or underbuilt, leaving the customer doing some functionality outside of the system, or some major expectation is missed, etc. What the customer wanted was a system that satisfied their needs, reduced the cost of operations, and created organizational value. What they wanted is Figure 1.13. The rest of this

FIGURE 1.9
IT project installation.

FIGURE 1.10
IT project support.

FIGURE 1.11
IT project billed.

FIGURE 1.12
After installation vendor visibility.

book will focus on how to go straight to Figure 1.13, without making many of the mistakes that we currently make along the way.

IT ISSUES TO AVOID

In the preface we learned that 54% of the energy generated in the United States is wasted. Unfortunately we also know that we personally increase that percentage when we race the engine of our car, or when we take an extra long shower, or if we leave the light on in a room after we depart, or when we forget to turn the stove off after using it. In reality, the energy wasted is probably closer to 75%. So why am I talking about energy in a book about information technology? As stated in the preface, in my 30 years of working with, installing, and sometimes even pulling out IT systems, I have never found an IT environment that I would consider to be 100% efficient. There always exists one of the many IT plagues:

FIGURE 1.13
Customer expectations.

- Systems overconstruction—a system that covers all possible conditions is a waste, because it creates extra work for the 95+% of cases where the exceptions do not exist.
- Systems forced upon a user that do not fit—too often we buy the system and force users to adapt to it, rather than finding a system that adapts to the current work environment. A basic principle here is that we "optimize the process first;" then we find the IT application that will facilitate this optimized process—never the other way around.
- Work-arounds—this is where a new system does not handle a specific situation correctly and the user has to use some type of backdoor methodology to accomplish their task.
- Systems that miss the boat and part of the process has to be done by hand—often the author has encountered situations where a new system is implemented and the users now have to do more manual work than before, preparing the data for input, because the new system did not handle every situation in the process correctly.
- Duplicate data entry—I cannot count the number of times where employees have to spend their time reporting data three, four, and sometimes even five times because of different systems requirements,

like a time card, an expense report, a job activity log, etc.—and often the information recorded in each case is identical.

- Systems that miss timelines—IT is cursed with repeatedly missing time schedules. Projects within any organization in a company other than IT are expected to be completed on time. Unfortunately everyone seems to assume that IT is exempt from this requirement, because they just do not know how to accurately predict the effort behind a project. This should be humiliating to IT managers. The guys with all the technology cannot predict their own workloads. The company's customers would never be as patient with the time and cost overruns that IT expects its internal customers to tolerate.
- In extreme cases we find systems where the process is completely performed manually and then the data is input into the computer so that the data can be maintained on some kind of corporate database—unfortunately this happens far too often. I have seen hand recordings and spreadsheet recordings that are later manually input into the computer so that the ERP database can be maintained.

These are all areas where IT is filled with waste. No matter how technically perfect a system is, if it generates more work for the user, then it contains waste. IT should not be focused on creating the dream application, from a techie perspective. IT must focus on "user satisfaction." All systems within an organization must focus on the customer, and for IT, their customer is the end user of their applications. If the user's life is not made easier, more efficient, less time wasted, then the application is a failure! And the system is fraught with waste.

I recently attended a meeting where everyone was informed that the existing supply maintenance environment was being replaced with an Oracle database, and that everyone would need to adapt their processes to adhere to this new standard. Sadly, during the selection process of this system no one met with the users to see if this database would fit their needs. Would it be easier to use? No one asked about systems requirements. They were just "informed" that the change is taking place for "technology" reasons and that they would need to conform. The reality of the "informed" approach to implementing a new system is that users now:

- Keep their own manual (or spreadsheet) records for a period of time until they trust the new system, which may be years

- Stockpile critical maintenance parts for fear that the new system may not correctly anticipate their needs—which will, of course, make their supply maintenance usage information meaningless

In the end, the new system may be technologically better, but it has generated an enormous amount of redundancy and therefore "waste." Waste because of the "prima donna" effect, where IT "knows best." Waste because of the rework. And waste because of poor planning. In a later chapter of this book, we will discuss the "acceptance" tools of Lean, which are designed to help the reader introduce accepted change, rather than forced change.

I am not trying to beat up on IT. I am trying to increase awareness to the wastes that exist within the IT environment. IT is filled with opportunities for improvement. Here are a few more basic principles that IT needs to consider, as it moves toward becoming Lean.

1. IT is not always right, nor is the technologically optimal solution the best. You need a non-IT person involved in the IT decision making processes that will bring you back to reality or you will get dazzled by the "technobabble."
2. The role of technology is to enhance and facilitate a "good system," not replace it. First you need to optimize your system and create an ideal process. Then you need to automate it. Do not get the cart before the horse.
3. Do not solve a "systems" problem or a "process" problem by throwing technology at it. First fix the process, or you may end up with something worse.
4. IT does not always make the "system" more efficient. Far too often it drives unnecessary increases in complexity and therefore generates delays and confusion.
5. Be careful not to replace a manual system that can solve a problem within a couple of hours with an IT system that now requires several levels of approvals (standardized) and several days to accomplish the same thing.
6. Avoid the "system is down" excuse for nonperformance. Customers rarely buy it anymore.
7. Avoid the innate tendency to build an IT solution that covers every possible condition. Build a 95% solution, and then provide override access to everything on an exception basis. This should be a separate software entry point that does not force the user to bypass the

process on the 95% of the cases. Do not overbuild and make the system so complex that the 95% solution is too cumbersome to use.

8. Think "big picture" in terms of "integrated systems" where the IT portion is just one small portion of the overall solution. Ask questions like "What is the bigger problem that we are trying to solve?" IT should fit to the larger solution, not redefine it. Do not allow IT to force you to change your process. Use the following steps:

   a. Optimize the process using Lean/Six Sigma/Theory of Constraints (TOC) or other tools that are discussed in this book.

   b. Once the process is optimized, automate the areas of redundancy or integration or areas that need standardization.

A NEW DIRECTIVE FOR IT ORGANIZATIONS

For far too long IT has been treated as a hands-off organization of techies that bask in the aura of their exclusiveness. Management avoids them because they can effectively "technobabble" their way through most issues. But times have changed. IT needs to become a mainstream profit center that meets schedules and is accountable for improving the organization's performance. IT needs to realize that it does not always know the best way to solve systems or process problems. Not every problem is solved by throwing technology at it. Just because a solution is technologically easier does not mean it is optimal for the organization. Solving systems problems needs to be a team effort, using change management solutions like Lean. Then IT's role is to be a supporting function to help facilitate the optimized processes.

Over the years I have learned that, when IT says "It has to be done this way," what they are really saying is:

1. I prefer to do it that way because it is easier for me.
2. This taps the limits of my expertise, and we would have to find a different solution to accomplish this, and I do not know what that would be.
3. We in IT only know how to use this type of technology, and we would prefer to stay in our comfort zone.

That is simply not good enough. IT needs to support the objectives of the enterprise, not focus on building impenetrable walls around their existing IT organization.

SUMMARY

One more case example:

> Problem statement: The current time for in-processing of medical records is too lengthy, which causes clinic delays in patient care and interferes with appropriate accountability of the record.
> Performance gaps: Current large backlog of records to review is about 120 days.
>
> Improvement targets: Identify and reduce waste and establish improved process cycle times.
>
> Improvement results: Process cycle times are reduced to 3 days, which creates a 99% increase in efficiency.

In this example, by looking at the process using but not changing the existing IT solution they were able to increase data performance by 99%. Then they enhanced and wrapped their IT solution around this new process and found that minimal IT changes were needed.

IT is rampant with opportunities for Lean process improvements. And this book will help the reader:

1. Validate that the IT solution being selected is indeed the best solution
2. Minimize waste in the IT development and implementation process
3. Reduce the waste of IT changes, upgrades, and patches

Let us move forward Leaning out IT.

2

IT Background

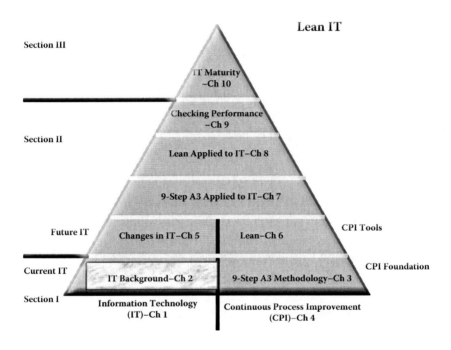

Lean IT

Section III

IT Maturity
–Ch 10

Checking Performance
–Ch 9

Section II

Lean Applied to IT–Ch 8

9-Step A3 Applied to IT–Ch 7

Future IT — Changes in IT–Ch 5 | Lean–Ch 6 — CPI Tools

Current IT — IT Background–Ch 2 | 9-Step A3 Methodology–Ch 3 — CPI Foundation

Section I

Information Technology
(IT)–Ch 1 | Continuous Process Improvement
(CPI)–Ch 4

Over the next five years, we are likely to generate about as much data as we have generated in the whole of mankind's history. The central task before human beings today is to teach the next generation to handle tsunamis of data.

"Top 75 Questions of Science,"
Discover Magazine, Spring 2008, p. 85

━━━━━━━━━━

THE TWENTY-FIRST CENTURY ENTERPRISE

It is no longer adequate to recognize that the current IT organization is desperately in need of change, as we saw in the last chapter. We also need to recognize that the twenty-first century enterprise has emerged with an entirely different set of needs from those that had existed in the past. These needs have created a set of initiatives that need to be addressed if the futuristic enterprise plans to retain world-class status. Some of the more critical issues include:

1. Futuristic thinking
2. Change management
3. Global markets
4. Geopolitical risks
5. Plethora of channels of data transfer
6. Pervasiveness of technology and the evolution of IT's role in the enterprise

Looking at each of these in more detail we see:

1. Futuristic thinking—Business in the twenty-first century is turning out to be different from that of the twentieth century in very significant ways, some of which are unanticipated. Extensive effort is being exerted in an attempt to predict these transformations. The rapid changes in hardware, software, and how technology is used, continue to grow at an alarming rate. When looking into the future, just 20 or 30 years out, we need to project the possibility that today's critical tools, like laptops, cell phones, and the Internet, will probably be obsolete. But what will replace them? What will make them obsolete? One effect of this futuristic look has been the emergence of the "futurists" as a distinct profession. Technological and social upheaval is anticipated. But what form will it take?
2. Change management—The "nervous nineties" was also a period when businesses went through multiple waves of initiatives aimed at improving internal operations and productivity. These took different forms, often with the unfortunate impact of unnecessary layoffs that eliminated core capabilities of the company. For example, the offshore migration of United States manufacturing capability

has resulted in the offshore transfer of its manufacturing engineering capability, leaving the United States technologically starved in this area. Change management tools like BPR (business process reengineering), TQM (Total Quality Management), Six Sigma, the Toyota Production System, and other management philosophies and approaches have sprung up. Lean was leveraged, initially starting on the shop floor and later migrating throughout the organization. Prominent focus areas for improvement now include procurement, warehousing, back-office operations, logistics, and IT.

3. Global markets—New global markets have emerged. Changing classifications reflect the emerging geopolitical and economic realities in a new world order. Thus we had the Asian Tigers in the 1990s (Malaysia, Singapore, Japan, Hong Kong, Indonesia), more recently the "BRIC countries" (Brazil, Russia, India, and China), and now the "flat world" showing up in business discussions. These distinctions segregate the world's economies into a tiered structure (notably "first world and third world countries") or the "developed" vs. the "developing." In addition to operational globalization we now have the rising specter of high fuel costs, which is a basic cost driver in almost every aspect of a company's function. Transportation and logistics managers have to balance low-cost operations with dramatically increased transportation costs.

4. Geopolitical risks—The globalization of operations was viewed as a natural evolution of business triggering the migration of most basic manufacturing to lowest-cost locations like China, Mexico, the former Soviet Bloc, and Vietnam. This reduces the direct cost of fabrication, but it also created the global supply chain where a product may travel many miles from fabrication/manufacturing to test/assembly and then again to some distribution hub before finally coming to rest in a distributor's warehouse, thereby servicing a local market. Time-in-transit and distances covered (ton-kilometers) became very significant, and variable in nature. Supply-side uncertainties have since become magnified, fueled by geopolitical risks. The sensitization of enterprises to their environmental impact is a relatively new and significant phenomenon. It causes changes in operational decision making, as well as creating new market opportunities and increasing corporate overhead. (Please review the author's book *Reinventing Lean: Introducing Lean into the Supply Chain*.)

5. Plethora of channels of data transfer—Twenty years ago we had a very limited number of data channels. We had one phone line and one mailing address. Today we have multiple land lines, multiple cell lines (one for work and one for home, and each member in the home has their own), fax lines, and pagers. For mail we have the postal services, FedEx, UPS, several e-mail addresses, LinkedIn, Twitter, Facebook, text messaging, etc., and we need to check all these sources regularly or we may miss something important. And each of these channels is plagued with spam. The future opens the door for even more channels of communication—more data. We spend more time processing more data, most of which is less and less useful for making meaningful decisions. IT of the future will need to create gatehouses and security mechanisms far beyond the antivirus, anti-spam software of today. Executives need the right information at the right time to make meaningful decisions. And the ever-increasing plethora of data transfer channels is making meaningful decision making harder, rather than easier.

6. Pervasiveness of technology and the evolution of IT's role in the enterprise—With all these changes, companies are changing at a fundamental level. The organization is no longer working on a quasi-military command-and-control structure with direct charge for all activities within buy-make-move-sell-support. Instead, there are extensive partnerships and alliances. We see the outsourcing of activities within core operations to specialized service providers (from product design and R&D to marketing, distribution, channel partnering, customer service, and even IT services). The enterprise has become an orchestration of collaborative activities. As a direct result of this, there are significant changes in operating processes. There is a need for operational visibility and financial transparency. This is enabled by information availability in a combined manner. This is something that has been enabled by IT and its evolving role as a key strategic element.

Enterprises continuously seek to accomplish more with less. This is increasingly true in the twenty-first century, and more so in the context of IT. Increased operating environment expectations reflect the new global reality, which includes global opportunity, global markets, and global resource access. While leaders seek ways to leverage all of these for strategic advantage and shareholder value, the role of IT is increasingly that of a strategic enabler for the enterprise, as opposed to just being confined to the nuts and bolts for information and data management along with communications and infrastructure. To use a biological analogy, IT has evolved from just being the base neural network that is responsible for survival in a living organism. It is now the enabler for independent thought and stimulus response, hence the need for a "higher level" of IT utilization. Organizations need to transform from information technology (IT) generators to information processing organizations (IPO), and the tool that will help them achieve this goal is Lean.

THE IT EVOLUTION

At this point we need to look at the businesses perspective of IT. The understanding and expectations around IT differ tremendously between practitioners of IT and the business community in general. There are also significant operational differences within the enterprise. For example, the needs differ between corporate functions and business units, and across functional areas like operations, sales, marketing, etc. This section discusses these differences and their impact on the role of IT.

Historically, the business community has played a passive/arms-length role in IT decision making, as shown in Figure 2.1. They would get involved during the implementation cycles where they tried to articulate business requirements. Unfortunately, this level of involvement was often too late, especially in enterprise resource planning (ERP) implementations. Since

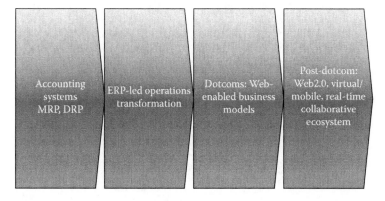

FIGURE 2.1
IT evolution.

then, complexity has continued to increase in both business operations and IT technologies, creating huge implementation problems. The result is that the business side had to become more involved in the IT decision making process. But the focus was still on the operational aspects. Some high-level thinking organizations received some strategic benefits through successful integration and transformation programs. The most significant shift in the role of IT was realized during the dotcom boom, with very significant strategic impact on business models, often changing the way companies made money (the "what" along with the "how" of operations).

The result is that IT migrated out of the back office, and business has never been the same since. In the post-dotcom era, senior business executives and managers are often visible sponsors and often even leaders in defining and selecting ERP programs. This is a far cry from the 1990s, where we routinely assigned junior-level, relatively inexperienced functionaries to participate in IT programs.

Mature organizations (typically Fortune 1000 companies) tend to also rely on centralized business reengineering or corporate development teams that collaborate with IT teams on the current and future initiatives. These groups also act as a vehicle for bringing Lean or Six Sigma thinking into process redesign. As seen in Figure 2.2, counting business process owners and actual business users of systems, there are five different IT perspectives from a business standpoint.

Each group brings its own unique set of expectations to IT, with some areas of overlap. However, experience tells us that most IT-enabled business transformations tend to fail if all of these constituencies have not been involved appropriately.

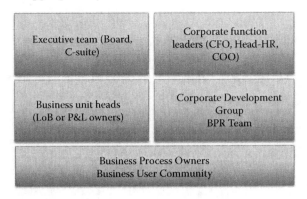

FIGURE 2.2
IT from a business perspective.

1. Executive team and board—The focus here is on the big picture strategic view and IT's role. More advanced companies have an executive team that recognizes the operational transformation of IT and the potential use of IT for strategic leverage. This may also involve customers and markets, product propositions, and competition. Thus, while the COO's primary focus will be supply chain operations and customer-facing processes, the CEO and CFO may focus on the role of IT in strategic market positioning and financial and regulatory compliance.

2. Corporate function leaders—Leaders of corporate functions such as strategic planning, finance and controls, human resources (HR), and legal typically have very focused interests in IT. Strategic planning is primarily a consumer of IT outputs including consolidated reporting and executive dashboards. In some cases, strategic planning will own IT tools to assist them in performing scenario-based planning or macro-level business forecasting. HR has a deep involvement here, particularly if people management and performance measurement are considered. In such situations HR is a significant user of information which is derived from core transactions which are the backbone of the system. HR also uses specialized tools and applications that must interface with the main enterprise systems.

3. Corporate development/BPR (business process reengineering)— Corporate development teams typically drive inorganic business growth through acquisitions. In some situations the same team will also focus on carve-outs and divestitures. Thus, the group tends to drive a unique set of expectations that corporate IT must fulfill including, for example, enabling rapid operational integration for acquisitions, smooth transitions, and migration in the case of carve-out/divestiture. In cases where the company has active process change initiatives (BPR/process improvements, standardization and/ or outsourcing), the centralized team shapes the IT agenda in a very significant way (for example, from identifying key needs and prioritization all the way to business requirements definition and assistance in change management during actual systems implementation).

4. Business unit heads—Business unit heads are P&L (profit and loss/ income statement) owners. This means that most investments are eventually paid for by these leaders. The expectation for IT is to focus on ROI (return on investment) as a first priority. Secondary areas

include operations enablement, market advantage, and minimization of business disruption risk.

5. Business process owners/user community—The majority of requirements for IT come from the business process owners and the user community. These are individuals who take direct responsibility for ensuring that the investments in IT systems actually bear fruit. Process changes required for execution and their associated management, along with decision making and reporting, all go hand in hand at this level.

With such a diverse combination of perspectives spread across investors, owners, and users in the twenty-first century organization, the relationship between business and IT has become fairly complex. Both sides must recognize the multilayered nature of expectations and interactions, as outlined in Figure 2.3.

The interdependencies must be recognized as well (Figure 2.4). Market success and effective operations drive the capability to invest in IT, and IT must in turn be an effective enabler of operations. Dysfunctional situations arise when key aspects of this interplay are not recognized.

Aspect	Business	IT
Investment	ROI - impact on operating processes	ROI - impact on systems environment
Intrinsic nature	Typically leads	Typically lags
Cost impact	Reduction in headcount and other costs through automation	Application pricing and predicted Total Cost of Ownership (TCO)
Broad focus areas (performance parameters would be within these)	Market share, gross margin, customer response, supply chain effectiveness, production efficiencies	Scope of deployment and adoption, information availability, data quality system uptime and robustness (integrity, security)
Operations effectiveness	Business process enablement, scalability, adaptability/ flexibility of operations	Scalability, business disruption risk minimization, system uptime

FIGURE 2.3
IT/business interactions.

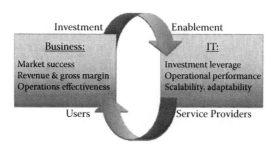

FIGURE 2.4
IT/business interdependencies.

All the information in this section should be taken as guidelines for business–IT interactions. However, there are a few situations when a company can and should step outside of this box. Even though these changes may be revolutionary, they should be carefully evaluated before we jump in with both feet, and the methodology for this evaluation will be the subject of the next chapter. These revolutionary changes may include:

1. Major breakthroughs in information technology could impact the way we do business, like blackberries and laptops.
2. Evolutions in the business model or the operating model may change the way we do business, for example, offshore production or international supply chains.
3. Unfavorable economic environment may cause waves in our demand or supply curves, thereby affecting the types of business decisions that we make.
4. The way IT development work is handled has changed, to where IT development work or even processing work can be offshored using the flat world concept, thereby reducing the sizes of the internal business IT staff and significantly effecting the IT–business relationship.

The business user–IT relationship must become integral in the enterprise. Business is the customer, and IT is the information supplier. And "Lean" teaches us that organizational optimization requires the customer and the supplier to work closely together if they are to achieve world-class status.

THE ENTERPRISE ROLE OF IT

Enterprise operation revolves around five business processes (see Figure 2.5 and Figure 2.6). Each of these processes places its own distinct set of requirements on the IT organization. In each of these processes there is a dependency on the performance, reliability, and quality of the IT service, even more so than we find in many of the other functions of the organization. For example, if a delivery mechanism fails, like UPS, we can go to FedEx. But if our IT process fails, the entire enterprise goes into a standstill. In many cases, all the employees may as well go home. Reviewing some of these key business processes we learn:

1. Product and services—This is the collection of deliverables that our enterprise provides for its customer. The deliverables can come in several forms. If we deliver a "product," then the business processes that need to be managed include the scheduling, quality management, packaging, delivery, product performance management, product service, product tracking, and possibly product storage. If we deliver a "service," then we need to track the level of service, who is performing the service, the scheduling of the service, any materials associated with the delivery of the service, the documentation of the service, the delivery mechanism for the service, its tracking, and service performance.

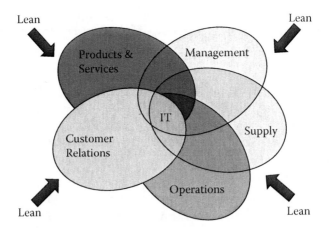

FIGURE 2.5
Five business processes.

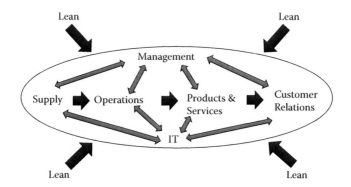

FIGURE 2.6
The flow of the five business processes.

2. Operations—This is the business mechanism that takes the raw input that our enterprise receives and converts it to a deliverable product or service. The IT functionality needed for this process includes forecasting of demand for output, forecasting of supply availability, production/operations planning, capacity analysis, inventory tracking, routings, bill of materials, lead times, real-time scheduling, and tracking the performance of the productive activity.

3. Supply—The supply side of the enterprise is the sourcing of the materials (the raw materials input). This business process focuses on what the enterprise needs to acquire from outside sources in order to accomplish its operations functions. The IT functionality needed includes procurement, delivery scheduling, delivery service tracking, supplier and delivery performance tracking, the receiving and inspection process, and the inventory tracking process. Many organizations incorrectly refer to this as the supply chain of the product, or supply chain management (SCM). Actually, SCM includes all the steps from the initial materials creation to the final product delivery, all the steps listed in the complete business process, as outlined in Figure 2.6.

4. Management—The management business function is the decision making function wherein lies the ultimate responsibility for the overall success of the enterprise. IT needs to provide them with information about customer satisfaction, investor satisfaction (stock price), enterprise profit and loss, cost, or operations, and performance statistics. At middle management we find the need for demand management and capacity management information.

5. Customer relations—The customer relations business function involves sales, marketing, branding and imaging, and the customer service functions of the enterprise. In this category IT needs to provide sales performance history, customer sales history, marketing cost and performance statistics, and customer satisfaction survey and feedback data.

The five business processes each have a critical expectation from IT, and a lack of IT performance can result in poor decisions being made based on bad information. IT is no longer a technological luxury or a corporate toy like the Wii or the Xbox. IT needs to wake up to its role as a critical piece of the process within an enterprise. And any enterprise process can be enhanced and improved through Lean tools, including the traditional no-man's-land/techies-only-land of IT.

THE TWENTY-FIRST CENTURY ENTERPRISE AND IT

The author had a long conversation with General Wong of the Hawaii Air National Guard (HIANG), and the general gave some incredible insights into organizational management. He told about how he blew out his knees and had to find a sport that would not put stress on his knees. He chose canoeing. A canoe team is typically made up of five individuals: the first is the stroker, who sets the pace for the canoe, the middle rower is the strongest rower, and the last is the one who steers. The general explained how he is the stroker, and he normally works with a team of men. But the night before our conversation he had been practicing with a team of women, who tend to have a softer, smoother stroke than the men's more abrupt and deliberate stroke. When he was practicing with the ladies, he soon realized that if he used his regular manly stroke, he would be pulling ahead of the team. He would be "pulling the team along." And his stroke would be the main driver of the canoe. He learned that he needed to back off and change his stroke to match the stroke of the rest of his team. And, when he did this, the canoe moved faster. Rather than his stroke being the one that by itself moved the canoe, by backing off, the team's combined stroke moved the canoe. The lesson he learned was that he had to "go slower to go faster." This is also true of organizations. If the manager is too strong, too domineering, to controlling, then the entire organization moves at the speed that he or she can pull it along. However, if the manager becomes a leader and works at the speed of the organization, taking advantage of the strengths of each individual in the organization, then the combined strength of the organization can push the organization forward at a faster speed. This story also teaches us that the strength of the organization is in the middle of the organization. If the top manager is too domineering, the "strength of the organization" is never allowed to "pull its weight."

So what does this mean for information technology (IT)? It tells us that sometimes we need to "go slower to go faster" when it comes to data collection and information generation. We need to get away from the mindset that all data is good data. We need to realize that collecting unnecessary data is a "waste" and consumes valuable resources that could be used in more productive ways. We need to slow down and ask questions like

Why are we doing that?
Does it help to satisfy the customer?
Does it make the product better?
Does it help management to make better decisions?

If the answers to the last three questions are "No," then what we are doing is generating "waste."

In IT we need to look at the "team" that we are working with. We need to optimize the capabilities of the team and use the team to generate optimal IT output. We need to take an enterprise perspective, and not an individual needs perspective, as we develop IT requirements and expectations.

What is the status of enterprise IT performance today? Not good! For example, the failures of private sector organizations like GM and Ford and the banking systems demonstrate poor management decisions. Commercial banks, or the failure of public sector organizations like Fannie Mae, Freddie Mac, FEMA, or the Federal Reserve Bank, demonstrate poor lending decisions. "Friendly fire" killing Canadians in Afghanistan demonstrates poor military execution decisions. Stimulus and bailout spending demonstrates poor economic decisions. Ironically, in today's world we have better data and more readily available information than at any time in the world's history. So why are we making such poorly informed decisions? Because we are not managing IT correctly. We live in a world that claims that data is good, and more data is better, and most data is best. But that is not what our failures are telling us. They are telling us that large volumes of poorly managed data are impeding our decision process rather than improving it. Excessive "waste" data is not good. It encumbers our decision process and causes us to make poor, reactionary decisions. Failures are also telling us that the IT processes are not in place which will facilitate our ability to determine which data is good, what information is valuable, and what is needed to make better, more informed decisions.

Figure 2.7 shows the IT integration model. In this diagram we see the three key components that make up any enterprise:

Systems (IT)
Processes (manufacturing)
Organization (resources)

Driving the optimal balance of these three pieces is what creates an efficient, smooth-running enterprise. The diagram also shows the inundation of data that surrounds these three components. Most of this data is extemporaneous. Traditionally, Lean, as an optimization tool, has been applied heavily to the processes. More recently it has been used to squeeze out inefficiencies in the organization. It looks at how best to utilize resources throughout the supply chain. But the last piece, the systems piece, has just recently started to receive Lean pressures. This is because we have learned that an organization is no more efficient than its weakest link. Inefficiencies in the IT area drive inefficiencies throughout the

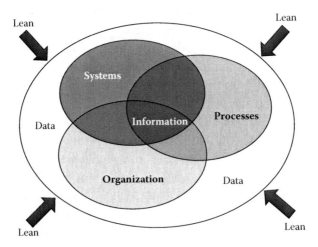

FIGURE 2.7
IT integration model.

organization. However, the balanced application of Lean principles to all three enterprise components will result in an optimally performing organization. This integration is what this book is looking for, driving the information technology (IT) organization into a world-class information processing organization (IPO).

Realizing that the traditional enterprise IT environments are dramatically failing, we need to find out why. What is the root cause behind these failures? To answer this question, we need to investigate several symptoms, any of which may point us at root causes. These include:

1. What is the value of information to the enterprise?
2. What are the threats to information accuracy and information value?
3. Why we are data rich (saturated) and information starved?
4. How do we classify information as credible and valuable?
5. What does it take to assure that we are receiving the right information in the right format and that it is going to the right person in the right location at the right time?

1. The value of information is determined by the customer, never by IT. If the customer perceives value, and can use the information to make decisions, then it has value. This customer may be an internal customer (which includes the entire enterprise which IT services), or it may be an external customer if the information is a component of the product that the enterprise sells. If the information is value-added for the customer, then IT is producing a value-added product. Otherwise, the product is a waste. I can remember installing ERP systems where a mountain of reports were generated each week. If we asked the users if they wanted to keep getting the report, they would always say yes. But it was like having a newspaper delivered to your home every day, even though the only thing you ever looked at was the comics on Sunday. They wanted the reports "just in case" there was something worth looking at. That is not information, and it is definitely not value-added. One week we decided to test the usefulness of the reports. We quit distributing the reports and waited to see who screamed. Those that screamed received their report. And everyone else was informed that the report would only be generated for them on request. This exercise eliminated about 75% of the reports that we generated. And we proceeded to improve upon the rest, by identifying what parts of the report they really needed, and

only gave them the needed portion. IT needs to provide value to the customer (internal or external). IT needs to Lean out its non-value-added processes and eliminate the waste.

2. When we talk about threats to information, we initially think of viruses and spam. But there are subtler threats as well. These are internal threats to information accuracy and information value which include obvious things like data recording and data entry errors. Also included are data redundancy and data duplication, where data comes from multiple sources and provides multiple, conflicting answers. Poor data management. And inaccurate report generation. This is an environment where small errors can have enormous cumulative repercussions. For example, the United State Air Force Supply Maintenance Logistics Support System, one of the most complex inventory management systems in the world, reports an aggregate information accuracy level of only 11%. There are also less obvious information corrupters which seem contraintuitive, like data control mechanisms which were instituted to validate data accuracy, but which result in increased systems complexity and end up opening the door for additional errors. These are all system wastes, and Lean is a tool to help you identify and weed out these non-value-added pieces.

3. We are data rich (saturated) and information starved because of tradition. Ten years ago we were told that all data is good. Even if we do not use it now, someday it will have value, and storage is cheap, so collect it all. Unfortunately, that is working backward. Data is inventory. And all inventory has a carrying cost associated with it, which includes data acquisition cost, data transfer costs, data storage costs, etc. As specified earlier, the only good data is data that adds value to the customer. Otherwise it is a waste and uses up valuable resources. The correct way to approach data collection is to look at the end product: the information output produced from the data. If the data facilitates value-added output in the form of customer-focused information, then it is of value. Otherwise it is waste and needs to be Leaned out.

4. Information is credible and valuable if the customer finds it so thrilling and so viable that they cannot live without it. Unfortunately, most of the information generated by IT still requires some level of "reading between the lines" in order to get the full meaning or the full impact of the information. This suggests that the customer is not getting the best information. Rather, they are getting adequate information, enough to make a decision, but not necessarily everything they would like to make the best

possible decision. Unfortunately, many of the "COTS" (commercial off-the-shelf) systems, which we are eager to install because of their lower cost and shorter implementation time, will require information users to do a lot of "reading between the lines" rather then providing them the best possible information for their decision making process. IT's job should be to make their customer's life easier, rather than just giving them a "tolerable" set of decision making tools. Lean has the mechanism to help get you from "tolerable" to "thrilling the customer."

5. To assure that we are receiving the right information in the right format and that it is going to the right person in the right location at the right time, we need to go to the customer and identify their expectations. Unfortunately what happens is that we go to the software vendor and ask them who gets the report, and then we tell the user, "This is what you get—like it or lump it." IT often forgets that they are working for the user, rather than the other way around. IT is just a tool designed to facilitate improved decisions. If it becomes a structured mechanism that drives the operation of an organization, or if it becomes the operating vehicle that everyone in the organization needs to conform to, then IT has made itself a non-value-added "waste." IT needs to break out of its elitist silo and become an integral, value-added part of the enterprise.

In searching for a common root cause, the threads found in all the above five symptoms seem to focus us toward:

1. A disconnect with what the customer (internal or external) considers to be value-added
2. A disconnect between the data that gets collected and the end product information that is generated

The role for IT should be to distinguish themselves within the enterprise as the generators of "information superiority" by eliminating these root causes and therefore eliminating the symptoms that result from root cause failures. In the following chapter we will find ways that "Lean" can be used to address these root causes.

CASE STUDY: WIPRO

Wipro Technology is an India-based global supplier of technology services of about 108,000 employees (more than tripled in 5 years), the majority of which reside in India. They perform a variety of IT services for their international client base. Wipro recognized the need for process performance efficiencies in IT and implemented Lean throughout their internal IT process. Later they expanded their Lean IT capabilities to include external clients. Their Lean IT journey started in 2005, and by 2008 Lean was mainstreamed in the organization (Figure 2.8).

The Lean process at Wipro has been so successful that it is now an integrated part of their culture. The number of Lean improvement initiatives has skyrocketed, as can be seen in Figure 2.9.

But the surge of successes has not been an accident. A team of trained and available Lean experts has been developed within Wipro, and they, in turn, developed a detailed methodology to support their Lean practice. The author has chosen to present Wipro's methodology in their own words, rather than describe it in detail. For example, Figure 2.10 shows some of the phases and challenges in the software development life cycle.

Wipro is a shining star amongst the IT technology service providers. There will be several references to Wipro in future chapters. The reader will find the success stories especially interesting.

SUMMARY

We have enormous IT performance challenges. IT frequently misses schedules and is plagued with cost overruns. Any other functional area of the enterprise with the poor historical performance of IT would have been eliminated or outsourced long ago. But the security and privacy elements of IT have prevented enterprises from sending their data outside of their internal "black box." But it will not be long before cost pressures force organizations to consider other alternatives for satisfying IT needs. This book offers a way for IT to bring itself in line with enterprise expectations. If we do not "Lean" out our IT process, we may find ourselves too heavy to stay afloat. If we do not fix ourselves, we are going to sink.

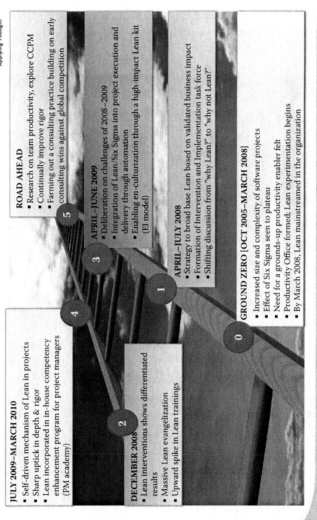

WIPRO
Applying Thought

JULY 2009–MARCH 2010
- Self-driven mechanism of Lean in projects
- Sharp uptick in depth & rigor
- Lean incorporated in in-house competency enhancement program for project managers (PM academy)

DECEMBER 2008
- Lean interventions shows differentiated results
- Massive Lean evangelization
- Upward spike in Lean trainings

ROAD AHEAD
- Research on team productivity, explore CCPM
- Continually improve rigor
- Farming out a consulting practice building on early consulting wins against global competition

APRIL–JUNE 2009
- Deliberation on challenges of 2008–2009
- Integration of Lean/Six Sigma into project execution and delivery through automation
- Enabling en-culturization through a high-impact Lean kit (EI model)

APRIL–JULY 2008
- Strategy to broad base Lean based on validated business impact
- Formation of Intervention and Implementation task force
- Shifting discussion from "why Lean?" to "why not Lean?"

GROUND ZERO [OCT 2005–MARCH 2008]
- Increased size and complexity of software projects
- Effect of Six Sigma seen to plateau
- Need for a grounds-up productivity enabler felt
- Productivity Office formed; Lean experimentation begins
- By March 2008, Lean mainstreamed in the organization

FIGURE 2.8
The Wipro Lean roadmap.

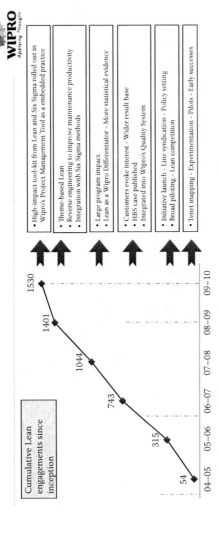

FIGURE 2.9
Lean @ Wipro—A timeline.

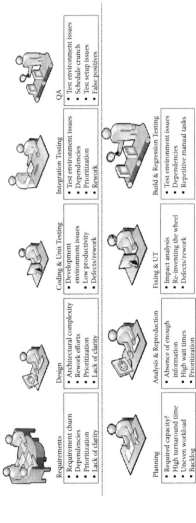

FIGURE 2.10
Applying Lean: the Wipro way.

3

Are We "Doing the Right Things"?

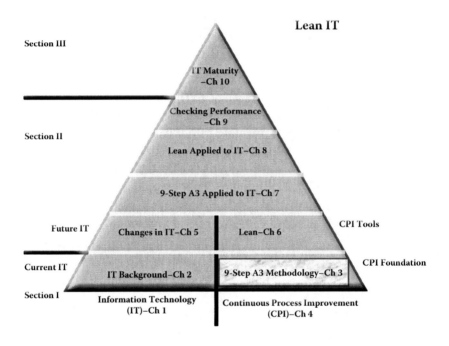

Caught in the headlights of infologic, it occasionally feels as though we have met the man with the proverbial hammer to whom everything looks like a nail.

John Seely Brown and Paul Duguid
The Social Life of Information, *HBS Press, 2000, p. 19.*

A3 PROBLEM ANALYSIS

The author was brought in to consult on a hospitality industry customer satisfaction project. One of the Six Sigma events was to analyze the performance of the elevators of a large hotel. Customer service had received a large number of complaints on the poor performance of the elevators, and so a project, lasting several months, was in process. The IT department in conjunction with the Six Sigma team collected data on elevator travel times, elevator rider wait times, and the costs associated with increases in elevator speed. After four months, the conclusion was that it would cost too much to increase the speed of the elevators and that this could not be justified based on the minor difference it would make in wait times. Therefore, no change should be made.

The author took a slightly different approach to the problem, a more sociological and systems-oriented approach. He suggested that the problem was not the length of the wait, but that the potential riders were bored; they needed a distraction. The author suggested putting mirrors on either side of the elevators. That way the women could check on their appearance, and the men could also check on the women's appearance without being direct and obvious about it. Although this was a rather sexist approach, and some would consider it offensive, in the end the complaints went down by 80 percent. And the change did not require extensive data collection, research, and months of waiting. Maybe the IT and Six Sigma teams were trying to solve the wrong problem. Maybe they were throwing data analysis at a problem where it did not fit.

Before we go any further in our discussions of Lean and its application to IT, we need to discuss one of the foundational tools of the Toyota Production System (TPS) or, as it is more commonly referred to, "Lean." This tool is the A3 report. This tool is important because it precedes IT. It asks the question, "Why are we even doing this IT project at all?" This is an important step because IT tends to get into a "we can do anything" trap, many times triggered by a spurious comment. That is the wrong way to engage in an IT activity. IT is a critical enterprise resource, not a company toy where we challenge the resolve and the capability of the IT team to correct any problem.

Using the A3 in the TPS environment we see multimillion-dollar projects approved or rejected based on the information from this one simple tool. It is referred to as the A3 report because of the size of the paper that the report is created on. The entire report is on one sheet of paper. It is not presented in a 200-page document, or a 100-slide "death by PowerPoint" deck. The entire analysis is performed and reported on one sheet of A3 sized paper. But it is not the size of the paper that is important; it is how the paper is organized and what information it contains.

My recommendation is this:

> As soon as you are done with this chapter, do not initiate another IT project without first going through an A3 analysis to make sure the project is justified.

In fact, it would probably be smart to review many of the projects that have already been started. This A3 tool becomes a critical methodology to make sure you are not wasting time, that you are doing the right things. Later in this book we will discuss if you are doing things right.

THE A3 STEPS

The A3 methodology outlined here is not the only A3 format available. There are many others, and you can find them in a variety of Lean books. However, the author has experienced a great deal of success using the example of the tool presented here for both opportunity analysis (the first 7 steps) and later for reporting progress (steps 8 and 9). Other change management process options will be discussed in Chapter 4.

In the A3 that this book is recommending for IT, there are nine A3 steps. In Chapter 4, which discusses change models, you will see some of the roots of where the A3 originated. For IT the author has found this 9-Step A3 to be the most successful. The report itself looks much like the example in Figure 3.1. This same report format is used for opportunity analysis, project presentation, project justification, and project performance review. When you use the same format consistently, the entire team (management and users) becomes familiar with the format and you do not waste time explaining each box. Everyone knows what they are looking for, and they go right to the box that interests them.

A second formatted example is shown in Figure 3.2, which is the way you would actually use the report to fill in the boxes. The size of each box is irrelevant. If you need more room for Box 3 and less for 4, just move the line down. Do not reduce the font and make it harder to read. Remember, this is an A3 sheet of paper, not a regular sheet of paper.

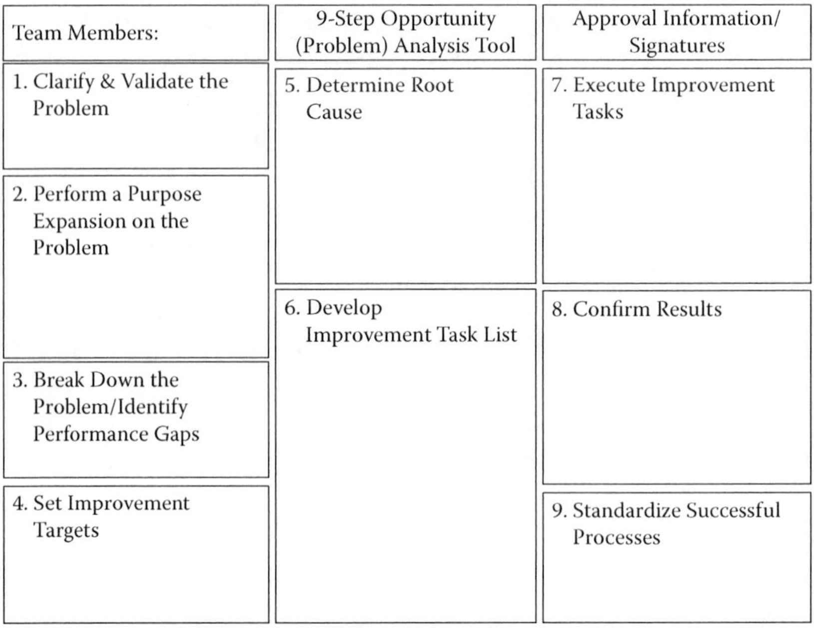

Team Members:	9-Step Opportunity (Problem) Analysis Tool	Approval Information/ Signatures
1. Clarify & Validate the Problem	5. Determine Root Cause	7. Execute Improvement Tasks
2. Perform a Purpose Expansion on the Problem		
	6. Develop Improvement Task List	8. Confirm Results
3. Break Down the Problem/Identify Performance Gaps		
4. Set Improvement Targets		9. Standardize Successful Processes

FIGURE 3.1
9-Step A3.

At this point we will go through each of the boxes in the A3. In this discussion you will hear about a variety of tools and techniques. A cursory explanation of each tool will be presented in this chapter. However, these tools and techniques will be discussed in detail in Chapter 6, and an example of their application can be found in Chapter 7. But first we need to take a "big picture" look at the 9-Step A3 tool and see how it works.

Figure 3.3 offers a brief description of the purpose of each of the boxes, and this can be used for reference purposes once you are familiar with the tool. Let us move forward with a more detailed description of how to use each box.

"Team Members" Box

When analyzing a problem or opportunity it is important to include all the relevant subject matter experts (SMEs). This includes:

Team Members	9-Step Opportunity (Problem) Analysis Tool	Approval Information/Signatures
1. Clarify & Validate the Problem	5. Determin Root Cause	7. Execute Improvement Tasks
2.Perform a Purpose Expansion on the Problem		
3. Break Down the Problem/Identity Performance Gaps	6. Develop Improvement Task List	8. Confirm Results
4. Set Improvement Targets		9. Standardize Successful Processes

FIGURE 3.2

9-Step A3—blank.

Team Members: Who are the individuals that worked on this 9-step report	9-Step Opportunity (Problem) Analysis Tool	Approval Information/Signatures Who are the Champions for (Signers of) this Project
1. Clarify & Validate the Problem State the basic overall fundamental problem that needs to be solved and validate that it is strategically aligned with the enterprise objectives. 2. Perform a Purpose Expansion on the Problem Confirm that we are doing the right things.	5. Determine Root Cause Define the root-causes of the current problem and the reason for current performance gaps. What caused the need for this change?	7. Execute Improvement Tasks Prioritize the actions listed in step 6, time sequence them, identify specific completion dates, assign responsiblility for the completion, and state where help is needed in order to complete the action. What are the deliverables and their due dates?
3. Break Down the Problem/Identify Performance Gaps What are the facts? List what specifically needs to change to solve the problem and what are the performance gaps to be closed to realize required performance. Prove it!	6. Develop Improvement Task List List the specific actions that need to be implemented to create change and close performance gaps. Validate that all the root causes listed in step 5 have been accounted for and resolved. What needs to change in order to eliminate the root cause?	8. Confirm Results Report progress made on the improvement targets listed in step 4. Confirm that we are doing the right things in the right way by improving the desired performance areas. Did you achieve your desired results? (At-a-glance status)
4. Set Improvement Targets Set improvement targets. Identify annual and long term stretch targets as appropriate		9. Standardize Successful Processes List ways to institutionalize best practices and processes learned from implementing this change. How can we institutionalize this "best practice?"

FIGURE 3.3
9-Step A3—with definitions.

a. The technical IT expert who will own the process from a hardware and software capability perspective and the software from an execution perspective
b. The end user, both from an analysis perspective and from a decision making perspective
c. The supplier who is the source of data that will be processed

The "Team Members" box lists the individuals that were involved in the analysis work that went into the creation of the 9-Step A3 document.

"Approval Information/Signatures" Box

Every improvement project must have a champion(s). This is the individual who controls the purse strings. This is the individual that is responsible for scheduling and allocating the resources (people, money, time) that will be needed to execute this improvement project. This champion must be willing to sign his or her name on the dotted line approving this effort. If you do not have a champion, then do not waste your time on the project.

"Clarify and Validate the Problem" Box

This box defines the opportunity or improvement project that you are about to engage in. In this box we state the fundamental opportunity that we want to work on and define it sufficiently so that anyone looking at this A3 will know what you are talking about. This is where we challenge ourselves to make sure that this project meets our strategic objectives. Ask the question, "Will this improvement help to drive the enterprise toward its vision/mission/objectives?" If not, for example if this is more in the category of "nice to have," then do not waste your time on it. Here are some questions that should be resolved in this box (if some of these tools are unfamiliar to you, do not worry; they will be covered in more detail in Chapter 6—see Figure 3.4):

a. Does solving this problem (executing this opportunity) help meet needs identified by the organization?
   - Is solving this problem linked to the vision/mission of the organization?
   - Does it help satisfy customer needs (VOC—Voice of the Customer—Technical Tool #5 in Chapter 6)?
b. What opportunities were identified or observed by "walking" through the process (Gemba Walk—Technical Tool #7 in Chapter 6)?

1. Clarify & Validate the Problem

Problem Statement: IT Set-up time for New Customers to access the order processing system is too long and customers are complaining

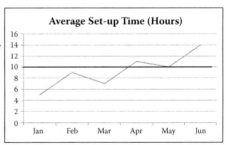

Strategic Alignment: Solving this problem supports the enterprise mission statement of "Thrilling the Customer"

Gemba Walk: We walked the process by observing the installation of an order processing system with a new customer and found that at numerous stages there were disruptions to the process and the customer had to call in to get additional information

Supporting Information: The data shows that we are significantly exceeding the allowable 10 hours installation time

Desired Future State: Automatic installation without user involvement – transparent to user – significantly less than the 10 hour standard

FIGURE 3.4
9-Step A3—Step 1 example.

Observing the process in context is a highly effective way to confront previously made assumptions/misconceptions/biases.

- What is happening that should not be happening, or what is not happening that should be happening?
- Where the problem is discovered is not necessarily where it originated. Dig toward the root cause.
- Will addressing or improving these issues deliver the desired results?
- Will addressing or improving this problem deliver the desired future state?

c. If it is a problem, where did it occur? When? Under what conditions?

- Once traced back to the point of cause, then quantify the extent of problem, frequency, percent affected, cost impact of problem (these answers can later be used as metrics to set improvement targets [Box 4] or to check performance improvement results [Box 8]).

d. Use the holistic systems perspective.

- What does this opportunity (problem) say about the Strengths/Weaknesses/Opportunities/Threats (SWOT—Technical Tool #4 in Chapter 6) of the organization from an overall enterprise perspective?

e. Tools that are available to help develop Box 1 (again, if some of these tools are unfamiliar to you, do not worry; they will be covered in more detail in later chapters):

- Strengths/Weaknesses/Opportunities/Threats (SWOT—Technical Tool #4 in Chapter 6) analysis—Used to analyze the internal condition and the external environment of the enterprise.
- Supplier/Input/Process/Output/Customer (SIPOC—Technical Tool #3 in Chapter 6) analysis—Applied to the problem/opportunity to determine who is involved in the process. This analysis defines what the *customer* expects, what *output* we produce to satisfy those expectations, what *process* we use to achieve those outputs, what *inputs* we need in order to execute that process, and which *suppliers* provide those inputs for us.
- Voice of the Customer (VOC—Technical Tool #5 in Chapter 6)— Used to identify the customers and their needs/expectations.
- Gemba Walk (Go and See Analysis—Technical Tool #7 in Chapter 6)—Gemba is Japanese for "the physical place." This tool is used to go out and physically see how the process is done. We walk

the process and see or experience every step that occurs in the process. We question and challenge each step as we observe it.

This box seems simplistic, but it is critical. If you cannot define the problem, then you cannot fix it. It is important to make sure that everyone listed in the "Team Members" box and in the "Approval Information/ Signatures" box have the same understanding of what you are trying to accomplish. Far too often you will find that there is disagreement at a very fundamental level, and until this is resolved, moving forward toward a solution is a "waste."

"Perform a Purpose Expansion on the Problem" Box

Mitsubishi had all their employees log all the activities, every day, for one week. After this exercise, they had each type of activity analyzed by adding three columns to the right of each activity. The columns were as follows:

First column: What was the purpose of doing this activity?
Second column: What was the purpose of the purpose listed in the previous column?
Third column: Does the purpose in the previous column achieve either of the following:

1. Increase customer satisfaction?
2. Increase the quality or performance of the product or service we perform?

If the answer to the question in this last column was "No," they were told to quit performing that activity. Approximately one third of the activities of the enterprise were eliminated.

This may seem like a radical example, but the message should be clear. Why do we engage in activities which do not support the goals and objectives of the enterprise? In Mitsubishi's case, the goals were customer satisfaction and product/service excellence. In another enterprise the goal may be profitability or shareholder wealth. But whatever that goal is, we should not engage in activities that do not bring the enterprise closer to its goals.

In very simple terms, the concept of purpose expansion says that we ask "Why" looking upward in the organization. Why are we doing this activity? What is the purpose of doing it? The purpose expansion brings us to

---

2. Perform a Purpose Expansion of the Problem

> Problem Statement: IT Set-up time for New Customers to access the order processing system is too long and customers are complaining
>
> What is the Purpose of Solving this Problem?
> To make it easier for the customer to get access to our order processing mechanism – fewer customer complaints – more customer satisfaction
>
> What is the Purpose of Solving this Problem?
> To help the customer place more orders – increased revenue
>
> Does this satisfy the strategic objectives of our enterprise?
> Yes

FIGURE 3.5
9-Step A3—Step 2 example.

a higher-level, systems perspective, where the entire enterprise is looked at as a system that is trying to accomplish a specific set of goals. Through purpose expansion we often learn (see Figure 3.5):

1. What we are trying to do is not value added to the goals and objectives of the organization.
2. Changing what we plan to change should be integrated into a different or larger improvement process within the enterprise.
3. Expanding the purpose of this improvement opportunity would easily encompass other needed changes, which helps create a broader, more encompassing solution.
4. We are not working on the right problem from a systems/enterprise perspective.
5. There are more solution options than we initially assumed by looking at the problem from too low a level.

The purpose expansion tool is part of a broader concept known as breakthrough thinking, which focuses on the tools needed for identifying creative solutions. The concept of breakthrough thinking is outlined in slightly more detail in Chapter 6—Acceptance Tool #1. There are numerous books available that go into breakthrough thinking in great depth. These include:

- *Breakthrough Thinking: The Seven Principles of Creative Problem Solving* by Gerald Nadler and Shozo Hibino

- *Creative Solution Finding* by Gerald Nadler, Shozo Hibino, and John Farrell
- *Making Innovation Happen: Concept Management through Integration* by Gerhard Plenert and Shozo Hibino
- *Reinventing Lean: Introducing Lean Management into the Supply Chain* by Gerhard Plenert

"Break Down the Problem/Identify Performance Gaps" Box

Box 2 of the 9-Step A3 report had us look upward in the organization. Box 3 and onward has us looking down deeper into the problem or opportunity that we are exploring. The objective of Box 3 is to answer the questions, "What makes this problem a problem?" and "Prove that it really is a problem." Here are some questions that should be resolved in this box (if some of these tools are unfamiliar to you, do not worry; they will be covered in more detail in later chapters—see Figure 3.6):

    a. Does the problem require more analysis, or does leadership have enough information to execute a solution?
- Is this simply a leadership directive?

    b. If more data is needed, how do we measure performance now?

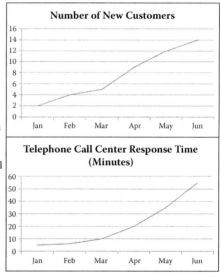

3. Break Down the Problem/Identify Performance Gaps

Analysis of the data indicated that there had been a surge in the number of new customer setups. Further drilling into the data demonstrated that our call center response time had geometrically increased because of the increased number of calls coming through the center.

There seems to be a clear bottleneck in the call center whose delayed responses is causing longer installation times.

FIGURE 3.6
9-Step A3—Step 3 example.

- What are the key performance indicators (KPIs)?
- What is the performance gap?

c. Does other "nonexistent" data need to be gathered?

d. What do the data indicate are the potential root causes?

e. Does the data review indicate a bottleneck or constraint?

f. Tools that are available to help develop Box 3 include (again, if some of these tools are unfamiliar to you, do not worry; they will be covered in more detail in later chapters):

- Gather and review key process indicators and metrics (see Chapter 9)—problem solving and process improvement begins with data. Relevant and meaningful data is critical if we are to identify the true "root cause" of the problem we are trying to solve.
- Performance gap analysis—Once the data has been gathered we need to analyze it in order to identify the gaps between the current state and the desired state.
- SIPOC—Discussed in Box 1 tools
- Information flow diagrams (see Technical Tool #6 in Chapter 6)—Drawing out a detailed process flow based on the actual steps that occur in a process is extremely insightful. An information process flow diagram should be created from several perspectives, including:
  1. Database perspective
  2. User perspective
  3. Software execution perspective
- We need to look at the number of interactions/transitions/exchanges of information that occur between users and the system, between systems, with the database, etc. and ask questions like: "Is this a reasonable number of transitions?" "Does this make sense?" "Can this be done in a quicker/easier/more efficient/more user-friendly way?"
- Bottleneck analysis (see Technical Tool #26 in Chapter 6)—Bottlenecks are process flow inhibitors which can be critical to the overall flow. They need to be identified and understood. The broader concept relating to bottleneck analysis is called "theory of constraints," and there are numerous books and articles available that offer a better understanding of how this works. These include:

- *Reinventing Lean: Introducing Lean Management into the Supply Chain* by Gerhard Plenert
- *The Goal* by Eliyahu M. Goldratt and Jeff Cox
- *The Haystack Syndrome* by Eliyahu M. Goldratt
- *The Race* by Eliyahu M. Goldratt and Robert E. Fox
- "Optimizing Theory of Constraints When New Product Alternatives Exist" (in the *Production and Inventory Management Journal*) by Gerhard J. Plenert and Terry Lee

"Set Improvement Targets" Box

The key question that we need to answer in this box is "What is the goal? What do you want to achieve by making this change?" In this box we utilize some of the KPIs or metrics that we identified in Box 3 and set targets that we hope to achieve. Here are some questions that should be resolved in this box (if some of these tools are unfamiliar to you, do not worry; they will be covered in more detail in later chapters—see Figure 3.7):

a. Is the improvement target measurable? Is it concrete? Is it challenging?
b. Is the target "Output Oriented"?
   - What is the new level of desired output?
   - This metric should include "things to be achieved" and should avoid "things to do."
c. The desired target should define:
   - Accomplish what? By how much? By when?
d. If it is a process problem, what is the future state?
   - How will it be realized?
e. Tools that are available to help develop Box 4 (again, if some of these tools are unfamiliar to you, do not worry; they will be covered in more detail in later chapters):
   - Value Stream Mapping (VSM—Technical Tool #2 in Chapter 6)—this is the primary tool and it works in stages:
     - Current state VSM—how does the process work now?
     - Ideal state VSM—in a perfect world, how should this work?
     - Future state VSM—given the constraints that we are restricted by, what is our best operating environment?
   - B-SMART targets—B-SMART (see Technical Tool #8 in Chapter 6) is an acronym for the characteristics of all good goals:
     - B = Balanced

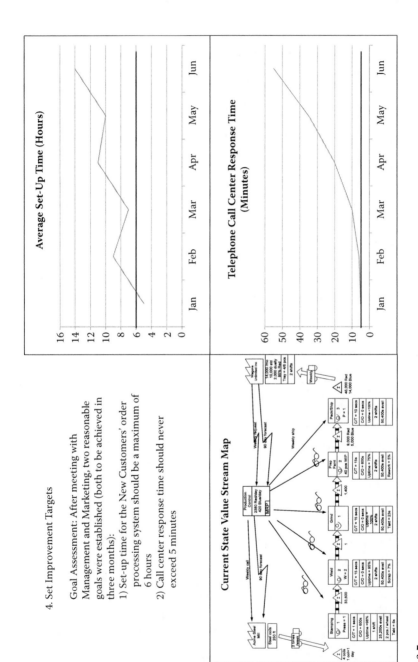

FIGURE 3.7
9-Step A3—Step 4 example.

- S = Specific
- M = Measurable
- A = Attainable
- R = Results oriented
- T = Time based

"Determine Root Cause" Box

In this box we focus on defining the root causes of the current problem and the reasons for the current performance gaps. We try to answer the question, "What caused the need for this change?" We look to find out what is the immediate thing that is happening or not happening that is creating the problem. Here are some questions that should be resolved in this box:

a. What root cause analysis tools are necessary?
- Why are these tools necessary?
- What benefit will be gained by using them?
- Who will need to be involved in the root cause analysis?
  - 10 heads are better than one.
  - Remember "cultural" issues related to problem.
b. What are the root causes according to the tools we used?
c. How will the root cause be addressed?
d. Will addressing these root causes address the performance gap?
e. Can the problem we are trying to solve be turned on or off by addressing the root cause?
f. Does the root cause make sense if the 5 Whys are worked in reverse?
- Working in reverse, say "therefore" between each of the "whys"
g. Root cause analysis results should describe a clear and coherent cause-effect chain that demonstrates an in-depth understanding of the problem in context, showing how the root cause is linked to the observed problem. Root causes may result from a poorly specified activity, an unclear connection, or a complicated or undefined pathway. Tools that are available to help develop Box 5 (again, if some of these tools are unfamiliar to you, do not worry; they will be covered in more detail in later chapters—see Figure 3.8):
- 5 Whys (see Technical Tool #19 in Chapter 6)—Reiterative process of asking "why" to go beyond superficial analysis. Start with "Why is this problem occurring?" Then, using that answer, ask

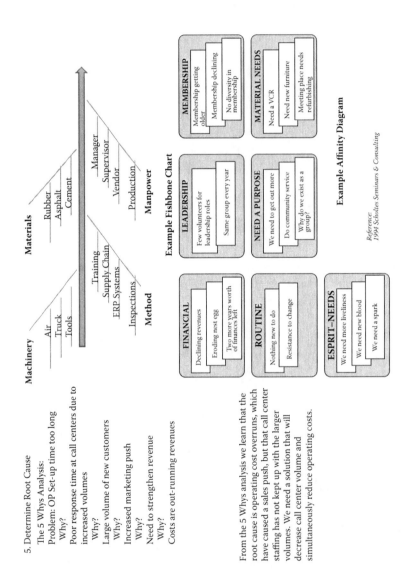

5. Determine Root Cause
The 5 Whys Analysis:
Problem: OP Set-up time too long
Why?
Poor response time at call centers due to increased volumes
Why?
Large volume of new customers
Why?
Increased marketing push
Why?
Need to strengthen revenue
Why?
Costs are out-running revenues

From the 5 Whys analysis we learn that the root cause is operating cost overruns, which have caused a sales push, but that call center staffing has not kept up with the larger volumes. We need a solution that will decrease call center volume and simultaneously reduce operating costs.

Machinery
Air
Truck
Tools

Materials
Rubber
Asphalt
Cement

Training
Supply Chain
ERP Systems
Inspections
Method

Manager
Supervisor
Vendor
Production
Manpower

Example Fishbone Chart

LEADERSHIP
Few volunteers for leadership roles
Same group every year

MEMBERSHIP
Membership getting older
Membership declining
No diversity in membership

NEED A PURPOSE
We need to get out more
Do community service
Why do we exist as a group?

MATERIAL NEEDS
Need a VCR
Need new furniture
Meeting place needs refurbishing

FINANCIAL
Declining revenues
Eroding nest egg
Two more years worth of finances left

ROUTINE
Nothing new to do
Resistance to change

ESPRIT–NEEDS
We need more liveliness
We need new blood
We need a spark

Example Affinity Diagram

Reference:
1994 Scholtes Seminars & Consulting

FIGURE 3.8
9-Step A3—Step 5 example.

"Why?" about the answer. And iteratively repeat this process five times to see what this teaches us about the cause of the problem.

- Brainstorming (see Technical Tool #20 in Chapter 6)—This is a simple tool where we get several people into a room and start writing on a chalkboard, or a whiteboard, and start asking "Why?" to the group to see what they come up with.
- Fishbone charts—A fishbone chart (see Technical Tool #21 in Chapter 6) is a tool that is used to organize brainstorming ideas into categories.
- Pareto charts—A Pareto chart (see Technical Tool #22 in Chapter 6) tries to identify those factors with the greatest impact on the problem using bar charts.
- Affinity diagrams—The affinity diagram (see Technical Tool #23 in Chapter 6) is an alternative way to group, prioritize, and organize the results of the Brainstorming exercise.
- Control charts—Control charts (see Technical Tool #24 in Chapter 6) are a statistical tool which analyzes performance data in an attempt to identify out-of-control processes. Control charts are used over a period of time to monitor performance and to track data movement.

"Develop Improvement Task List" Box

Up to now we have been focused on making sure we are doing the right thing. Are we fixing the right problem? Are we focused on the correct opportunity? Starting with Box 6, we shift our focus away from "doing the right thing" and look at "doing things right." But we did not do Boxes 1 through 5 in a vacuum. As we worked our way through the last five steps we identified improvement opportunities. Particularly in Step 4, when we developed the current state Value Stream Map (VSM—Technical Tool #2 in Chapter 6), we noticed a large number of things that did not make sense. Now, in Box 6, we record all these "opportunities for improvement" and identify tasks showing how we should improve this process.

As we develop our list of improvement tasks, we should observe a few rules:

a. The root cause(s) must be corrected.
b. We should avoid trying to fix symptoms.
c. The tasks should be designed to prevent the reoccurrence of the problem.

    d. We should be able to predict the extent to which the proposed change will alleviate the problem.

    e. Activities shall be specified according to content, sequence, timing, and outcome.

    f. Customer/supplier connections shall be clear, direct, and binary.

    g. Pathways that deliver a product shall be simple and direct.

    h. Understand the resource impact (financial, labor, materials, capacity, etc.) of your recommended tasks.

Here are some issues that should be resolved in this box (if some of these tools are unfamiliar to you, do not worry; they will be covered in more detail in later chapters—see Figure 3.9):

    a. Develop a list of potential corrective action steps (task list).

    b. Brainstorm specific changes to the current process that address the root cause(s).

    c. Select the most practical and effective corrective actions.

    d. Build consensus with others by involving all stakeholders appropriately.

       • Communicate, communicate, communicate.

    e. Create a clear and detailed action plan.

       • Use project management tools as appropriate.

6. Develop Improvement Task List

Task	Task List	Issue Resolved	Resource Demands
1	Review the reasons for Customer Calls to the Call Center and eliminate the need for the calls	Reduce delays caused by excessive call center volume	1 person 1 week
2	Improve the software so that customer interaction is minimized	Shorten software implementation time	2 software developers 2 months
3	Give the call center a list of documented standard solutions to the most frequent problems	Reduce delays caused by excessive call center volume	1 tech writer 1 month
4	Develop a website alternative with solutions to reduce call center volume	Reduce delays caused by excessive call center volume	1 web developer 1 month

FIGURE 3.9

9-Step A3—Step 6 example.

"Execute Improvement Tasks" Box

This box answers the question, "Why aren't we there yet?" This box takes the tasks that were identified in Box 6 and performs the following activities:

a. Prioritize them based on their impact on the organization and effort to install.
b. Assign a due date.
c. Assign a department or person of primary and secondary responsibility (you cannot commit someone who is not present—if they are not part of the team, they need to be contacted and be brought into the team).
d. Identify areas where specific help is needed that goes beyond the scope of this team (this will become the responsibility of the team champion who was listed in the upper right-hand corner of the 9-Step A3 document).

Here are some issues that should be resolved in this box (if some of these tools are unfamiliar to you, do not worry; they will be covered in more detail in later chapters—see Figure 3.10):

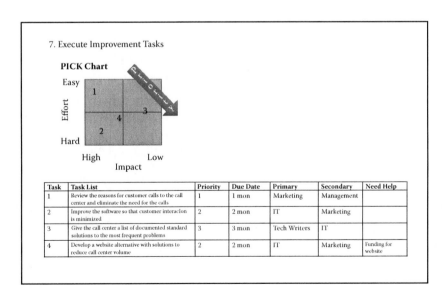

FIGURE 3.10
9-Step A3—Step 7 example.

a. Develop a PICK (possible, implement, challenge, kill) chart, sometimes referred to as an impact/effort matrix (see Technical Tool #5 in Chapter 6), which is used to prioritize the identified tasks. On the horizontal axis we have "effort." Is the implementation of this task easy or hard? On the vertical axis we have "impact." Will the impact of this change be low or high? Prioritize the tasks, starting from the upper left-hand corner of the matrix (high priority) to the lower right-hand corner (low priority).

b. Select which method should be used to implement the tool and improvement needed.

   - Rapid improvement event (RIE)—this is the Lean event process that will be discussed in detail later in this book in Chapter 8.
   - Improvement project—this is a project, like a construction project or a move to a new location.
   - Point improvement or "just do it"—this is a task that is easily accomplished, for example, writing a letter.

c. If this is an RIE or project, create a project "charter" (see Technical Tool #27 in Chapter 6) for that task.

d. What training or education is needed? By whom?

e. Who does the task? What do they do? When do they do it by? Etc.

f. Document "standard work" where appropriate.

The purpose of this box is to make sure that a clear path to implementation has been laid out. Improvements often fail to realize their potential because the implementation plan, not the improvement, was flawed. We need to ensure that the anticipated outcome of each task is made explicit from the description. As part of a successful implementation, we need to develop a follow-up plan. We need to determine how the actual results will be verified against predicted outcomes. This should be accomplished through regular (monthly) status reports by the implementation team (upper left-hand corner of the A3) to the champion (upper right-hand corner of the A3). During this report-out, the following items should be discussed:

a. The status of each activity or task.

b. Performance on the metrics (Box 4 and Box 8), which determines whether the implementation had the desired effect.

c. Have we solved the problem (advanced the opportunity)? Have we targeted the right tasks? Has our defined corrective action been effective? Did we solve the correct root cause? How do you know that the problem is actually resolved?

"Confirm Results" Box

The purpose of this box is "governance," which is to prove that we are working on the right things, that we are actually having the impact that we discussed in Boxes 1 through 5. We start with the improvement targets that were set in Box 4, and we monitor and measure our performance to those targets. Questions we should be asking are:

a. How are we performing relative to the "Doing the Right Thing" phase (Boxes 1, 2, and 3)?
b. How are we performing relative to the improvement targets set in Box 4?
c. Are we seeing the correct improvements to the root cause in Box 5?
d. If we are not meeting targets, do we need to return to Box 5 and reevaluate?
   - Most problem solving "breakdowns" result from improper root cause identification.

This box is the accountability box. It is where we report back the metrics that demonstrate improvement. As already mentioned in the Box 6 discussion, these numbers are then used to report performance back to the project champion.

"Standardize Successful Processes" Box

This box is about communication. It focuses on sharing the lessons that we learned during this 9-Step A3 exercise. An important part of any Lean effort is to make sure that improvement efforts are not occurring in isolation. The lessons learned should be standardized and shared. Some key questions that should be asked are:

a. What is needed to standardize the improvements?
   - Procedural changes?
   - Executive decreed changes?
   - SharePoint database for storing the A3 reports?
b. How should improvements and lessons learned be communicated?
   - Continuous process improvement database?
   - Key meetings?

c. Were other opportunities or problems identified by the problem solving process? Often, in going through a 9-Step A3 exercise we identify areas that need further investigation, but which are out of the scope of this project. These opportunities are tracked on a document referred to as the "parking lot" and are given to the champion for further consideration, or for referral as appropriate.

- Run additional 9-Step A3s as appropriate for the "parking lot" opportunities.

USING THE 9-STEP A3 TOOL

By now you should have realized that this chapter is the most important chapter in this book. This chapter has been a short overview. A deeper discussion is needed, and the remainder of this book will deep dive into the areas that surround the 9-Step A3 process and help you become a successful user. At this point we should have seen that the 9-Step A3:

a. Is a tool for organizing projects/opportunities/problem resolutions
b. Goes way beyond just the IT world, but is critical within it
c. Identifies responsible parties (champions and team members)
d. Identifies that we are working on the right problem (Boxes 1 and 2)
e. Forces us to validate that the problem needs fixing (Boxes 2 and 3)
f. Forces us to prove that by fixing the problem we will have a positive impact on enterprise performance (Boxes 2 and 4)
g. Makes sure that we are addressing the root cause of the problem and not just the symptoms (Box 5)
h. Helps us build a plan of attack for resolving the problem (Boxes 6 and 7)
i. Forces us to be accountable for the progress we predicted (Box 8)
j. Forces us to share our understanding and lessons learned with the remainder of the enterprise (Box 9)

The first 5 steps (boxes) are focused on "Are we doing the right thing?" (analysis of the opportunity/problem). Steps 6 and 7 are focused on "Are we doing things right?" and "How do we fix it if it is broken?" Steps 8 and 9 are focused on reporting what we have done. Step 8 gives us a quick, at-a-glance status (Figure 3.11), and Step 9 shares what we have learned (Figure 3.12). What is left is for us to define when, where, and how we share this information.

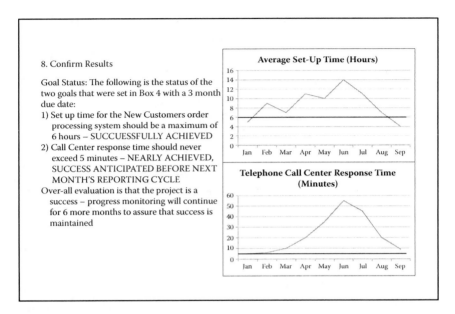

8. Confirm Results

Goal Status: The following is the status of the two goals that were set in Box 4 with a 3 month due date:
1) Set up time for the New Customers order processing system should be a maximum of 6 hours – SUCCUESSFULLY ACHIEVED
2) Call Center response time should never exceed 5 minutes – NEARLY ACHIEVED, SUCCESS ANTICIPATED BEFORE NEXT MONTH'S REPORTING CYCLE
Over-all evaluation is that the project is a success – progress monitoring will continue for 6 more months to assure that success is maintained

FIGURE 3.11
9-Step A3—Step 8 example.

9. Standardize Successful Processes

Standardization Actions Taken	Due Date	Responsible
Review the reasons for Customer Calls to the Call Center and eliminate the need for the calls	L mon	Marketing
Improve the software so that customer interaction is minimized	2 mon	IT
Give the call center a list of documented standard solutions to the most frequent problems	3 mon	Tech Writers
Develop a website alternative with solutions to reduce call center volume	2 mon	IT

FIGURE 3.12
9-Step A3—Step 9 example.

The champion (senior leader) that is involved with the project needs to do regular status checks on the progress of the project. This should occur:

1. At project inception where he or she asks questions like:
   a. Did the team walk the process (Gemba Walk—Box 1)?

2. During the development of the 9-Step A3 there should be regular status out-briefs which should answer questions like:
   a. Do the root causes make sense (Box 5)?
   b. Does the improvement task list address the root causes (Box 6)?
   c. Is the implementation plan realistic (Box 7)?
   d. Is the follow-up plan substantive (Box 7)?
   e. Did the Team talk with the right people during the problem-solving process (Box 1 and Box 3)?
   f. Are all the right people agreeable to the proposed change?
3. After the analysis has been completed, a regular status check should occur, usually on a monthly basis. During this meeting, the following questions are appropriate:
   a. Are we seeing the improvements that we projected (Box 8)?
   b. If not, do we need to revisit the root cause and the improvement task list (Boxes 5 and 6)?
4. At some point the champion should be reporting the results of the 9-Step A3 exercise to his executive board. For that meeting, the A3 document is the desirable out-brief document, not some "death by PowerPoint presentation." It is appropriate for the executive board to challenge the improvement process in much the same way as the champion challenged it. Everyone should be focused on the two big questions:
   a. "Are we doing the right things?"—Are the things that we are doing helping us to achieve the goals of the enterprise?
   b. "Are we doing the things that we do in the right way?"—Are we eliminating non-value-added "waste" everywhere possible?

WHAT LOOP AM I IN?

Problem solving is a series of never-ending loops. We are never done. There is always something that can be improved upon. Circumstances change. Customers change. Technology changes. And as long as something is changing, we open the door for improvements.

If you search the change management literature, you will find a never-ending collection of loops. We have the Lean PDCA (Plan-Do-Check-Act) loop, also referred to as Deming's Quality Wheel (see Figure 3.13); we have the Six Sigma DMAIC (Define, Measure, Analyze, Improve, Control) loop (see Technical Tool #16 in Chapter 6); we have the TOC (Theory of

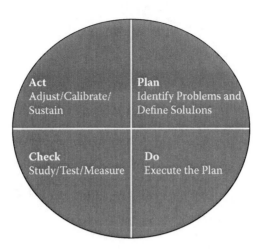

FIGURE 3.13
Deming's Quality Wheel—PDCA.

Constraints) loop (see Technical Tool #26 in Chapter 6); and now in this book we have the 9-Step loop. The bottom line is that all these loops are basically the same. Table 3.1 shows how each of these tools parallels the other in the change management cycle. So, when you hear conversations about the different loops and tools, remember that nearly all of them are variations of the Toyota Production System, which is the foundation of Lean, Six Sigma, and the 9-Step A3.

CASE STUDY: WIPRO (CONTINUED)

Continuing the Wipro story from Chapter 2, and integrating some of the principles learned in this chapter, we can see in Figure 3.14 how Wipro highlights some of the areas of waste that occur in the IT life cycle. *

Additionally, Figure 3.15 is extremely informative in suggesting areas where Lean IT has been exceptionally successful at Wipro. For example, the diamond areas of the chart show that key areas for success. These include:

Consistency (Standard Work)
Quality (Six Sigma/DMAIC)

---
* The charts used in this case study come from a Wipro presentation on Lean implementations created by Seema Walunjkar in the Wipro Global Delivery Organization.

TABLE 3.1

"Loop" Comparison

9-Step	PDCA	DMAIC	TOC
Step1—Clarify and validate the problem	Plan	Define	Identify the constraint
Step 2—Perform a purpose expansion on the problem		Measure	
Step 3—Break down the problem/ identify performance gaps			
Step 4—Set improvement targets			
Step 5—Determine root cause		Analyze	
Step 6—Develop improvement task list	Do		Exploit the constraint
Step 7—Execute improvement tasks		Improve	Subordinate the processes
Step 8—Confirm results	Check	Control	Repeat the process—find another constraint
Step 9—Standardize successful processes	Act		

Waste Category	Examples (Software)	Waste Category	Examples (Software)
Transport	• Searching for required information (document, email etc.) • Changing requirements, evolving requirements • FTP/copy	Over-Production	• Duplicate test cases • Extra features • Unused features
Inventory	• Frequent task switching results in half-baked inventory & loss of context • Backlog, Over skill	Over-Processing	• Redundant reviews, Irrelevant training, Duplicate builds • Obsolete test cases • Duplicate test cases • Unnecessary meetings • For every code drop, every engineer initiates FTP & does a build
Motion	• Customer deliverable going through multiple hands – customer, onsite co-ordinator, offshore team • Frequent travel between locations for reviews • Test setup	Defects & Rework	• Defects • Rework • Poor documentation • Incomplete documentation • Efforts spent in tracing the test setup (Other members disturb the setups to fill the equipment shortage in their setups)
Waiting	• Waiting for customer feedback, information, resources • Waiting for completion of predecessor tasks, clarification on requirements • Delayed reviews		

FIGURE 3.14

Waste categorization in IT.

Business Challenge	Impact
Application Development	
Consistent Quality	◆
Productivity Improvement	■
Adherence to Plan	◆
Handling Requirement Volatility	☐
App Maintenance	
Improvement in Cycle Time	◆
Improvement in Productivity	■
Application Re-engineering	◆
Backlog Reduction	■
Production Support	
Improvement in SLA Adherence	◆
Backlog Reduction	■
Ticket In-Flow Reduction	■
Optimal Capacity Planning Based on the Demand	◆

High - ◆
Medium - ■
Low - ☐

FIGURE 3.15
Areas where Lean has worked.

Adherence to Plan (Standard Work)
Improvement in Cycle Time (VSM and the supporting processes)
Application Reengineering (Brainstorming/5 Whys/Fishbone)
Improvement in SLA adherence (Standard Work)
Capacity Optimization (VSM and 5S)

SUMMARY

At this point we have had an overview of the most powerful Lean change management tool that exists. With the 9-Step A3 process, anyone can analyze the validity of a change opportunity or problem, determine its viability, and find the appropriate corrective action. The remainder of this book will drill down into the pieces of this tool and help you to get a better understanding of its components. However, there is still one key piece that is missing. And that is the cultural change that is necessary that will make an organization want to use the 9-Step A3 tool. Without a cultural "buy-in" that change is a good thing within the enterprise, none of these tools will be successful. Cultural change is the subject of the next chapter on change management.

4

The Art of Managing Change

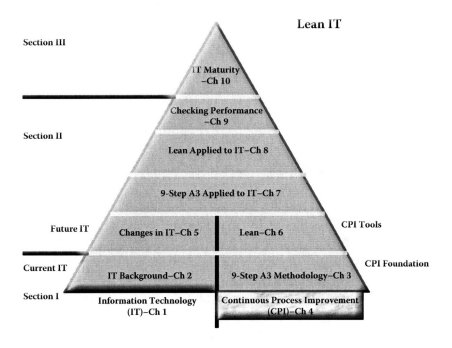

The definition of Insanity is continuing to do the same things and expecting different results.

Gerald Nadler and Shozo Hibino
Breakthrough Thinking: The Seven Principles
of Creative Problem Solving

A DISCUSSION OF CHANGE

One day a man was leading his donkey down the street. After a short distance, the donkey decided he did not want to travel any farther. He stopped in his tracks, put his rump on the ground, and would not budge. The man tugged at the donkey's rope and tried to coax it along to get up and walk. The coaxing soon turned to name calling and threats involving glue factories. The donkey did not move. A neighbor was passing by and stopped to help the frustrated donkey owner.

"The only way you are going to get that donkey to move is by talking nice to it," the neighbor advised. Indignantly the donkey owner challenged his neighbor to see if he could do any better with the stubborn critter. The neighbor picked up a two-by-four that was lying by the side of the road and proceeded to give the donkey a swift, hard wallop right between the eyes. Then he pulled on the rope softly and asked the donkey to get up. The donkey immediately stood up and followed the neighbor down the street.

"Didn't you say I should talk nice to the donkey?" the donkey owner protested.

"Of course! And I did," said the neighbor, "but first I had to get his attention."

Sometimes we managers are like donkeys. Sometimes we need to be hit by a two-by-four on the side of the head before we will start paying attention. Often "change" brings out the donkey in all of us. Remember:

Change and Innovation are not stifled by the way things are
But by the way we incorrectly perceive things

Change is as old as time and as leading-edge as the future. Even the rate at which changes are occurring is changing. But as prevalent as change is, we often want to resist it with all the effort we can muster.

Let us contemplate the two sources of changes:

1. The changes that come from us
2. The changes that happen to us

Treating the second source of change first, we need to be prepared for changes that will happen to us. We need to watch for these changes and manage them into opportunities. This brings us to another thought:

It does not matter how far
in front of the pack you are,
If you are not moving fast enough,
you will get run over.

Change is innovation; it is developing leading edge competitive strategies; it is moving forward. Remember (this goes along with the previous thought):

It does not matter how fast you are moving,
If you are not moving in the right direction,
You will never achieve your goal!

The first type of change, change that comes from us, requires us to originate the change. We are required to come up with the changes. For some managers, this type of change is a little harder to manage because of the effort involved in creating the changes. It suggests that we need to find and generate our own opportunities for change, our own innovations. This is harder to achieve because most organizations tend toward bureaucracy, which suppresses change. Too many organizational structures are motivated by measurement systems that stifle and often punish change. We need measurement systems that motivate the discovery of change. The search for change opportunities can mean a structural reorganization as well as a mental reorganization of your enterprise.

This book focuses on systems that will facilitate both types of change. It also discusses how your organization needs these changes, not only to stay ahead, but also to survive in a competitive environment. The purpose of this book is to help you become a leader who can help your organization manage optimal change in your IT organization and in the greater enterprise. Its goal is to motivate you to find and implement positive changes in a goal-oriented direction and to turn you into a leader who motivates and directs changes. Finally, the purpose of this book is to help you become world class.

To get the most out of this book, carefully read the Preface, Introduction, and all the chapters. What you are doing is hunting for ideas. Mark the ideas that fit you best, and, after reading the book, reread those ideas that impressed you the first time through. Then search for ways to implement these ideas into your management style. The last step in the use of this book is to TQM (Total Quality Management) the review process by repeating this process every six months to one year. As your goals and job function "change," so will the information and tools you need to help you through the change process. Reviewing this book regularly will help you reanalyze your position and put it into perspective, both for you individually, and for you within your role in the company as a whole.

> The single greatest power in the world today is the power to change. . . . The most recklessly irresponsible thing we could do in the future would be to go on exactly as we have in the past ten or twenty years.
>
> **Karl W. Deutsch**
> *Professor of International Peace, Harvard*

MODELS FOR CHANGE

There are numerous models for implementing change, from the slow and systematic, such as Total Quality Management (TQM), to the fast and radical such as Process Reengineering (PR). There are models that motivate change through their measurement process, and there are measurement systems that discourage change. Correctly implemented change models give us an entirely new focus on what change can do for us.

When we manage change, rather than letting change manage us, our focus becomes global, technology oriented, flexible, and customer responsive. We need to focus on competitive, customer-oriented areas of change.

The author has spent many years dealing with technology transfer to industrial settings all over the world. One of his favorite questions to ask is, "How do you deal with change and innovation, such as the implementation of new technology in your environment?" Another question he often asks is, "How do you motivate innovation?" Many answers are similar to this: "Innovation is great and we like it, as long as it has already been tried somewhere else." The attitudes of most people in response to these questions are similar to:

> The innovator makes enemies of all those who prospered under the old order, and only lukewarm support is forthcoming from those who would prosper under the new.
>
> **Machiavelli**
> The Prince

Innovation is seldom rewarded, and only in the case of extreme success is the innovator thanked for his or her risk-taking. The result is a fear of innovation and change, as shown in the following model where we see that time causes change to occur, which builds uncertainty, which causes fear.

$$\text{Time} \Rightarrow \text{Change} \Rightarrow \text{Uncertainty} \Rightarrow \text{Fear}$$

We need to conquer the fear by demonstrating that the model can be changed to one where time causes change which is viewed as an opportunity for innovation.

$$\text{Time} \Rightarrow \text{Change} \Rightarrow \text{Opportunity} \Rightarrow \text{Innovation}$$

Change is forced upon us through problems and errors, but problems and errors are also the seeds of opportunity and innovation. A world-class manager (WCM) focuses on the opportunities rather than the problems. Problems and errors bring the opportunities to our attention, but the WCM will resist solving the problem and will prefer to focus on the opportunity for change. Alone, these statements sound idealistic. However, what this really means is that problems or errors occur because there is some basic need that is not being taken care of properly. The "problem" can be solved by measuring and identifying the root source of the problem more effectively. The "opportunity" to fix the root cause offers us the chance to build a better mousetrap that avoids the cause of the problem. One example of this is the creation of Post-it notes, which started as a problem (attaching notes to a letter, book, or report without damaging it the way staplers or tape do). The problem was converted into an opportunity (develop a new adhesive that allows for easy removal), and the opportunity has now been translated into a major product and market segment.

We need to establish an environment of motivated innovation within our organizations by removing the fear of change. We need to FOCUS on innovation in our enterprises, and this can only be achieved with properly motivated changes.

Small companies and countries, which are often the companies and countries that are innovating, are upsetting large companies and countries, which tend to be slow to move. For example:

1. If you want process innovation, where do you go? For a long time Japan has demonstrated its international competitiveness through its ability to reduce production lead times and production costs. The Japanese were considered small at one time.
2. If you want to introduce a new product into the market quickly, where do you go? Taiwan has become the time-to-market innovation leader.
3. Minimum cost and maximum flexibility steel production has been taken over completely by the small steel companies in the United States which have, for a long time, been successful in beating out the big guys, both foreign and domestic, in competition and quality.
4. And the examples go on endlessly.

We have defined world-class management in terms of the style of management, and the role of change. Let us next take another look at world-class management, this time addressing the role of innovation and creativity.

INNOVEERING

A world-class IT organization is an innovative, creative, goal-oriented organization. A world-class manager motivates the positive innovative and creative thinking process referred to as *innoveering,* which means, "creatively innovated changes." Changing, just for the sake of changing, only creates turmoil. Changing, to move positively forward toward a goal without sacrificing the integrity of the organization, is world class.

Recently the topic of creative thinking has become very popular. Books such as *Breakthrough Thinking: The Seven Principles of Creative Problem Solving* and *A Whack on the Side of the Head* have stressed the importance of imagination in the change process. For example, von Oech stresses the need for creativity to discover new solutions to problems and to generate new ideas when old ones become obsolete. Stephen R. Covey, in his book *The Seven Habits of Highly Effective People,* focuses his second habit on creativity. Peters, Waterman, and Austin, in their search for eight common characteristics of excellent companies, focus on employee innovation within the corporate value system.

Innoveering is innovative change engineering. It is change that uses technology, integration, and innovative strategies and focuses on a continuous improvement model. Again, change, in and of itself, is not necessarily good. We need positively directed, goal-oriented, innovative, creative change. Then we have innoveering. That is when we become world class.

One of the best examples of innoveering is the Toyota Just-In-Time production system. Just-In-Time (JIT) is a production planning philosophy developed in Japan that focuses on waste minimization through inventory reductions. But JIT did not exist before being developed by Toyota. JIT was not copied; it was innoveered. Here is a brief summary of the story.

It was post-World War II, and Japan was trying to rebuild its industry. The Japanese tried copying Western (primarily United States) production methodologies, which were considered the best in the world, but they soon encountered four problems:

1. The Japanese lacked the cash flow to finance the large in-process inventory levels required by the US batch-oriented production systems.
2. The Japanese lacked the land space to build large US-style factories
3. The Japanese did not have the natural resource accessibility that the United States had.
4. Japan had a labor excess rather than a labor shortage, which meant that labor efficiency systems were not very valuable.

The Japanese innoveered these problems into opportunities. They realized that their competitive problem was a process problem, not a product problem. They proceeded to copy product technology and worked diligently to innovate *process technology* oriented around materials efficiency rather than labor efficiency. The result was the flow-through JIT production methodology for which Toyota has now become famous. But Toyota will be the first to admit that it was not easy. Toyota officials scoff at United States attempts to copy JIT after two or three years of implementation. They will readily say it took them 30 years to develop JIT. But they got into this position one innoveering change at a time.

The result was that the Japanese "Leaned" out their process. They built smaller factories (about one-third the size of their United States counterparts) in which the only materials that were in the factory were ones on which work was currently being done.[1] In this way inventory levels were kept low, investment in in-process inventory was at a minimum, and the investment in purchased natural resources was quickly turned around so that additional materials were purchased. The focus was on materials (inventory) efficiency rather than labor efficiency.

But the Toyota innoveering process has not ended. It continues, focusing on Lean-oriented changes and improvements, both in the product and in the process areas. Toyota continues its innoveering through a continuous improvement process referred to as *waste elimination*. The company views waste as anything that does not add value to the product. Waste can occur in labor, materials, machinery processes, or any other aspect of the company. Toyota's Lean strategy focuses on the following seven key areas of waste elimination:

1. Waste of overproduction—reduced set-up times, process synchronization, visibility
2. Waste of waiting—balance uneven workloads
3. Waste of transportation
4. Waste of processing—why is the product made?
5. Waste of stocks—inventory reduction
6. Waste of motion—motion for economy and consistency
7. Waste of making defective products

Toyota is determined to continue to improve. Innovative change is constant. Integration involving all levels of employees is critical.

However, we in the United States, or any other part of the world, are past the point of trying to copy Japan. We need to innoveer beyond what we can copy from anyone if we are to stay competitive. As long as we are playing copycat, the best we can ever do is to get caught up; and that is just not good enough! The only way we can get ahead is by innoveering. The Japanese will only stay ahead as long as we, by focusing on copying rather than innoveering, allow them to.

---

[1] This statement is a little idealistic. In reality, the Japanese work with single-digit batch sizes (one to nine units), whereas US batch sizes can range in the hundreds of units. For each batch, only one item in the batch is worked on at a time; the rest of the batch is inventory. Therefore, a batch of 100 units creates a continuous, ongoing inventory of 99 units. Unfortunately, the batch is often not being worked on and is just idle inventory. This batch size difference between the United States and Japan creates a tremendous difference in inventory levels.

HOW DO WE MANAGE CHANGE?

The biggest struggle in learning to manage change is identifying where, when, and how to begin. One purpose of this book is to give you the answers to these questions.

1. "Where do we begin?"—With you, the reader!
2. "When do we begin?"—IMMEDIATELY.
3. "How do we begin?"—By carefully laying out a "Lean" plan for innovation and change. This plan is developed by:
   A. Deciding on a focus or a vision for our change efforts
   B. Developing strategies for change that focus on our vision
   C. Solidifying each of the strategic areas around the vision (here we discuss how each of the strategies is defined and implemented):
      a. Quality vs. productivity
      b. Global management
      c. Timely technology
      d. Integration and measurement
      e. Value-added processes
      f. Training
   D. Discussing the characteristics, abilities, and traits that a world-class manager should use to motivate innoveering, including a discussion of the specific change tools available to the manager:
      a. Change models
      b. Management traits
      c. Management skills
      d. The role of teaming
      e. The integration of the manager in the enterprise
      f. The manager, the enterprise, and the environment
      g. The changes that affect the manager and the enterprise through time
   E. A wrap-up of whether or not you are working toward becoming world class.

Let us move forward. Let us learn about **world-class management** which uses goal-oriented, positive-change leadership to motivate and direct the change process. Let us evolve into effective masters of the change process.

Let us change, innovate, and improve ourselves, our family environment, our working environment, and our enterprise.

THE PEOPLE

Do we know anyone who resists change? We probably see them every day, every time we look in the mirror. So where does this stubborn streak come from? TRADITION! The greatest resistance to change comes from what we already know, and from what we already believe. Just look at the small child who is not yet hindered by tradition. The child will learn and believe anything. I am not asking you to be gullible, I am asking you to be open minded, like the little child. Learn and understand, before you hurry up to condemn.

Change is especially hard for managers. As we have learned from our quotes, the only thing certain in life is change. But we do not want change to happen to us, we want to utilize and control change to our advantage. A well-known anonymous axiom is:

> People like things to change, but they do not like to be changed.

Stated differently, this means that people like it when changes occur, if the changes are benefiting them. However, people do not like changes imposed upon them.

Federal Express (FedEx), a Malcolm Baldridge Quality Award winner, is the brainchild of founder and CEO Frederick W. Smith, who virtually invented the air express industry. The key focus of the FedEx quality program is to achieve 100% customer satisfaction through continuous improvement and change. The continuous improvement process involves the customer in the change process through a survey-feedback-action (SFA) program.

FedEx has based its quality program on three precepts, the first being:

> Customer satisfaction starts with employee satisfaction.

In order to make this precept effective, FedEx has implemented a program called the Guaranteed Fair Treatment Program (GFTP). The aim of the GFTP process is to maintain a truly fair working environment, one in which anyone who has a grievance or concern about his or her job, or who feels mistreated, can have these concerns addressed through the management chain, all the way to Fred Smith if necessary.

FedEx considers their employees as their most important resource and wanted to provide a fair and equitable process for handling grievances. The GFTP philosophy provides an atmosphere for employees to discuss their complaints with management without fear of retaliation. An employee is given seven days to submit a grievance, after which time management has ten days to respond. If the employee does not agree with the manager's decision, the employee has seven days to appeal the decision up the chain of the review process.

A key element of the GFTP program is that managers get evaluated from both directions, from the top down, and from the bottom up. The manager's boss evaluates the manager's ability to implement change through innovation and improvements. The manager's subordinates evaluate the manager's responsiveness to the needs of the employees. A manager must receive favorable ratings from both directions in order to get promotions, raises, or bonuses.

From the FedEx quality program we see both an emphasis on change (SFA) and an emphasis on the management–employee relationship aspects of how change is implemented (GFTP). I have had FedEx managers tell me that FedEx is the most challenging, while at the same time the most rewarding company they have worked for, because the FedEx program puts the manager into the challenging position of attempting to install change, while at the same time not allowing the manager to be excessively forceful in implementing the change. The best managers would be those who implement change by giving the employees ownership in the change. This reminds me of another quote (I hope you have enough wall space for all these pearls of wisdom):

I want workers to go home at night and say, "I built that car."

Pahr G. Gyllenhammar
Chairman, Volvo

At this point we have identified that change is inevitable; therefore it is important that change becomes a part of our life and the life of our enterprise. We have also learned that change management needs to be participative, not forced.

So what do managers need in order to be effective motivators of change? What do we need to do to become world class? Here is a list of nine key points:

1. The Circle
2. Goal Setting
3. Leadership
4. Values and Ethics
5. Add Value to Society as an Enterprise
6. Continuous Learning
7. Innovation and Change Creation
8. Measuring/Rewarding
9. Stakeholders

Let us take a look at what these mean:

Key Point 1: The Circle

> You can make more friends in two months by becoming interested in other people than you can in two years by trying to get other people interested in you.
>
> **Dale Carnegie**

The circle is a term used to refer to a group of cohorts working together to achieve a common purpose. There is the quality circle, the management circle, the family circle, etc. In order to be a world-class manager we need to define our "circles" and make them as effective as possible. And the first "quality circle" in the life of any manager should be the "family circle."

The family is the first and highest priority circle in anyone's life. The family is your reward structure; it is the reason for working; it is what brings quality into your life. A disastrous home life destroys your work life, whereas, a disastrous work life does not seem so bad if you have a successful home life. It is self-destructive to let your work life become your reason for living, because "change" can destroy that life in minutes.

Another important circle of everyone's life is the society they are members of. In the United States, success is measured by individual earning power. In most other parts of the world, success is measured by one's ability to contribute to society. Far too many of us are not contributing (adding value) to society; rather, we are only self-gratifying (trying to fill our own pockets at the expense of others). In reality, your own personal value is only increased by how much you work with and help others.

The third circles of importance in each of our lives are the circles we work in. These circles are often referred to as teams. But are we really forming teams, or are we just grouping? A group is a collection of people thrown together in a room for the propose of making some kind of decision. A team is a collection of individuals that have worked together over a long period of time and have found a creative harmony and synergy working between them. In teams we find sharing, not domineering, like we do in groups.

In all the circles in our lives, we need to establish quality. The author is bothered by terms like "quality time" when referring to our children, as if this phrase is some kind of excuse for spending as little time as possible time with them. There is no "quality time" if an insufficient amount of time is spent, whether it is with the children, the spouse, or the employees. The biggest challenge of a world-class manager is to prioritize his or her time in order to achieve "sufficient quality time" to the extent that it will make a difference in the circles that are important in the manager's life.

Key Point 2: Goal Setting

> IF YOU DO NOT KNOW WHERE YOU ARE GOING,
> YOU WILL PROBABLY GET THERE

If you cannot see a target, how can you expect to hit it? Unfortunately, far too many people and companies go through life without targets to shoot at. They let changes affect the road they take in life without ever identifying why they are traveling down the road to begin with. If we are only working for money, then money is all we will ever get out of our work. However, if we work for some greater purpose in life, like a successful family and marriage, or to be the best at whatever it is we do, we will find that the money comes along as a nice added benefit, and we will have a lot more fun doing it.

We need goals at many levels and at many time frames. Here are just a few areas in which we should have long-range (20 years +), mid-range (5 years +), and short-range goals (1 year):

Family goals—Sit down with your spouse and children and determine what is important to the family.

Personal goals—What do you want out of life? What will give your life meaning?

Career goals—Where do you want your career path to go, realizing that most people change professions on the average of about four times during their life?

Corporate goals—What does your company's business plan state the goals of the company are?

Job function goals—What do you want to accomplish in the job function you are performing? Are you hoping to build better relationships in your "circles"? Do you want to become world class? Far too often I have encountered people that, when asked, "How do you decide what areas of your job function you want to perform well in?" give an answer like, "Whatever it takes to keep my job and get a raise." My reaction is, "I'm glad you don't work for me!"

After you have collected these goals together, you now need to do two things:

A. Develop an action plan that will work toward the achievement of the goal.
B. Communicate the goal to all involved. For example, I have encountered numerous organizations where the corporate goals are pretty much kept secret amongst top management. Yet the employees are expected to achieve this goal, which they cannot see. You can never overcommunicate your goals.

Your personal success needs to be defined. Even playing the lottery requires the selection of numbers and the purchasing of a ticket. Most other goals, like family or work goals, need a more clearly defined game plan. There are several good books out that help in the development of life and work goals. Let me highly recommend the Covey and von Oech books if you have not already read them.

Recently we have discovered a slight reversal of the goal setting process in organizations. Previously the trend has been for the vision and mission of the organization to be defined by top management. However, we have seen a reversal of this process where the employees are defining the mission of the organization, and then a top management vision statement is developed from this employee-defined mission statement. For example, Tridon-Oakdale brought a team of managers together and had them establish the mission statement of the corporation. This gave the managers an ownership in the goals and an added commitment in achieving the goals of the organization.

Goals define success. Without defined goals, how will you ever know if you were successful in achieving them?

Key Point 3: Leadership

The most powerful teaching tool has always been the power of example. Every parent has learned this principle the hard way. The children always seem to "do as I do" rather than "do as I say." And the principle is just as correct in the workplace as it is in the home. If you are grumpy about changes that are being passed down to you, do not expect your employees to be motivated by changes you pass to them.

Mojonnier highlighted that top management's role in fostering positive organizational change fell into four essential elements:

1. Create a detailed vision statement. This is done with a vision and mission statement, and a strategic plan.
2. Assess your current organization's total culture. This is done as part of the core competency assessment and vision statement process.
3. Develop a strategy for achieving your vision.
4. Establish midpoint goals to motivate your troops. Midpoint goals are part of the short-term strategy and the plan of operation.

Leaders run their organizations using respect, whereas the manager drives his/her people by intimidation. Just ask yourself what environment you would prefer to work under. Then give your employees the same level of respect. A leader positively influences and motivates changes. An effective leader helps to position an organization for success.

Key Point 4: Values and Ethics

The integrity of men is to be measured by their conduct, not by their professions.

Junius

Values are the glue that keeps us together. We need a value system built on virtue, integrity, and ethics if we want to grow old feeling good about what we have done in life, whether it was successful or not. It would be helpful to have Webster's define some of the terms we are using here:

Values: Worth; that which renders anything useful or estimable; excellence

Virtue: Worth; moral excellence

Integrity: Completeness, wholeness; honesty, sincerity, etc.

Ethics: Standards of right and wrong; system of conduct or behavior; moral principles

The lack of ethics and integrity in the United States has resulted in such a large number of non-trust systems, and often the non-trust systems are more complex than the systems they are trying to protect. A non-trust system is a system established specifically for the purpose of making sure that the original system is not abused. For example, antifraud systems like financial auditing systems exist in every organization.

From a psychological perspective, we develop non-trust systems to protect us from having others do to us the types of things we are likely to be guilty of. Otherwise, we probably would not have thought of setting up the non-trust system to begin with. It has been estimated that the non-trust systems that are in existence are costing us more than if we were to just eat the occasional fraud that might happen. Our lack of ethics and integrity leaves us morally and financially bankrupt.

We can get into a long, drawn-out discussion about whether a bribe is less ethical than a tip. However, it really is not that complicated. If we feel good about ourselves, and if the results leave everyone involved in a win–win situation, chances are the activity was ethical. It is like pornography; we have difficulty defining it, but we know it when we see it.

Internationally, ethics gets very confusing. The United States citizens seem to see everything in life as black or white in the decision making process, whereas most of the rest of the world sees a lot of gray. For example, Malaysia and Thailand were having a border dispute in a region where a large reserve of oil was discovered. The American solution would be to battle it out. But the Malaysia–Thailand solution was to draw a line around this region and to bring in a private developer to develop the oil reserve. Then both countries shared equally in the profits. So which is more ethical, the US way or the Southeast Asian way?

We are obsessed with the legalistic. The handshake is worthless because our legal system has declared it as worthless in court. Technically (on the books), the handshake has value, but in practice (in the courts) it has no value. This has destroyed our ability to trust each other. If it is not written down and spelled out in fine print, it legally does not have to happen. This brings to mind another interesting ethics example from the Southeast Asia region. North America and Southeast Asia both have a free trade agreement. For North America it is the North America Free Trade Agreement (NAFTA), which binds three countries, the United States, Canada, and Mexico, in a free trade arrangement. For Southeast Asia it is the Association of Southeast Asian Nations (ASEAN) that has formed a trade agreement involving six countries: Indonesia, Malaysia, Singapore, Philippines, Brunei, and Thailand. The NAFTA agreement is 2,200 pages long, whereas the ASEAN agreement, with twice as many countries, is 16 pages long. It is pretty obvious that our lack of integrity and ethics has made us obsessed with non-trust systems. Show your employees a little more trust and respect, and they may surprise you by trusting and respecting you in return.

Levi Strauss considers the company's most important asset to be its people's "aspirations." This organization has become famous for combining strong commercial success with a commitment to social values and to its workforce. They developed the famous "Levi Strauss Aspirations Statement," a major initiative that defines the shared values that will guide both management and the workforce. This Aspirations Statement is reshaping occupational roles and responsibilities, how performance evaluations are conducted, how training is handled, and how business decisions are made. This aspirations statement, and its focus on the people and their values, is credited with making Levi Strauss a flexible and innovative company. More importantly, Levi's has an exemplary record on issues like workforce diversity and worker dislocation benefits.

The Levi Strauss aspirations statement focuses on people that are proud and committed; an environment where opportunity exists to contribute, learn, and grow; a place where people are respected, treated fairly, listened to, and involved. It talks about friendship, balanced personal and professional lives, and "to have fun." Levi Strauss' Aspirations Statement identifies a new type of leadership focused on:

New behaviors—directness, openness, honesty, commitment to the success of others, willingness to acknowledge problems and errors.
Diversity—diversity in age, sex, ethnicity, etc. in the workforce.

Recognition—financial and non-financial recognition for individuals and teams that contribute to success. "Recognition must be given to all who contribute."

Ethical management practices—Leadership that epitomizes the stated standards of ethical behavior.

Communications—Employees must know what is expected of them and receive timely and honest feedback.

Empowerment—Leadership should increase the authority and responsibility of those employees closest to the products and customers.

Levi Strauss has demonstrated the importance of people values and ethics and has taught that these values are critical to world-class management (leadership) status.

> A company's values—what it stands for, what its people believe in—are crucial to its competitive success.
>
> **Robert Haas**
> *CEO, Levi Strauss & Co.*

Key Point 5: Add Value to Society as an Enterprise

Being world class refers to two opposite but equal activities:

Eliminating all waste
Focusing on value-added functions

Identifying non-value-added activities on a factory floor has always been relatively easy. But this section is focusing on people. This section is focusing on us. How do we identify non-value-added activities in our own lives? Here are a couple of guidelines:

Does the activity help achieve any of the goals that we established?
Does the activity we are engaged in benefit society or our family (our "circle") in any way?

Let me give you a story that will help your understanding of this concept. One time when the author was working overseas he got into a discussion of "What is wrong with the United States?" Outsiders always have lots of ideas about what we should be doing differently. However, sometimes, as in this occasion, these insights are thought provoking. The answer was, "The economic decay of the United States is being caused by the fact that you are graduating more and more non-value-added graduates than you ever did before." So the author asked for a definition of a non-value-added graduate. The answer was, "Anyone working in a profession that does not increase the output of the nation." Individuals who work at professions that simply move the existing resources of the nation around, placing some of them in their own pocket during the process, without adding any value, are non-value added.

On a smaller scale, a lot of the activities we are engaged in only benefit our own pocketbooks on the short term. We are not creating anything of value to society. And if we are engaged in activities that add no value, then we are actively engaged in creating waste. In our private or corporate life, we need to refocus our activities, and the activities of our employees, on adding value. We need to eliminate non-value-added processes. We need to add value to society as an enterprise, through the efforts of our employees.

Key Point 6: Continuous Learning

> It is only the intellectually lost who ever argue.
>
> **Oscar Wilde**

There are a million quotes that could be selected for this section. The author picked the Oscar Wilde quote because he believes that you cannot learn if you have your mouth open. You can only learn if you have your ears open and your mouth closed. In this section, what we need to focus on is people learning, or sharing between each other.

We have a lot of people that are filled with good ideas, and we need to listen to them if we are to benefit from their wisdom. Additionally, being world class means realizing that improvement only comes about if we open ourselves to changes in the form of new ideas. We need to learn new ideas in order to incorporate them into the things that we do. World class is giving everyone in the organization opportunities and the appropriate motivation to learn and develop through education and training. We need to build a learning organization.

In this category belongs the need for self-renewal, otherwise known as vacation time. Creativity is improved when pressure is removed, and drudgery is relieved. Employees need time to "get away from it all," and they need to be encouraged to get away from it often.

Key Point 7: Innovation and Change Creation

Chaos often breeds life when order breeds habit.

Henry (Brooks) Adams
American Historian

World class is breaking out of the ritualistic, mundane things in life. It is realizing that:

Professionals built the *Titanic*—amateurs the Ark.

Frank Pepper

Just because an employee is not an expert at something, does not mean he/she does not have worthwhile and valuable ideas. And the expression of all ideas, whether by the professional or the amateur, needs to be encouraged. The trick in managing ideas is to not allow egos to get wrapped up in the innovation process. Every idea has to be considered valuable, even if you really think it stinks, because you are a prejudiced observer, and you do not want to discourage the creative process. Additionally, you need to be careful that the "professional" is not offended if the ideas of an amateur contradict his or her professional opinion.

World class is also the ability to laugh at yourself.

For the wisdom of the world is foolishness with God.

1 Corinthians 3:19

The books by the authors von Oech, Nadler, and Hibino stress this point as being critical in the creative process. Allow your ideas to be destroyed. In fact, do your best to destroy them yourself. How else can you be sure they are foolproof?

Employees need to be involved in and to understand the change process in order to effectively initiate changes. This process is explained in many models similar to the following:

1. Identifying/recognizing the need or opportunity for change is the first step in making any change.
2. Define the problem or opportunity that needs to be addressed.
3. Identify the current company position relative to the problem—you need to know where you are before you can determine where to go.
4. Identify alternative destinations.
5. Identify the desired destination.
6. Define a road map to get from where you are to where you want to be.
7. Unfreeze the organization and prepare it for change—this includes training and empowerment.
8. Change implementation.
9. Stabilize the organization under the new order—this includes the establishment of a new feedback mechanism that will monitor the new status quo.

With an understanding of the change process, organizations and their employees are now ready for innovation and change creation.

This brings us to a critical element of world-class employee innovation and creativity. We need to develop empowered work teams that work together as teams, not groups, and have the authority to implement their ideas. Creativity works best through the synergy of effectively developed and empowered teams. We saw an example of this earlier in this chapter in the Levi Strauss story. Another example can be seen if we look at the Antilock Braking Systems Division (ABS) of General Motors in Dayton, Ohio (formerly Delco Products Company). They did what they were told would be impossible, they developed a world-class empowerment program, called employee involvement (EI), starting with a traditional United Auto Workers (UAW) contract. A covenant was established between the union and ABS. They felt this was the only way they would be in business in two years and that this was necessary if they were to stay even with the continuous improvement programs of their competitors.

ABS supervisors were given new responsibility based on communication and training. A system of trust was established with the workers. This trust is at the core of the EI program. Based on this trust, a set of guiding principles was established which included:

1. We will establish and maintain innovative systems that can compete in a world-class climate.
2. We will enact cultural change necessary to insure profitability and job security at the Dayton plants.
3. We will run the business as a joint activity seeking contribution from and sharing benefits with all.
4. We will provide mechanisms and incentives which promote continual improvement in customer satisfaction.
5. We will approach this covenant as a living agreement, continually reviewing our progress and proactively adjusting to maximize our competitiveness.

ABS truly has a world-class empowerment program that is worthy of study and emulation.

Key Point 8: Measuring/Rewarding

Innovation and creativity need to be stimulated. Recently the author was working for a company that had an elaborate Total Quality Management (TQM) program. TQM is a tool for implementing change into an organization. However, the TQM program was failing, and they could not understand why. I reviewed their measurement system and quickly learned that they were evaluating employee performance based on units per hour efficiency. Bonuses were being paid when employee performance exceeded the standard rates of production. Why would any employee want to spend time implementing changes through TQM if:

1. They were being rewarded based on historical rates and historical methodologies.
2. There was no reward for implementing the change.
3. Changes would, in effect, decrease their productive output on the short term and therefore reduce their bonuses.

Explaining point number three in more detail, when change is implemented, the first thing that happens is a drop off in efficiency. As we see in Figure 4.1, we are working away at a certain level of output, and immediately, as change is introduced, a loss of productive output occurs. Then, through the process of the learning curve, employees slowly become better and better at the new process, eventually achieving a new, higher

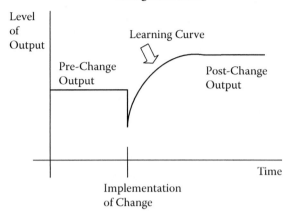

FIGURE 4.1
Change function.

(hopefully) level of output. Unfortunately, in the short term, efficiency suffers, and so does the paycheck.

This company was asking the employees to sacrifice their paycheck in order to implement changes. The company did not want to lose output, but they still wanted the employees to initiate improvements. They were giving the employees mixed signals, and the signal that motivated the employees the most was the paycheck signal.

To understand this concept completely, here is a "hang on your wall" statement:

> A Measurement System Is Not for Management Information.
> It Is for Motivating Employees.

Any measurement system that exists simply for "accounting purposes" or "information-gathering purposes," is probably countereffective and is destructive to the company's ability to achieve its goals. A measurement system that is not focused on the goals of the organization is distracting employees away from the goal of the organization. This is because, whether it is true or not, employees believe they are being graded by what they are being measured on. And they will focus their performance in those areas that they are being measured on. So, select your measurement systems wisely; they may motivate the wrong actions.

Key Point 9: Stakeholders

As a world-class manager you need to identify all the PEOPLE involved in your circles. These include:

Family
Friends
Employees
Peers
Bosses
Customers (both internal and external)
Vendors
The community

Taking it from the top, can you satisfy your spouse's needs? Are you making him or her happy? Do they enjoy being with you? How about your children? How about your friends?

Do the people you work with come to you for help, or do they avoid you like the plague? Do your customers consider you as someone that can get things done, or as someone that puts things off, or blames things off? Do you identify both your immediate customer (the one you pass product to) and your final customer (the eventual end user) as some who need satisfaction?

Do you get involved? Do you look to help out your fellow employees and your family and friends, or do you avoid challenging situations? Are you willing and eager to change? Simply put:

ARE YOU WORLD CLASS?

In Hawaii the native Hawaiians have a sense or feel for each other that supersedes the words of the conversation. They refer to this as the "*ha*," which can best be translated as the "breath of life." When Westerners started to visit the islands, that "*ha*" did not seem to be present. The warmth of the relationship, which is a comfort or a knowing where the other person was coming from, was not there. The Hawaiians started to refer to these people as "*ha-ole*" which is translated "without *ha*." They felt distanced from these foreigners because of this lack of feeling for each other. This lack of feeling created a lack of trust. Today's manager must learn what Hawaiians already know well. They must learn to have "*ha*."

Without people who are willing and motivated to change, there can be no world-class organization. It is "We the People," which includes you the manager, your bosses, your employees, your customers, and your vendors, that make your enterprise world class, and just like Steve Young or Michael Jordan, you cannot get there without your "circle."

Man is here for the sake of other men.

Albert Einstein

SUCCESSFUL CHANGE MANAGEMENT

The business functions of an organization have, for a long time, focused on stability rather than on change. For example, IT, accounting, finance, personnel, the legal department, most upper management, and marketing would love nothing more than to have a steady stable growth. Operations, traditionally, would love a perfectly balanced operation with just the right amount of inventory, just the right workforce, and no problems. However, one of the competitive lessons we have learned is that stability breeds failure. If we try to stay where we are, we will get run over. Just ask the American passenger railroads.

Operations have learned the new competitive lesson, which the remaining functional areas are just waking up to:

The only way to competitive success
is through change management!

The function of the IT organization has changed from one of seeking stability to one of managing change: change in products and their components, change in demand, changes in resources and their availability, changes in operational technology, changes in competitive product makeup, changes in competition, etc. And this is a lesson that needs to be shared with the remainder of the organization.

Continuous improvement (change) is critical in a global economy. Changes should include:

Product innovation
Process innovation (what the Japanese are good at)

Technology innovation
Time-to-market innovation (Taiwan)
Marketing innovation
Etc.

But uncontrolled and undirected change can be as disastrous as no change. What we need is to be able to stay ahead of the change process. We need to change ourselves faster than external forces have a chance to change us. We need the change to be focused on a target. And we need to maintain our corporate integrity as we institute change.

To manage change we need to incorporate change models into our business which facilitate the change process. Some of these change models, like Total Quality Management and Process Reengineering, will be discussed in this chapter. The problem with the change models is that they are often thought of as another fish story.

Company (and change models) are like fish—after three days they stink.

Most change models contain some label of quality in them. Quality has become the flag behind which the battle for continuous change is most often fought. But "quality" does not fully define everything that is wanted by the change process. Nevertheless, terms like Total Quality Management (TQM) and Quality Functional Deployment (QFD) are change processes that look like they focus on quality; however, in reality, like all change models, they focus on positive, goal-direct changes in all the measurement areas including quality, productivity, efficiency, financial improvements, etc. Before we discuss some of the change models specifically, let us first discuss some of the psychology behind change.

SOME MODELS FOR CHANGE

Remember the change function shown in Figure 4.1. We start by operating at a steady-state, stable level of operation. Then change is implemented. The level of efficiency drops, and a new learning curve kicks in. The growth stage is the most critical stage, because this is the time when many changes are dropped. If the growth stage takes too long, the change may be dropped. This is what has occurred with Florida Power & Light, with the United States Air

Force, and in many JIT, TQM, or Process Reengineering implementations. Unfortunately, when a change process is dropped during the growth phase, the organization wastes the growth that has occurred and which would have brought them to a newer, higher level of performance. Most United States companies do not want the growth stage to take more than a few months, and often, with larger changes, this short time span is impossible.

Eventually, after the growth has leveled out, we start to see a return on the change process. The final phase of the learning curve has kicked in. Finally, we have once again achieved stability, hopefully at a higher level of output.

Another model for IT change shows us as having to work our way through the phases of growth in a change process. They are:

Phase I—Recognize the need for change. Invest in new technology or processes. Motivate innovation and experimentation. Encourage learning about new technologies just for the sake of learning.

Phase II—Learn how to adapt technology beyond the initial sought-after results. Keep the ideas flowing.

Phase III—The organization goes through structural changes as process changes occur.

Phase IV—The broad-based implementation of change occurs, affecting all aspects of the organization.[2]

The Japanese model for the continuous change process is called kaizen. It suggests that every process can and should be continually evaluated and continually improved. The primary focus of the improvements is on waste elimination, for example:

Process time reductions
Reducing the amount of resources used
Improving product quality
Etc.

Kaizen problem solving involves:

---

[2] Gibson, Cyrus F., and R. L. Nolan, "Managing the Four Stages of EDP Growth," *Harvard Business Review*, January-February 1974, page 76.

1. Observing the situation
2. Defining the changes that need to take place
3. Making the changes happen

One example of the implementation of the Kaizen continuous improvement process is at the Repair Division of the Marine Corps Logistics Base in Barstow, California. Utilizing the Kaizen focus on continuous improvement, they ran a pilot project, and they received results like:

63% reduction in final assembly lead time
50% reduction in work-in-process inventory
83% reduction in the distance material traveled
70% reduction in shop floor space requirements

The process and the system which controls it represent the real problem facing business today, not the people who work within the boundaries set for them by management. . . . The improvement efforts and their supporting systems must be directed at the process and not the individual.

H. James Harrington

The focus of any change model should be on continuous improvement in the broad sense which includes both the Japanese incremental step perspective and the United States breakthrough business process improvement perspective. The need for change is rarely argued. What is different between the various change models is the speed of the change and the depth at which the change occurs. This is where the Japanese and the United States change methods bump heads. In comparison;

The United States
    Fast change.
    Fast return on investment.
    Radical and dramatic change.
    Deep and extensive changes feeling the need to redefine the whole
        process.
    On the hunt for the one big change that will fix all the problems.
    Process Reengineering which is characterized by rapid/radical
        changes and focuses on change implementation and high-tech
        solutions.

Slower to get around to making any change, because the change process is viewed as being so extensive, dramatic, and upsetting. The result is that there is more resistance to any change process.
Change ownership belongs to some change "hero" who quite often is the CEO.

The Japanese
Slow change.
Long-term return on investments.
Carefully planned out changes.
Think the change through carefully.
Plan before you implement.
Small step changes.
Total Quality Management which focuses on analysis and planning in the change process and technology-that-fits-the-situation solutions.
The change process is much less painful, because change involves small, undramatic steps. Therefore there is much less resistance and stepwise, small changes are continuously occurring.
Change ownership is shared.

Einstein was asked, if he had 60 minutes left in which to save the world, what would he do. His answer was that he would spend 55 minutes planning and 5 minutes implementing.

Some methodologies have attempted, unsuccessfully, to combine the Japanese and United States approaches by suggesting the implementation of "radical changes without being radical." What they are hoping to do is implement big changes without upsetting the entire organization and developing enormous resistance to the change process. But no one has come up with a good way to accomplish this (probably because no one really understands it). So the conflict between the two changes approaches remains. Total Quality Management (TQM) continues to be viewed as "too slow" by the United States, and Process Reengineering (PR) continues to be viewed as "too destructive" by the Japanese.

Let us now consider the several of the most popular models for change (excluding the Lean management process which will be discussed in detail later in this book) and discuss the procedures used in implementing these models. The ones we will consider are:

I. Quality Functional Deployment (QFD)
II. Total Quality Management (TQM)
III. Process Reengineering (PR)
IV. ISO 9000
V. Change Acceleration Process (CAP)
VI. Kotter
VII. USAF 8-Step

Some of these models only supply us with focus areas of improvement. Others have specific procedures for the change process. The models should not be thought of as exclusive in that, if you pick one, you cannot use any of the others. Rather, they should all be considered as stepping stones toward your development of your own successful change program. Later, in our discussion of Lean management, we will also see that these change management programs can be used as tools in your Lean management collection of tools.

Model I: Quality Functional Deployment (QFD)

QFD is the implementation of a continuous improvement process focusing on the customer. It was developed at Mitsubishi's Kobe Shipyards and focuses on directing the efforts of all functional areas on a common goal. In Mitsubishi's case the goal was "satisfying the needs of the customer." Several changes were instituted in order to accomplish this, such as increased horizontal communication within the company. One of the most immediate results was a reduced time-to-market lead time for products.

QFD systematizes the product's attributes in a matrix diagram called a house of quality and highlights which of these attributes is the most important to a customer. This helps the teams throughout the organization focus on their goal (customer satisfaction) whenever they are making change decisions, like product development and improvement decisions.

QFD focuses on:

1. The customer
2. Systemizing the customer satisfaction process by developing a matrix for:
   a. Defining customer quality
   b. Defining product characteristics

    c. Defining process characteristics

    d. Defining process control characteristics

3. Empowered teaming
4. Extensive front-end analysis which involves 14 steps in defining the "house of quality"

    a. Create and communicate a project objective.

    b. Establish the scope of the project.

    c. Obtain customer requirements.

    d. Categorize customer requirements.

    e. Prioritize customer requirements.

    f. Assess competitive position.

    g. Develop design requirements.

    h. Determine relationship between design requirements and customer requirements.

    i. Assess competitive position in terms of design requirements.

    j. Calculate importance of design requirements.

    k. Establish target values for design.

    l. Determine correlations between design requirements.

    m. Finalize target values for design.

    n. Develop the other matrices.

Implementing and using QFD is not an easy process. A great deal of commitment throughout the company is required for the process to be successful. The results of effective implementation are well worth the effort. Reduced product development time, increased flexibility, increased customer satisfaction, and lower start-up costs are just a few of the benefits that can be expected through the use of QFD.

Gregg D. Stocker

QFD has been widely recognized as an effective tool for focusing the product and the process on customer satisfaction. A lot has been written on the subject. However, as discussed earlier, QFD is a Japanese approach to focused change and therefore focuses on extensive analysis, utilizing the philosophy that we need to:

Make sure we are doing the right things,
Before we worry about doing things right!

Detailed analysis through the matrices is time consuming, conceptual planning time is much extended by QFD. However, the overall design-to-market time should be cut because the design effort focuses on the most important areas.

Dave Henrickson

Model II: Total Quality Management (TQM)

Simply put, TQM is a management approach to long-term customer satisfaction. TQM is based on the participation of all members of an organization in improving the processes, products, services and the culture they work in.

Karen Bemkowski[3]

As mentioned earlier, Total Quality Management (TQM) focuses on careful, thoughtful analysis. However, the analysis should be creative, innovative, and innoveering oriented. The carefulness comes in when it comes time to implement. We want to make sure that we are implementing positive, goal-focused changes before we move a muscle.

TQM is much broader than QFD. TQM is a change model that is enterprise wide. Some people define TQM in general terms as simply making the "entire organization responsible for product or service quality." This is the way TQM is defined in many organizations, and it encompasses everything and anything. However, there is also a specific, proceduralistic version of the definition of TQM. Perhaps the best way to understand TQM is to look at this TQM process. Afterward we can consider the significance of TQM and its process.

The TQM Process

TQM is not just a tool, it has an entire philosophy about how businesses should be run. The philosophy of TQM is filled with ideas and attitudes, like:

Attitude of desiring and searching out change
Think culture—move from copying to innovating
Do the right things before you do things right
Focus on the goal

[3] Bemkowski, Karen, "The Quality Glossary," *Quality Progress*, February 1992, pages 19–29.

Measurement/motivation planning
Top to bottom corporate strategy
Companywide involvement
Clear definition and implementation of quality
Education, training, and cross training
Integration and coordination
Small, step-by-step improvements

In TQM, the philosophy behind change is that we become excited about changes. We look for opportunity to change, especially because change should mean that we are becoming better. To be a TQM organization is to become an organization that wants to be the best and realizes that there is always room for improvement.

The success stories for TQM can be found in settings all over the world. TQM success is measured in terms of the successful implementation of change. This change can take the form of the implementation of new technology, or the correction and improvement of old technology. Often, a successful TQM project results in the ability of employees to work more effectively together. The result is that the measurement of TQM success tends to be an internal success story, and not always externally comparable.

In operationalizing TQM there are several points of importance. They are:

The TQM coordinating team (quality council)
The three "P" teams—cross-functional teams
The TQM project implementation steps
Training programs
Measurement and feedback
Showcasing
Team building
Systematic problem solving (SPS)

TQM implementations start with a *coordinating team,* often referred to as a quality council. This is a team composed of high-level corporate leaders from all the functional areas. This team is appointed by the CEO and operates under his/her direction. The CEO takes an active part in directing the activities of the team. This quality council is then responsible for organizing and measuring the performance of the other TQM teams within the organization. It oversees the installation, training, performance, and measurement of the other teams. This team focuses specifically on the corporate goal/vision and definition of quality.

The quality council will organize three different types of teams referred to as the cross-functional *three "P" teams*. These teams are process, product, and project teams. The process teams are ongoing, continuous improvement teams set up at different levels of the organization. They look for improvements in the organization's functioning processes. These teams should be composed of both "insiders" and "outsiders." The insiders know and understand existing functions and operations. The outsiders challenge the status quo.

The second of the three P teams are the product teams. These teams are cross-functional but focus on a specific product, product line, or service. They are customer and vendor interface teams that are specifically oriented toward the development of new products and the improvement of existing products. Their life span is the same as the life span of the product they represent.

The third of the Three P Teams are the project teams. These teams are limited-life teams set up to specifically focus on a specific project, like the construction of a new plant, or a computer installation. These teams may be the result of a specific process or product that is being targeted, or they may be set up to research something that the general management team is interested in developing or improving.

The TQM project implementation steps are as follows:

Identify problems (opportunities).
Prioritize these problems.
Select the biggest bang-for-the-buck project.
Develop an implementation plan.
Use operations research and MIS tools where appropriate.
Develop guide posts and an appropriate measurement system.
Training.
Implementation.
Feedback—monitoring—control—change.
After successful project implementation and on-going status, repeat cycle.

The first function of the team is to identify their function and charter. If you are on one of the three P teams, your team's charter is laid out for you by the quality council. If you are the quality council, this charter is laid out for you by the CEO and is aimed at the focused goals of the organization.

After understanding their charter, the team will then search for and identify problems that exist and that prevent the organization from achieving this charter. The word "problems" has a negative connotation. A better wording would be to say that we search for "opportunities for improvements." We are not just trying to correct negative effects, we are looking for techniques or tools that will allow us to become better and possibly even best.

Next we take these problems (opportunities) and prioritize them based on their effect on the charter of the team (which should be focused on the goals of the organization). We do a type of ABC analysis (80-20 rule or Pareto principle) to determine which change would have the greatest effect. Then we select the biggest bang-for-the-buck project and develop an implementation plan for this project. This implementation plan needs to contain guideposts that are based on an appropriate measurement systems that points the team toward achieving its charter. The book *Breakthrough Thinking* does an excellent job of discussing opportunity identification techniques.

Training of the implementers and users is critical, or else the planned project is doomed to failure. This training makes future users comfortable with the changes. It also offers a bit of ownership because the planned users will now feel comfortable with the changes.

The next step is implementation. The implementation should be a trivial process, if all the planning and training steps are preformed carefully. Part of the implementation is the installation of feedback, monitoring, and control mechanisms, as laid out in the implementation plan. Careful monitoring allows for corrective changes to occur whenever necessary.

After successful project implementation, and seeing that the ongoing status of the project is functioning correctly, the team repeats the implementation cycle, looking for more new opportunities for change. If this process is performed correctly, the list of change opportunities should become longer with each iterative cycle. This means that your team is now open for newer and broader opportunities for change.

Training programs need to exist before and after project selection. In the before case, the TQM team needs to understand what tools are available to them. This training would involve an understanding of tools and techniques. Initial training could include programs in areas like operations research/management science tools and techniques, motivational/philosophical training, semitechnical and technical education, the operation of the systems approach, etc.

Training programs after TQM team implementation should be user training focused on the changes being implemented. These programs need to be defined (and often conducted) by the TQM team which has the best understanding of the change.

The issue of *measurement and feedback* has already been discussed several times. It is critical to realize the motivational role of the measurement system and that the proper implementation of an effective feedback (reporting) mechanism will assure the ongoing success of the changes implemented.

Showcasing is one of the best techniques for expanding implementation time. Here we use the quality council to develop and implement a "sure thing" TQM implementation project. What we are doing is attempting to demonstrate the successes of an organization-wide TQM implementation. In the United States, where short-term, quick benefits need to be demonstrated, showcasing becomes a critical part of the selling job of TQM.

There are several types of *teams* required in a TQM environment, like the quality council and the three P teams. Understanding which teams need to be organized is just a small part of the problem of team construction. A much bigger problem is making the team effective. For example, team training and team relationship building are necessary for effective interaction and for the synergy of the team.

One of the biggest downfalls of a TQM system, as far as the United States is concerned, is the implementation lead time of changes (how long it takes to implement the change). Often a decision is made to change, and then we start worrying about how to implement the change. *Systematic Problem Solving (SPS)* is a procedurization of the change process. There is no one perfect model for how this change procedurization should be set up. However, there are a few good examples. Let us take a look.

Systematic Problem Solving (SPS) at AT&T

AT&T uses a methodology that includes tasks which are to be performed in four distinct stages. These are:

Ownership—Team responsibility for the activities.

Assessment—Clear definition of the process.

Opportunity selection—Analyze how process problems affect customer satisfaction and rank them in order of opportunity for improvement.

Improvement—Implementing and sustaining the change.

The ownership, assessment, and opportunity selection stages are considered management processes. Then, based on the overall four stages, grouped under management and improvement, AT&T developed a series of steps called the management and improvement steps, which focus on the SPS process. They are:

1. Establish process management responsibilities.
2. Define process and identify customer requirements.
3. Define and establish measures.
4. Assess conformance to customer requirements.
5. Investigate process to identify improvement opportunities.
6. Rank improvement opportunities and set objectives.
7. Improve process quality.

Note that the AT&T process follows the Japanese model closely. More detailed information is available about this process through publications put out by AT&T.

> Quality excellence is the foundation for the management of our business and the keystone of our goal of customer satisfaction. It is therefore our policy to:
>
> - Consistently provide products and services that meet the quality expectations of our customers.
> - Actively pursue ever-improving quality through programs that enable each employee to do his or her job right the first time.
>
> **Robert E. Allen**
> *Chairman and CEO, AT&T*

The Good News about TQM

TQM was the first stage of realizing that we need to take "quality" (or the search for positive change) out of the quality department and make it a company-wide program. TQM is a strategy toward continuous, corporate-wide change, it is a philosophy, it is an operationalized process, and it is a fad. It becomes a fad if we expect quick results and become disenchanted because we are not "like the Japanese" in the first two months. TQM is a strategy toward becoming leading edge and world class.

TQM differs from the other quality tools like TQC (Total Quality Control), SPC (Statistical Process Control), or ILQC (In-Line Quality Control) in that it is not as focused on a specific procedure. Rather, TQM is a continuous search for problems (opportunities) that eliminate waste and add value in all aspects of the organization, and makes these improvements one small step (5% to 10% improvements) at a time.

In spite of its slowness, TQM has been internationally extremely successful. References to TQM and its leadership abound. TQM is a very specific process improvement step in a drive toward world-class status.

Model III: Process Reengineering (PR)

> Wisely, and slowly. They stumble that run fast.
>
> **William Shakespeare**
> *Romeo and Juliet*

Process reengineering (PR) is rapid, radical change. It is not downsizing, which many companies are using it for, rather it is work elimination. It is positive, growth-focused change, looking for opportunities to eliminate waste and improve value-added productivity, often through the implementation of technology like image processing.

In 1994, $32 billion was invested in reengineering, of which 2/3 of the reengineering projects will fail. Why? Because the change process builds up a lot of resistance, thereby forcing its failure. Secondarily, because PR is used as an excuse for downsizing, often the downsizing results in the elimination of critical employees that will be difficult to replace. The downsizing process was not carefully thought through, it is rushed through, and the results are disastrous.

However, just like any tool, there are some extremely positive aspects to Process Reengineering that make it worthy of our attention. The first is that PR focuses on change implementation at the top of the corporate hierarchy. It generates more of a top-down change culture. And it focuses on process-oriented changes.

PR's focus on the process emphasizes that the process, not the products, holds the secrets for the most dramatic improvements within an organization. PR focuses on an "all-or-nothing proposition that produces impressive results." PR is defined as:

The fundamental rethinking and radical redesign of business processes to achieve dramatic improvements in critical, contemporary measures of performance, such as cost, quality, service, and speed.[4]

The principles of reengineering include:

Organize around outcomes, not tasks.
Have those who use the output of the process perform the process.
Subsume information processing work into the real work that produces information.
Treat geographically dispersed resources as though they were centralized.
Link parallel activities instead of integrating their results.
Put the decision point where the work is performed, and build control into the process.
Capture information once and at the source.

The three Rs of reengineering are:

Rethink—Is what you are doing focused on the customer?
Redesign—What are you doing? Should you be doing it at all? Redesign how it can be done.
Retool—Reevaluate the use of advanced technologies.

Some characteristics of Process Reengineering include:

Several jobs are combined into one.
Workers make the decisions—empowerment.
"Natural order" sequencing of job steps.
Processes with multiple versions depending on the need.
Work is performed where it makes the most sense.
Checks and controls are reduced.
Reconciliation is minimized.
"Empowered" customer service representative.
Hybrid centralized/decentralized organizations.

Like TQM, the focus of the reengineering effort is the team. Departments are replaced by empowered process teams. Executives change their role

[4] Hammer, M., and J. Champy, *Reengineering the Corporation*, Harper Business, New York, 1993.

from scorekeeper to leaders. Organizational structures become flatter. Managers change from supervisors to coaches.

PR has the following steps or phases in the change management process:

1. Mobilization
   Develop a vision.
   Communicate the vision.
   Identify champions and process owners.
   Assemble the teams.
2. Diagnosis
   Train and educate.
   Current process analysis.
   Select and scope the process.
   Understand the current customer.
   Model the process.
   Identify problems.
   Set targets for new designs.
3. Redesign
   Create breakthrough design concepts.
   Redesign the entire system.
   Build prototype.
   Information technology.
4. Transition
   Finalize Transition Design.
   Implementation Phase.
   Measure Benefits.
   The Role of Communication to Avoid Resistance.
   You cannot overcommunicate.

PR has many of the procedural characteristics of TQM; however, it is more philosophical than TQM. PR focuses on being competitive via the rapid and the radical, and it stresses the process as the key to successful change.

Model IV: ISO 9000

ISO 9000 is a model that is often advertised as a model for change and improvements. However, the ISO 9000 process tends to focus on stability. The ISO standard was developed by Europe in an attempt to standardize the quality of goods coming into Europe. For many companies it seemed like a trade barrier attempting to keep companies out of Europe. The reason why is because ISO 9000 focuses on quality in the internal process of the organization, assuring that what was designed is what is actually built. It does not focus on the customer. Nevertheless, the ISO standard has become an international standard for quality and systems performance that many companies are utilizing.

ISO has come to define quality, not change. It is a set of standards for quality based on two main foundations:

Management responsibility and commitment to quality which should be expressed in a formal policy statement and implemented through appropriate measures

A set of requirements that deal with each aspect of the company activity and organization that affects quality

ISO can be used as a standard for improvement, and the ISO quality system requirements can become the focus of change systems. In this way, ISO criteria can be integrated into a change process. However, in and of itself, ISO is not a change model, as frequently believed.

Model V: Change Acceleration Process (CAP)

MainStream Management, a leading Lean consulting company, uses an adaptation of the Change Acceleration Process (CAP) model (see Figure 4.2) for their change model. This was adapted from the model used by GE, which was originally developed by Noel Tichy and which is similar to Kotter's change model. The model indicates several stages of change in the change management process. The first section is about selling the Lean change process to the organization. The second section focuses on sustaining the Lean change process so that the process continues even after the facilitator discontinues his oversight activities.

In the selling phase of the CAP change model, we first see the creation of a need for Lean within the organization. This is accomplished by the identification of a need for change. We ask questions like: What are some large problem areas, or strong growth needs, that the organization has? Without the proper change management driver, the problem may never get resolved or, worse yet, it may not get resolved in the best

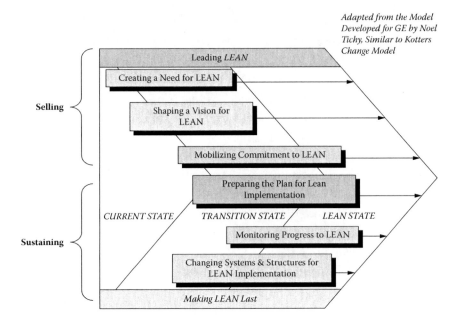

FIGURE 4.2
Change Acceleration Process (CAP) Model.

possible way. We need to identify opportunities where the Lean change process can be effective.

Shaping the vision for Lean requires us to look first at the goals of the organization and then to look for ways to help the organization optimize those goals. This requires a Lean look at both growth opportunities and at error correction opportunities.

Mobilizing the commitment to Lean requires team identification and team building. It means identifying and setting aside the resources that will be required for this effort. It means getting management commitment to facilitate the Lean effort.

Preparing a plan requires timelines and schedules. It requires a plan of attack with specific steps. It requires the agreement and support of management all the way to the top so that there are no delays or disruptions to the change management process.

Monitoring the Lean process requires checkpoints and measures. It requires checklists and action items to make sure that all the concerns of the team are resolved and that action is taken on every identified activity or task.

Change systems and structures for Lean implementation require ownership and commitment from top management down to the workers on the floor. The teams need to own the change process and need to be excited about it so that they will maintain it even after the facilitator leaves. This is about putting structures and systems in place that continue to facilitate the Lean change management process by having all the necessary people properly trained in order to avoid future doubt or confusion about the process. And it is about making Lean a lasting cultural change within the organization.

Model VI: Kotter

Another change model that can be used is the one designed by Kotter (see Table 4.1). This model can be used in place of the CAP model and has also been found to be a very effective tool. It contains an eight-stage process for implementing major change and can be seen in Table 4.1.

Model VII: USAF 8-Step

One last model for change, which has been heavily utilized by the United States Air Force (USAF) and many other organizations throughout the Department of Defense (DOD), is referred to as the "8-Step Problem Solving Model." Its roots come from several change management methodologies:

a. The PDCA (Plan, Do, Check, Act) change management steps of the Toyota Production System (TPS)
b. The DMAIC (Define, Measure, Analyze, Improve, Control) steps that are a part of the Six Sigma change program
c. The OODA Loop (Observe, Orient, Decide, Act) which was developed in the 1950s by Col. John R. Boyd of the USAF.

Each of the eight steps of the 8-step problem solving tool can be mapped into one of the steps from these above methodologies. The 8-step problem solving tool successfully integrates TPS, Six Sigma, and the OODA loop together, taking the best of each methodology. A summary of the eight steps is shown in Figure 4.3. The advantage of this tool is that it serves several purposes:

1. Problem analysis
2. Problem strategic alignment
3. Problem root cause identification

TABLE 4.1

The Eight-Stage Process of Creating Major Change

1. Establishing a sense of urgency
   Examining the market and competitive realities
   Identifying and discussing crises, potential crises, or major opportunities
2. Creating the guiding coalition
   Putting together a group with enough power to lead the change
   Getting the group to work together like a team
3. Developing a vision and a strategy
   Creating a vision to help direct the change effort
   Developing strategies for achieving that vision
4. Communicating the change vision
   Using every vehicle possible to constantly communicate the new vision and strategies
   Having the guiding coalition role model the behavior expected of employees
5. Empowering broad-based action
   Getting rid of obstacles
   Changing systems or structures that undermine the change vision
   Encouraging risk taking and non-traditional ideas, activities, and actions
6. Generating short-tem wins
   Planning for visible improvements in performance, or "wins"
   Creating those wins
   Visibly recognizing and rewarding people who made the wins possible
7. Consolidating gains and producing more change
   Using increased credibility to change all systems, structures, and policies that do not fit together and do not fit the transformation vision
   Hiring, promoting, and developing people who can implement the change vision
   Reinvigorating the process with new projects, themes, and change agents
8. Anchoring new approaches in the culture
   Creating better performance through customer- and productivity-oriented behavior, more and better leadership, and more effective management
   Articulating the connections between new behaviors and organizational success
   Developing means to ensure leadership development and succession

4. The development of an action plan for improvements
5. A reporting mechanism used to report back on the improvement process
6. A plan for sharing the knowledge gained with other organizations

The entire 8-step report is made on one sheet of A3-sized paper and is referred to as an A3 report. Using this as the standard, all commanders and leaders follow the same lexicon and understand what they are looking

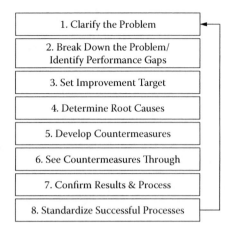

FIGURE 4.3
Air Force 8-Step Problem Solving Process.

at. The process eliminates the "death by PowerPoint" that many of the continuous improvement reporting processes are plagued with.

The A3 tool is a Toyota Production System tool. The 9-step A3 tool that was discussed in Chapter 3 is a combination and integration of several of the change tools already discussed, including the Air Force's 8-step problem solving tool and the CAP model. It also integrates some tools that have not yet been discussed like breakthrough thinking and concept management.

UNDERSTANDING CHANGE

The one thing that is consistent in life is change. You can either manage the changes, or you can let them manage you. And Lean focuses on continuous improvement, or managed change. Within organizations we find those that:

- Resist change—Unfortunately we find these people everywhere. They require conversion to the process. They need to feel confident and secure that the change will not detrimentally affect their role or station in life. And they are the primary reason why change management is important.
- Lead change—This is often a small number—These are early adaptive and innovative people.

- Walk a balancing act between the opposing forces to see which is going to win—This is where the majority of a company's employees have positioned themselves. These people are focused on their longevity and permanence and on being politically correct. They need tools like Lean to give the change process structure and to show them that a meaningful and appropriate end state is coming out of the change process.

The success of Lean has created a competitive pressure and therefore a desire for fence-sitting companies to want to realize the benefits of Lean. Knowing that Lean works, these companies now look for change management opportunities and tools that can help their cultures adapt. They want to succeed in transforming themselves using Lean principles. The Lean process tries to generate a change transformation process that results in a sustainable change culture.

Traditionally, the change management process has been top down, with top management owning and driving the change process. With Lean, all employees become owners of the change process. It is the working ranks that determine what changes need to be made, and management's role becomes one of being the provider of resources and tools so that the desired changes can rapidly take place. With Lean management, everyone becomes a thinker and a creator.

Figure 4.4 shows how an IT organization needs to drive itself toward Lean maturity. Without an aggressive, leadership-directed change management program, the initial enthusiasm for Lean can stall out. This is where change management kicks in and reinvigorates it toward world-class success. Without a structured change management approach, the enterprise culture can become disillusioned, and Lean will become just another passing "top management fad" without any meat.

Some organizations try to drive Lean down through edicts. However, with Lean we learn that:

- Lean is not something you do to people.
- Lean is a set of tools that you provide people with in order to meet the organization's objectives.
- Lean is best served when it is supported from the leadership and then is implemented by the workforce.

Some of the common pitfalls found in the implementation of a Lean change process include:

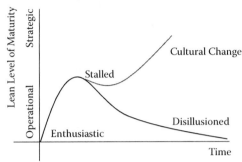

FIGURE 4.4
Lean IT maturity.

- Organizations think of Lean as an event and not a new business paradigm.
- Organizations fail to seek expertise regarding cultural change and development.
- Organizations maintain "business as usual" while attempting broad transformations.
- Organizations tend to avoid dealing with active or passive resistance in their leadership group.
- Organizations do not always "get the right people on the bus." The process owners need to be involved, not just staffers.

In order to achieve Lean leadership success, the organization needs to:

- Establish a clear vision and direction
- Create top-down support (dealing with detractors)
- Engage in bottom-up implementation
- Manage complex change
- Run interference—eliminate or reduce barriers
- Continually train and add momentum

IT PITFALLS

This book has highlighted and will continue to demonstrate that IT is plagued with numerous pitfalls. A solid change management structure based on Lean will strengthen and build a world-class IT organization. Some of the unique challenges that affect IT include:

- An IT change management team needs a different set of tools to analyze and identify root causes, because they are often looking for these causes in a world of bits and bytes.
- IT programming resources are not always readily available because IT is maxed out with other projects. Unfortunately this argument can be heard in many areas of the organization where change is critical. But within IT, it takes on unique characteristics. IT management needs to be convinced that the time spent developing a 9-step A3 report will be worth the lessons learned.
- The acceleration of technology causes server hardware to change, desktop computers to change, upgrades to operating systems, the addition of the latest ERP module, etc. These changes have forced the IT organization to build a monster that it cannot get its arms around. It is afraid to make any changes. Deconstructing this environment without wrecking the business can be an enormous challenge. This reinforces the need for a high-level look at the organization to see how this environment can be restructured and managed. This is just the type of project that Lean is exceptionally good at.

IT is often described as "having to change all four tires on the Mercedes while driving at 80 miles per hour." It is hard to improve this environment on the run. It is critical that every IT organization build a change management process built on Lean so it can review, evaluate, and reconstruct (if necessary) its processes. Without this evaluation it will become impossible to manage the next revolutionary wave, which may possibly be even more complex and have a larger impact on IT than the PC or the Internet.

CASE STUDY: WIPRO (CONTINUED)

Continuing the Wipro story from Chapters 2 and 3, we find that Wipro performed an extensive amount of work to develop a proprietary framework

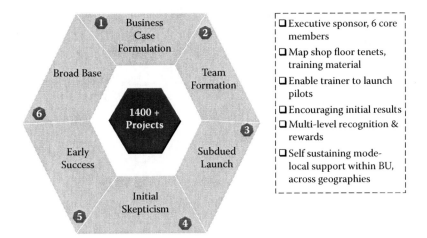

FIGURE 4.5
Methodology adopted for launching Lean at Wipro.

for productivity improvement. It required numerous iterations to come up with a framework that worked for them. Because the specific framework is a Wipro intellectual property, its details cannot be included here. The framework starts with the "as is" condition and performs a Lean process analysis, starting with defining the current state and looking for ways to eliminate waste and ultimately to streamline the process through an iterative continuous improvement process. The end result is a transformed IT application that incorporates value engineering.

Figure 4.5 shows details on how Wipro has developed a change management approach for launching Lean throughout the organization.[5]

SUMMARY

In conclusion, before change management and Lean transformation can achieve significant improvements, there must be an acknowledgement and commitment from the organization's leadership. There needs to be leadership acceptance throughout the organization that the current process that they are now running either does not, or in the future will not meet the needs of customers and therefore will not ensure the continued survival

---

[5] The figures used in this case study come from a Wipro presentation on Lean implementations created by Seema Walunjkar in the Wipro Global Delivery Organization.

of the organization. Once this acknowledgement is made, then we can get the organization committed to change. And with that commitment to change, Lean is the mechanism that will facilitate the change process.

Section II

Bringing Lean into
Information Technology (IT)

5

How Can Lean Help IT?

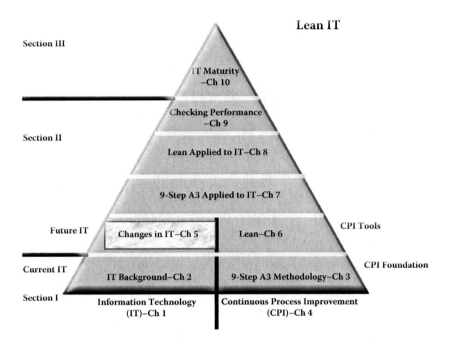

The way forward is paradoxically to look not ahead, *but to look around.*

John Seely Brown and Paul Duguid
The Social Life of Information, *HBS Press, 2000, p. 8.*

When asked to define Lean, most experts would reply with a definition like, "A systematic approach to identifying and eliminating waste (non-value-added activities) through continuous improvement by flowing the product at the pull of the customer in pursuit of perfection." Lean is a change management tool. It was developed by Toyota over 40 years ago to help them standardize on a methodology for continuous improvement. Since then Lean has evolved through numerous iterations, primarily in the United States where everything needs to be Americanized. The result is that the version of Lean being used in many organizations is vastly different from the original Toyota version.

Most adherents see their Lean implementations as something that is "only useful for manufacturing." However, the author sees Lean as a company-wide tool. Across an enterprise, Lean practices can be used in engineering, in the front office, in the back office, in R&D, and even in IT to improve operations by driving waste from existing environments. Lean can be effectively applied within the IT organization.

Lean is both a management philosophy and a change methodology. Its management philosophy stresses the elimination of waste. Lean does not focus on making anyone work harder, or like its Six Sigma cousin, also derived from Toyota's production system, reduce variation in vertical processes (see Technical Tool #16 in Chapter 6). Lean focuses horizontally across the value stream of an organization.

As mentioned previously in this book, Lean is a methodology that is focused on the elimination of non-value-added processes or "waste." The author has found that nearly all organizations have a value-added content of less than 5%, and occasionally he has found a value-added content of less than 1%. As mentioned earlier in this book, his experience shows that by eliminating non-value-added wastes it is easy to double the capacity, throughput, and output of the organization while simultaneously reducing backlogs (the inventory of IT), regardless of whether it is for a single process or for an entire IT organization.

LEANING IT

In a recent study by Capers Jones, he identified the key factors for software and IT project success and failures. These are summarized in Table 5.1.

TABLE 5.1

Reasons for IT Failures

No.	Risk Factor	Root Cause	% of MIS Projects Failing
1	"Creeping" requirements	Lack of well-defined user requirements and control	80%
2	Excessive "schedule pressure"	Inadequate scoping of the project and process	65%
3	Low quality	Poor design, inadequate testing, lack of processes	60%
4	Cost overruns	Lack of design, inadequate testing, low skill set	55%
5	Inadequate configuration management	Lack of version control and rigorous process for integration	50%

Source: Jones, T. C. *Assessment and Control of Software Risks*, Yourdon Press, 1994.

From this table it seems obvious that poor project definition (Cause #1, 3, 4, and 5) and poor scheduling/planning (Cause #1, 2, 3) are primary factors in IT failures. We need to take a closer look at the overall IT organization and see where these failures may be occurring.

A typical IT organization can be broken down into a set of processes, all supporting a company's business. These processes can be further broken down into Level 1 and Level 2 processes that can have the Lean methodology applied and can be seen in Table 5.2.[1]

Each of these processes in the chart titled "Typical IT Organization Processes" can be subjected to a Value Stream Mapping (VSM) exercise that allows individuals to see what is actually happening in their organizations and what is possible (for a detailed discussion of VSM see Technical Tool #2 in Chapter 6). The objective of the VSM activity is to identify large non-value-added activities that can be eliminated. Often we find that what we thought was valuable to our process is in fact "wasteful" to our process.

Another area for reviewing IT effectiveness, which is primed for waste elimination, includes the three implementations that occur with all IT

---

[1] This table was developed by the author when he was employed by Infosys and is part of a larger article titled "Lean on IT: Apply Lean Management Principles across the IT Organization," by David Spencer and Gerhard Plenert. Sections of this chapter referencing this chart discuss similar principles that were also included in this article.

TABLE 5.2

Typical IT Organization Processes

Level 1 Processes	Manage Customer Relationships	Manage Business-IT Value Portfolio	Discover Business IT Potential	Deliver Business Solutions	Operate Business Systems	Manage IT Architecture	Manage Supply
Level 2 Processes	Understand business needs and priorities	Strategic planning (long term)	Discover and evaluate opportunities	Manage program/projects	Application maintenance	Manage application architecture	Manage strategic sourcing model
	Business advisement	Annual business planning	Propose solutions	Manage requirements	Manage business systems performance	Manage data architecture	Manage suppliers
	Nurture and maintain relationships	Portfolio management	Evaluate business solution initiatives	Design	Client support (repeatable requests)	Manage standards	Resource planning
		Governance	Initiation	Integrate/customize	Production system support	Integrate emerging technology	
		Manage funding model		Build	Post-project auditing	Review project architecture	
				Test	System sunsetting		
				Deployment/post implementation			
				Monitor compliance			

projects. These three areas tend to be very ad hoc with no standardization. They include:

- Physical implementation—facilities, servers, workstations, mobile devices, etc.
- Technical implementation—software, data, applications, mobile devices, security, data warehousing, disaster recovery, etc.
- Business implementation—workflows/process mapping, training, support, documentation, etc.

Still another way to identify wastes in IT can be accomplished using workflow classification. The foundation of this tool is the Impact/Effort matrix (see Technical Tool #25 in Chapter 6), which focuses on work creativity and work repetitiveness. The purpose of this matrix is to classify two things:

1. Work to be performed
2. Workforce

Using Table 5.3, an IT manager would classify all the tasks that need to be completed. Additionally he or she would classify all the employees in the department and classify them into one or more of these quadrants. Then, as tasks arrive, the table will assist the manager in assigning the tasks. Additional Lean tools like prioritization of the tasks can also be useful.

It is the author's experience that IT organizations are notorious for reinventing the wheel, with numerous redundant activities in development, maintenance, and documentation. Across all of the 7 Waste categories, typical IT organizations provide many examples, as illustrated in Table 5.4 (see also the detailed discussion of the 7 Wastes, which is Technical Tool #1 in Chapter 6).[2]

---

[2] This table was developed by the author when he was employed by Infosys and is part of a larger article titled "Lean on IT: Apply Lean Management Principles across the IT Organization," by David Spencer and Gerhard Plenert. Sections of this chapter referencing this chart discuss similar principles that were also included in this article.

TABLE 5.3

Workflow Classification

	Unique Work	Repetitive Work
Creative Work	Quadrant #1: Creative and unique tasks	Quadrant #3: Creative but repetitive tasks
Routine Work	Quadrant #2: Mundane but one-of-a-kind tasks	Quadrant #4: Mundane and repetitive tasks

MEASURABLE BENEFITS OF APPLYING LEAN TO IT

When applying Lean to IT, there are four specific measures that should be used. These measures define the success or failure of the Lean activity. Specifically applied to IT they are:

1. Cycle time—Cycle time is the time it takes to run through the entire process. For example, in the Level 2: "Manage requirements" process, documentation activities can be reduced by applying documentation standardization techniques. The result would be an overall through-put increase and reduced cycle time.

2. Inventory—For IT, inventory means backlog. If the backlog of work for the IT department is measured in terms of months or even years, the IT department is out of control. The workload between employees or between departments should be balanced. One should not have a larger backlog than the other, or you cannot have smooth workflow through the organization.

3. Value-added content—A value-added activity is one that either (1) directly adds value to the final product, or (2) directly satisfies the customer (also see Acceptance Tool #1—Breakthrough Thinking/ Concept Management/Purpose Expansion). Using this definition, some meetings or phone calls are value-added, and some are not. Code development is value-added, but discussing coding alternatives may not be, especially when the decision for these alternatives should already have been part of a standardized work set (see Technical Tool #18 in Chapter 6). A measure of the value-added content of the value stream is a good measure of ongoing improvement efforts (see

TABLE 5.4

The 7 Wastes in IT

7 Wastes	Examples Found within IT
Overproduction	• Overproduction is where "just-in-case" work is done in anticipation of some upcoming event. In IT this occurs when we have some "down time" and we feel the need to keep people busy, so we generate documentation, or we code some mini-systems which in the end will never be used. Lean thinking would suggest that it is better to not use resources than to waste them on non-value-added efforts which consume additional resources like computer or database capacity.
Waiting	• Delays occur between activities. For example, between coding and testing or between test and documentation, because the resources are not ready to perform these functions. These are wastes that increase total cycle time.
Unnecessary transportation	• Transport in IT equates to the amount of time it takes to navigate through a series of applications in order to accomplish a highly repetitive task. This can show up within internal support systems, but it is prevalent everywhere.
Overprocessing	• The big problem in this area is a lack of standardization. A lot of time is spent reinventing the wheel. There are a lot of similar activities, and the lead time (set-up time) for reinventing the process should be eliminated.
Inventory	• In IT, inventory is backlog. The workload throughout the organization is not evenly distributed. Rather, it is assigned by some predefined "area of responsibility." The result is that some individuals have enormous backlogs, while others have none. Backlog is expensive in that it equates to reduced results and lost revenue. Often this is seen in documentation reviews, support team queues, and finally in development projects not able to be initiated due to resource (money, people) constraints.
Unnecessary movement	• The flow and movement of individuals can be extremely inefficient. Accessibility to tools, like files, documentation, etc., can cause an IT employee to spend a lot of time walking around, which is nonproductive waste. • In IT we also find inefficient "movement" of data within the "system."
Defects	• Defects in IT occur both in the area of bad code and in inadequate documentation. The question to ask is "Does the product being delivered (including the documentation) satisfy the needs of the customer?"

Technical Tool #2 in Chapter 6). The value-added content can never be declared as "good enough." There is always room for improvement.

4. Throughput—The measure of quality (from the customer's perspective), complete, on-time customer delivery on or before the customer's original requested delivery date. From an IT perspective, this could mean anything from a business application required by the business to a solution to a customer's problem.

Beginning with Level 2 processes, the author believes that IT organizations can identify and initiate Lean related activities to demonstrate success using Lean measures and improve Lean's ability to support the overall business, as illustrated in Table 5.5.[3]

Obviously the challenges listed in the table are a reality in the world of IT, and nearly everyone has experienced them. Sometimes it feels as if the IT masterminds intentionally build "obsolescence" and "obscurity" into their world to guarantee future employment. But that is another topic for another book. In this book we are exploring the application of Lean principles to IT in the hope that some of the delays and quality problems can be reduced or even eliminated.

Any, and probably all, of the resource areas identified in the tables in this chapter which are part of the IT world contain waste. Lean is the methodology that identifies the waste and then utilizes a bag of tools to attempt to eliminate this waste. The more waste is eliminated, the greater the value-added time, resulting in greater throughput, lower costs, increased capacity, and reduced cycle times. Utilizing Lean principles provides an IT environment that is more efficient and more responsive to the customer, and therefore more competitive overall.

We find ourselves in a world that is saturated with data and starved for information. This book contains simplistic IT and Lean ideas that have been demonstrated and have proven to be enormously effective. Most of them will fit to any organizational environment from commercial sector to government, but they are not all intended to fit perfectly in every environment.

Lean adapts itself easily to the world-class Capability Maturity Models (CMM) so commonly used in IT to define world-class status. A major shortcoming of the CMM evaluation process is that they do not measure

---

[3] This table was developed by the author and David Spencer when they were employed by Infosys and is part of a larger article titled "Lean on IT: Apply Lean Management Principles across the IT Organization," by David Spencer and Gerhard Plenert. Sections of this chapter referencing this chart discuss similar principles that were also included in this article.

TABLE 5.5

Lean Measures

Lean Measures	IT Process Area 1	IT Process Area 2
• Cycle time	• All Level 1 processes	• Business assessment • Discover and evaluate opportunities • Design • Build • Test • Deployment/post implementation • Application maintenance • Review project architecture • Manage strategic sourcing model
• Inventory	• All Level 1 processes	• Design • Build • Test • Deployment/post implementation • Application maintenance
• Value-added content	• All Level 1 processes	• All Level 2 processes can have waste in their methodology and procedures • IT systems are user friendly and easy to use • IT is accessible and transparent to all, and you do not need a computer guru (or your 7-year-old daughter) to explain it
• Throughput	• Deliver business solutions • Operate business systems • Manage IT architecture	• Deployment/post implementation • Application maintenance • Manage business systems performance • Client support • Production systems support • Post-project auditing • System sunsetting • Manage application architecture • Integrate emerging technology • Manage suppliers • Resource planning • IT software development is completed on time and at or below cost • IT hardware installations are executed on time • IT hardware does not crash regularly

time, for example time to implement, time to change, or cycle time for the IT process. Lean drives an organization toward the world-class characteristics of the CMM and simultaneously accelerates their implementation and integration throughout the IT organization.

Lean opposes making changes based solely on financial measures. A focus on financial metrics causes inappropriate, nonstrategic activities to take place. Instead, the author's experience is that successful organizations make changes based on operational measures, and when these operational measures perform well, the financial measures easily follow suit. Do not get the cart (financial measures) before the horse (operational measures). For IT, this could mean operational measure improvements such as:

- Shortened lead time between project inception and initiation
- Increased customer on-time delivery performance
- Increased customer satisfaction from business teams
- Improved quality of products and services provided to internal and external customers
- Reduced cost of quality of products and services provided
- Reduced cycle time between project start and completion
- Increased capacity for other needed tasks that traditionally would be delayed
- Increased employee satisfaction
- Reduced cost of administrative processes

In summary, Lean has a history of excellent performance results. These results have been demonstrated in both production and nonproduction environments. Lean's capability to improve organizations can also be applied to a company's IT organization to reduce its own wastes and drive its own efficiencies. Given the challenges of improving product innovation, optimizing worldwide workforces, and constant cost pressures, IT organizations need to consider the improvement opportunities that are available to them through the use of both the Lean management philosophy and the Lean change methodologies. Superior IT organizations can no longer stay competitive in a rapidly changing twenty-first century organization. IT needs to join the Lean continuous improvement wave.

Those with tunnel vision [believers that technology is the end-all, be-all] condemn the foolishness of humanity for clinging to the past. Those exasperated by tunnel design tend to cheer the downfall of new technology as if it were never likely to come to any good.

> **John Seely Brown and Paul Duguid**
> The Social Life of Information
> *HBS Press, 2000, p. 3*

HOW IT IS CHANGING[4]

In this new economy of budget constraints we need to look at industry from several perspectives. These constraints are the driving factors that shape the thinking of CIOs (chief information officers) and the key enablers that allow CIOs and their teams to reshape IT operations. These concerns/trends are discussed below, as a precursor to optimizing IT operations:

- *Flip the spend*—Typically maintenance expenditures account for 70% to 80% of IT budgets, while development expenditures have dwindled to 20% to 30%. Flipping this expenditure allows IT directors and CIOs to move from being an IT cost center to a key enabler of revenue growth.
- *Smart and responsive execution enablers for business strategy*—The role of IT, as an operational tool, is simply incomplete. IT operations need to play a key role in enabling the execution of business strategy. Without responsive systems and operations that can adapt, we are left with poorly executed strategies. Responses to changes in market trends and new product bundling require rapid operationalization. IT operations are the key element to enabling these rapid responses.
- *The connected enterprise ecosystem*—Most enterprise operations include outsourced elements. In most cases, operational elements within an enterprise are poorly connected. Running a query against both temporary transactional data and permanent long-lived master data is almost impossible in most companies. This complicates many decision making processes. When this is extended to outsourced operations, the problem grows exponentially. In large, heavily siloed

---

[4] Portions of this section are taken from the thoughts of Romit Dey.

enterprises, these problems again get magnified. Connected enterprises that resolve these barriers to information connectivity are more agile in meeting market needs and keeping their customers happy.

- *Faster innovation cycles*—If you can "flip the spend" and create more responsive IT operations, the next issues come in delivering innovative value. This may require different forms of IT operations for different industries. For example, in pharmaceutical industries this could take the form of excellent search capabilities for a myriad of combinations of complex formulas. Or in the software industry this often takes the form of the intelligent processing of customer feedback shaped into "product feature set" recommendations.

But how should IT operations be successful in this world of concerns/trends? What are the "tools" that allow IT companies and CIOs to make their way through the jungle of differing requirements achieving increasing agility? Some suggestions include:

- *Next generation collaboration portals*—This is not a question of Web 2.0 or even Web 3.0. It is a new model of what portals can do. Product companies enable better collaboration among designers of different product lines. EMS (electronics manufacturing services) vendors and manufacturing companies allow their OEMs (original equipment manufacturers) to peer into the processing of their orders through firewalls. Large enterprises are creating a thin veneer over their federated BI (business intelligence) tools and warehouses. Online retailers are presenting different access/products to different customer categories offering a common look and feel. All of this is accomplished through what is called the "operating system for the enterprise" or the next generation portal.
- *Information enterprise resource planning systems (ERPs)*—Transactional ERPs are the basis for keeping the enterprises' lights burning. These perform the key operational activities that tie together elements of various processes. However, agility in decision making, thereby meeting customer demands, requires that we think of a new dimension in resource planning information. These include data warehouses, BI tools, MDM (master data management) systems, data set integrators, and data quality tools. How do they come together in a coherent

whole? What is it that ties them together? How do they help realize a better-connected and more agile enterprise?

- *ERP consolidation/iterative renovation*—ERP systems have gone through several different cycles. Traditional systems have given way to large single-instance ERP systems, and now federated ERP systems with best-of-breed packages are again making a reappearance. The number of CFOs (chief financial officers) that will sign up for large, expensive transformational upgrades is dwindling. Many will pay for extending the functionality of their existing systems through small upgrades and updates.
- *From enterprise architecture (EA) governance to governability*—Most IT operations end up wasting tremendous amounts of time and money due to poor decisions on the funding of projects and initiatives. A typical reaction is to create an enterprise architecture (EA) or program management (PM) body. Some groups typically form an advisory body to deal with such issues. Unfortunately, just focusing on the decision making process without understanding the overall technology and architecture across the enterprise is almost always going to result in failure.
- *Data models as an integration tool*—How does a business use and think about its data? The answer to this question requires analysis for systems and businesses that share data. Integration of semantics for interacting systems and businesses can only happen when the data and information they deal with mean the same to both. The extensive of use of data models and agreements on what they mean is a critical aspect of modern IT operations.
- *Enterprise service bus and service-oriented architecture (SOA) as a fabric*—Integration or EAI (enterprise application integration) is rarely considered the leading edge of an IT shop's technology issues. But, unfortunately, the amount of time and money we end up spending in alleviating or fixing problems introduced by poor integration decisions is enormous. In many cases, the strategic value that a CIO can present to his/her internal customers gets curtailed by integration roadblocks. A structured integrated EAI strategy is a key building block for all CIOs.
- *SaaS, IaaS, cloud computing, BPO*—Expensive up-front licenses are often difficult to get budgeted. The options for getting around expensive up-front licenses are increasing. Amazon's cloud infrastructure IaaS, replacing point-to-point integration, and customized SaaS

(software as a service) delivered applications are changing how we think of deployments and pricing.

- *Application development, the next generation*—The degree of collaboration in applications that we build and deploy is changing and must be recognized as a key driver for cost and development timelines. Mashups which are a critical part of Web 2.0 technologies are a perfect example of this. Mashups that pull together SOA-driven "apis" and deploy using resources available in a cloud are just one of the new models transforming app development.

- *Application portfolio management*—In the author's experience, there are very few organizations that "manage" their applications portfolios. It is not unusual to find numerous departments with duplicated versions of software, performing basically the same functions, but entirely incompatible with each other. The role of application portfolio manager would focus on the integration and standardization of applications across the enterprise.

- *Decision making and governance*—The selection of an IT alternative and then the monitoring of the success or failure of the installation often occurs uniquely on an application by application basis. A standardized selection process (the author recommends the 9-Step A3 described in Chapter 3) and then a follow-up/monitoring/governance process (Step 8 of the 9-Step) would clearly define everyone's expectations, assuring they are all focused on the enterprises' strategic perspective.

- *Analytics, BI (business intelligence), data models, MDM (master data management)*—Master data management is used to optimize data collection. Data modeling is used to facilitate the accurate and meaningful generation of information. But just generating information will not be adequate in the future. The future requires the use of business analytical tools that facilitate business intelligence. Better data gives us better information. Accurate information opens the door for intelligence gathering and optimized business decisions. The bottom line is that, if we do not improve the quality and accuracy of our data, then the intelligence is inaccurate, and the analytics that are performed at the top of the IT food chain are inaccurate and meaningless and a "waste" to generate.

- *Deployment strategies*—The implementation of IT programs lacks standardization throughout most enterprises. This causes a "reinvent the wheel" mentality for every implementation. Standard work for implementations can reduce this "waste."

- *App-development methodologies*—Lack of consistency and standards in the development of applications has generated large numbers of rogue applications that are quick fixes to specific issues. Unfortunately, this lack of standards generates a barrage of nonintegrated applications, which will in turn require "quick-fixes" every time data transfer or data consolidation is required. This problem is fraught with "waste."
- *Collaboration and integration strategies*—Interorganizational collaboration needs to become a strategic directive, and not the current hit-or-miss. A rapid improvement event (RIE) on collaboration has generated numerous successful tasks that have greatly improved overall organizational communication.
- *Rethinking ERP and large infrastructure*—ERP (enterprise resource planning) has become everybody's buzzword for any software application that claims to be enterprise centric. The result is that there is no longer a clear definition of what ERP really means. Comparing the ERP packages of two vendors turns into an exercise of comparing apples with oranges, and we often find that none of the ERPs are a very accurate fit for what we are trying to accomplish. Because it would be easier to move mountains than to get software vendors to standardize on a definition of ERP, each enterprise will need to define what ERP means to their organization, and how this integrates with the larger IT infrastructure.
- *Application portfolio rationalization*—Does our application portfolio make strategic sense? From a strategic perspective, what should our application portfolio look like? What are the performance gaps? What tasks do we need to execute in order to bring alignment back into our application portfolio? This set of questions should sound familiar. These are the types of questions we ask during the 9-Step A3 process that was highlighted in Chapter 3, and the Lean tools that are listed and discussed in Chapter 6, including the RIE and the VSM.

Application portfolio rationalization provides an objective, structured, and repeatable approach designed to map business requirements to technology decisions. It enables organizations to holistically assess technology assets (custom and ERP applications/ information sources and underlying platforms) in order to build a roadmap of IT investments. These investments need to align with current and future business needs, thereby achieving an acceptable balance of risk and reward. This approach also enables organizations to focus on end-to-end asset lifecycle management within the IT world. A periodic review of asset characteristics (in terms of location, performance, depreciation, maintenance, and support expenses in a standardized manner) is key to efficient portfolio management.

- *Asset management*—IT assets are unique within an organization. They are expensive, have a short life, and have nearly no salvage value. So are they really assets? In accounting terms that would be questionable. However, it also seems strange to think of them as a cost of doing business. Taking all of this into consideration, how do we manage the IT asset to maximize the value-add that we get out of every piece of equipment? Another excellent Lean exercise.

The next generation of changing competitive requirements highlights the need for IT organizations to become "Lean" capable, and possibly even Lean masters. The competitive and strategic power instilled within the IT organization places them in the position to become even more of a player facilitating organizational success. Considering the points highlighted in this chapter, and the Lean tools discussed in this book, we can see business value in organizations that:

- Are positioned for faster integration, future business growth, and flexibility
- Improve business process efficiency
- Enhance internal and external collaboration
- Improve decision making support

Similarly, we see IT value from:

- An IT organization that is aligned with architecture standards
- Reduced IT operations cost
- Improved service quality—availability, performance, and scalability

CASE STUDY: WIPRO (CONTINUED)

Continuing the Wipro story from Chapters 2, 3, and 4, we now look at success stories. A first example where Lean IT has been successfully applied with impressive results is found in a major global banker. The Lean effort focused on account interactions with the IT system. The current environment was insufficient in satisfying tight deadlines. The Lean process mapped the current state of user–system interactions and of data/information flow. Using traditional tools like spaghetti charting and system flowcharting, they were successful in improving overall systems responsiveness. The resulting benefits included a 10% productivity improvement and extensive error reduction.

A second example focuses on the optimization of IT maintenance support, specifically in the application of patches. The customer was a leading insurance provider. They were experiencing poor quality and a large number of post-delivery defects. This resulted in a large support staff which was utilized to correct 190 to 200 defect incidents per month. The Lean tools used included Value Stream Mapping and the establishment of some visual controls. The result was a process efficiency improvement driving efficiency from 11% to 29%, a 263% improvement.

SOME FINAL THOUGHTS

By now in this book we should feel confident in:

- Knowing how to focus your IT efforts strategically to maximize performance
- Knowing when to say NO if IT changes are not strategically aligned
- How to prioritize projects (Impact/Effort Matrix—Technical Tool #25 in Chapter 6)
- What types of processes could benefit from Lean (this chapter)
- How to evaluate the validity of a project and make sure it is worth doing (Chapter 3)
- A checklist approach to project evaluation and execution (the 9-Step A3 in Chapter 3)

By now in this book we should see that a world-class organization needs the support of a world-class IT organization, which will drive the entire enterprise to:

- Knowing how to focus your IT efforts strategically to maximize performance
- Being a strategically driven organization

At this point in the book we should have realized that Lean teaches us:
- How to get more from less
- Making sure you are doing the right things
- Eliminating non-value-added waste activities
- Creating and finding value
- Organizing information "pull"
- Making sure our IT efforts are strategically integrated and strategically aligned

The remainder of this book details out some of the concepts that have already been mentioned or discussed in this book. After going through the remaining chapters you should be able to "master" the Lean IT optimization methodology.

6

What Is Lean?

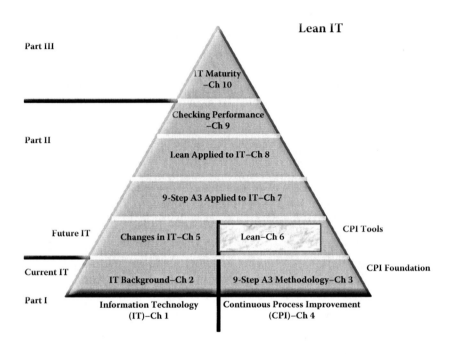

Lean IT

Part III

Part II

Part I

Future IT

Current IT

IT Maturity –Ch 10

Checking Performance –Ch 9

Lean Applied to IT–Ch 8

9-Step A3 Applied to IT–Ch 7

Changes in IT–Ch 5

Lean–Ch 6

IT Background–Ch 2

9-Step A3 Methodology–Ch 3

Information Technology (IT)–Ch 1

Continuous Process Improvement (CPI)–Ch 4

CPI Tools

CPI Foundation

For every problem there is a solution that is simple, neat, and wrong.

Mark Twain

DEFINING LEAN

Lean is the Westernization of a Japanese concept that has carried several names. It has been known as the Toyota Production System (TPS), Quality Circles (QC), Just in Time (JIT), Pull Manufacturing, TQM (Total Quality Management), etc. Each of these methodologies incorporates some aspect of Lean. One possible definition of Lean, taken from MainStream Management, a Lean consulting company, is:

> Lean is a systematic approach that focuses the entire enterprise on continuously improving Quality, Cost, Delivery, and Safety by seeking to eliminate waste, create flow, and increase the velocity of the system's ability to meet customer demand.

Another, briefer, but equally valid definition of Lean is:

> Lean is a focus on the elimination of anything not required in the delivery of a quality product or service, on time, at lowest cost, to customers.

What we call "Lean" today is a collection of tools and methodologies, very few of which are actually "required" in any specific Lean process. When working on a specific Lean project, one of the key roles of a Lean facilitator is to design and assemble the correct mix of tools to optimally facilitate the desired result. For example, if the goal is to improve the flow time for a production process, we would assemble one set of Lean tools. An entirely different set of tools would be used if we were trying to improve IT quality.

Historically, systems have maintained a "batch" perspective. This is true of manufacturing systems, and continues to be true in service and support environments like IT. In a "batch" environment we tend to group similar work together and do several of the same pieces of work at the same time. For example, if we are processing orders, one person would tend to do ten orders at one time, and then, in a "batch," move the ten orders on to the next work station. Utilizing the "batch" process leaves us with nine orders that are not being worked on while we are actively working on one. The result is that, in the end, it takes longer for one order to be processed (because of the wait time for the other nine) than if the "batch" only contained one order.

Traditionally we believed the "batch" process to be the more efficient methodology for processing orders. However, under Lean thinking, the time that the nine orders are not being processed is considered "waste." Lean thinking has moved us away from "batch" or "push" mentality and has moved us toward a "pull" approach to processing orders. Under "pull," each order is processed individually, and the "per order" processing time is significantly reduced.

Figure 6.1 shows us the historical development of the origins of Lean, going back to industrial pioneers like Frederick Taylor and Henry Ford. However, more recently, the Toyoda family, having become fascinated by the replenishment process of milk and bread in a grocery store, decided that it made a lot more sense to have materials become available "just in time" as needed. They saw only cost associated with having materials on the shelf that were not needed. From this they developed the Toyota Production System (TPS) which the United States has renamed "Lean."

Looking at Figure 6.1, we see the traditional "make to stock" production methodologies, which are characterized by "batch" processing. This fits one form of IT production, in that we occasionally tend to "push" a product out on the users whether they want it or not just because we know what is best. However the "make to order" production style only builds a product when it has an order in hand. This order processing type "pulls" and order through production. The pull trigger is the customer order. This same type of "push" vs. "pull" thinking works for all aspects of work, including service sector work, paper pushing, attorney's offices, government offices, military installations, and even IT. "Push" builds waste, and "pull," using Lean principles, attempts to eliminate that waste.

Lean has developed into its own entity, and along with that it has developed its own award process, the Shingo Prize for Excellence in Manufacturing (see Figure 6.2). In fact, the Shingo award program has become the international standard for what Lean should look like. Therefore, as we look at defining Lean it would be appropriate to reference the Shingo model.

The Shingo Transformation Model evaluates Lean performance in the following "dimensions:"

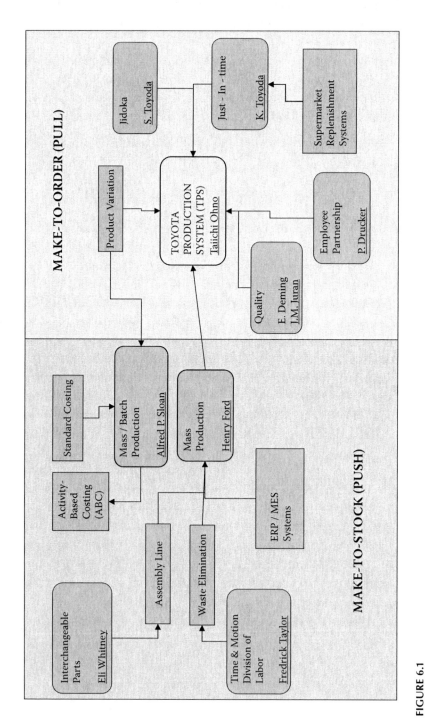

FIGURE 6.1

Origins of Lean: The Toyota Production System (TPS).

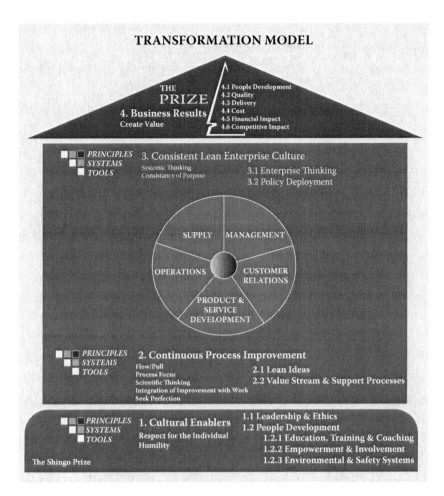

FIGURE 6.2
The Shingo Prize Model.

1. Cultural enablers (respect for the individual/humility)
    1.1 Leadership and ethics—Implementing world-class strategies and practices requires an enlightened leadership and organizational culture.
    1.2 People development—Respect for the individual and his or her development.
        1.2.1 Education, training and coaching—People development and knowledge transfer.
        1.2.2 Empowerment and involvement—Is the organization fully capitalizing on the knowledge base.

       1.2.3 Environmental and safety systems—Focus on the health and safety of the employees.

2. Continuous process improvement (CPI)—Focused on the deployment of the appropriate tools and techniques.

    2.1 Lean principles and ideas—Clarity and understanding of Lean principles. This section is quite extensive and goes through all the tools of Lean, including flow, pull, value, scientific thinking, and waste elimination.

    2.2 Value stream and support processes—This section reviews the areas where Lean can be applied. It checks the value streams in customer relations, product/service development/operations/supply/management.

3. Consistent Lean enterprise culture—Here they are evaluating the degree of integration between manufacturing and the nonmanufacturing functions of the organization, and the extent to which Lean improvement tools have been applied in nonmanufacturing settings. They look for systemic thinking/holistic thinking/dynamic thinking/closed-loop thinking/constancy of purpose.

    3.1 Enterprise thinking—Here they make sure the full potential of Lean is realized throughout the enterprise, including areas like financial reporting/other reporting/business development/organizational design and development/information management/leadership development.

    3.2 Policy deployment—This section validates that the proper leadership is in place to instill the principles that will execute strategic plans. They look for scientific thinking/catch ball/A3 thinking.

4. Business results—This is focused on creating and flowing value through the enterprise such that the customer is willing to pay for the product or service created.

    4.1 People development—Protecting and fostering the growth of the individual.

    4.2 Quality—Insure that there are no errors.

    4.3 Delivery—Ensure that the customer is getting what they want when they want it. Are customer expectations being met?

    4.4 Cost—Continuous improvement focused on cost reduction.

4.5 Financial impact—Consistent and predictable growth in cash flow compared to risk.

4.6 Competitive impact—Long-term growth market share growth.[1]

The Shingo Prize organization uses these criteria for applicant evaluation. They use a point system to evaluate the applicant on their Lean capabilities, and if their performance meets the standard, they are awarded the Shingo Award for Lean Excellence. However, these criteria are extremely valuable in a self-evaluation of your own Lean and continuous improvement performance. In a later chapter we will discuss the capabilities and maturity of your organization, and the Shingo Prize Criteria will become a valuable piece of that discussion.

Reading between the lines in all of these definitions and criteria for Lean, we see that Lean is primarily about team building, integration, and ownership. Someone commonly referred to as the Lean facilitator is tasked with organizing the appropriate teams and then giving them the appropriate guidance and training in the selected tools so that the Lean effort can progress with the greatest efficiency. The team is the one that makes the decisions about any changes in process, and they have ownership of these changes. It is the role of the facilitator to keep the team on task so that they develop and implement these changes in the minimal amount of time.

THE KEY PRINCIPLES OF LEAN

Drilling down to the roots of Lean, we can summarize Lean by focusing on some key principles.

1. Define "value" from the customer's perspective.
2. Define the process by looking at and analyzing all the pieces of the SIPOC (Supplier–Input–Process–Output–Customer). This should define the process value stream and identify opportunities for waste elimination.
3. Remove obstacles (bottlenecks) that disrupt the value flow.

---

[1] Utah State University, College of Business, The Shingo Prize for Operational Excellence–Model—Application Guidelines, 3rd ed., 2008, www.shingoprize.org.

4. Drive product and service flow at the "pull" of the customer.
5. Empower employees in the change process through teaming.
6. Build a strategic plan that focuses on the goals of the enterprise and which focuses on continuous improvement. Update the plan annually. Use this plan to identify strategic targeted areas of improvement.

Define "Value" from the Customer's Perspective

The customer's perspective should be the foundation for all value analysis. It is the customer who defines whether your product or service has value. Far too many industries feel that they, rather than the customer, have the best understanding of what defines value. This way of thinking is prevalent in the medical industry, in academia, and unfortunately, this is also true of technology industries. We need to break free from thinking that we are smarter than the customer and open our minds up to listening to what is important to the customer. Technology that adds no value to the customer is a "waste." And there is a long list of "good ideas" that have been poorly applied and which have resulted in technological disasters.

Define the Process by Looking at and Analyzing All the Pieces of the SIPOC

Defining the process by looking at and analyzing all the pieces of the SIPOC (Supplier–Input–Process–Output–Customer) (see Technical Tool #3 later in this chapter) should define the process value stream and identify opportunities for waste elimination.

When working on a Lean improvement process, we need to take a "systems" perspective. What is the system that we are analyzing? Where does the process start, and where does it end? Once we have drawn a circle around the system under consideration, we can then look at the internal process and the external influences to this system. SIPOC is a tool to help the Lean team work through this "systems" thought process. Typically, this is done by looking first at the "C," which stands for the customer. Who are the customers of the product or service that you are producing? Then we move on to the "O," which is the output. What output do we create which satisfies the customer? Does our output add value to the customer, from the customer's perspective?

Next, when working the SIPOC, we look at the "S" or supplier. Who supplies the inputs, including data, to our system? This is worked in conjunction with the next "systems" area, or the "I," which is the Input. Are we receiving the right inputs? Do they arrive on time and of the correct quality? Are we using the right supplier? And the last area of analysis is the "P" or process. To do this we develop a "current state Value Stream Map" or VSM (see Technical Tool #3 later in this chapter). This is a lengthy process of detailing out every step of the "system." There are numerous books that can help explain the VSM process, like *Reinventing Lean: Introducing Lean into the Supply Chain,* any of which would be helpful in understanding the methodology. VSM is an extensive process which requires further study, beyond the scope of this book. Once the current state VSM has been created, a future state VSM is developed. This is a similar diagram, focused on tearing a lot of the waste out of the current state process. The difference between the current state and the future state becomes the "gaps," and these gaps define the improvements that will need to be made.

There is also another tool which has been extremely valuable for IT process evaluations. The systems flowchart is a tool that most IT staff is familiar with, and it is an excellent tool for charting out information flow.

In the end, what Lean is trying to accomplish is not focused on making anyone work harder. Rather, Lean is focused on working smarter. Looking at the top of Figure 6.3 we see an example where the current value stream contains 95% non-value-added activities and 5% value-added activities. This is typical of most organizations. In the companies where we have worked, it is rare to find a process with more than 5% value-added content. The worst case has been about 0.5% value added, and the best case has been close to 9% value added.

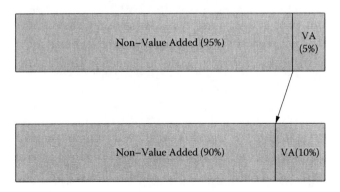

FIGURE 6.3
Eliminating 5% of the non-value-added content.

Following the thought process of Figure 6.3, if the current value stream has 5% value added, and we are able to identify removable non-value-added waste from the system, for example we remove an additional 5% non-value-added waste, as you see on the bottom of Figure 6.3, the impact is enormous. Moving from the top to the bottom of Figure 6.3 has the following impact:

a. Capacity has been doubled.
b. Throughput has been doubled.
c. The same labor resource is being utilized.

That is the power of Lean. By only focusing on eliminating 5% of the waste, we can have dramatic impacts on the overall productivity and efficiency results. This chapter will discuss the VSM process in more detail using specific examples.

Remove Obstacles (Bottlenecks) That Disrupt the Value Flow

The Lean tool that is extremely valuable for bottleneck elimination is called Theory of Constraints or TOC (see Technical Tool #26 later in this chapter). Eli Goldratt has authored a series of books explaining how bottleneck identification works and how bottlenecks are eliminated. The first of these books is *The Goal,* and it is strongly recommended. The focus is on recognizing that production "waves" exist and that these cause work clusters to occur, which then cause a bottleneck in the system. The bottleneck limits and defines the throughput of the entire system. The performance of the bottleneck needs to be maximized. This bottleneck needs to be supported with additional resources, or eliminated entirely.

Drive Product and Service Flow at the "Pull" of the Customer

Developing product for inventory creates backlog and waste. In a production environment, this is visualized by piles of finished goods at the end of the production process, which costs money to carry. In a service environment, this creates backlog of work "down the line," which results in throughput delays. IT is plagued with late deliveries and missed time schedules. A lot of this is the result of unbalanced workloads or work that has been generated that is not "value added" to the customer.

Empower Employees in the Change Process through Teaming

Lean is a participative process. It cannot be done effectively in isolation. It requires the involvement of everyone in the "system." Everyone in the "system" adds value to understanding and optimization of the process, including the customers and the suppliers. And enterprise leadership needs to empower the process improvement team to make recommendations that will in fact be implemented. If the team is going to invest time in analyzing and recommending improvements, they want to see the improvements implemented, or they will become discouraged and will consider the Lean process to be a failure.

Build a Strategic Plan

Build a strategic plan that focuses on the goals of the enterprise and which focuses on continuous improvement. Update the plan annually. Use this plan to identify strategic targeted areas of improvement.

Strategic plans need to be developed at the enterprise level and then cascaded down to organizations within the enterprise. An IT strategic plan needs to be built based on the objectives that are in the enterprise plan. Using the IT strategic plan, a set of tasks need to be created which are the executable activities that will make the IT strategy a reality. The execution of these tasks should be performed using Lean tools. End to end, Lean is used to drive the IT improvements that have enterprise-wide strategic impact.

LEAN TOOLS

Lean change management is not a specific methodology. It is more about adaptation, goal fulfillment, and sustainment. Lean tools and concepts will focus the organization on changing the "system" so that it is capable of adapting and flowing to changing customer needs. Because *"change is hard,"* we find that the technical implementation of Lean alone will not create the acceptance required to sustain the change. Looking at Figure 6.4, we see that the acceptance process is 80% of the effort in a Lean implementation, and that the technical tools are only 20% of the effort. We also see

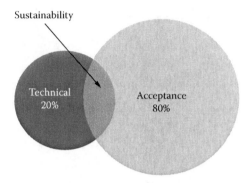

Sustainability = Technical • Acceptance

FIGURE 6.4
Technical and acceptance tools.

that sustainability cannot be achieved with only one or the other of these two elements. Both are required.

The book, *Reinventing Lean: Introducing Lean into the Supply Chain,* by Gerhard Plenert (2006), has an entire chapter on various acceptance tools that are designed to motivate cultural change. There are far too many of these tools to discuss them all in detail here. But a few of these tools that are worth investigating include:

1. Breakthrough Thinking/Concept Management/Purpose Expansion
2. Team Effectiveness Surveys
3. Change Readiness Surveys
4. Myers–Briggs Assessments
5. JoHari Window

Evaluate the effectiveness of each of these tools for your organization. They have been invaluable in Leaning out the IT process environments that I have worked in.

Additionally, this same book has a chapter describing some recommended technical tools. Technical tools are designed to analyze the existing process and to identify opportunities for systems changes. A recommended list of these tools that has worked well in the development of IT 9-Step A3s includes:

1. 7 Wastes
2. Value Stream Mapping (current state/ideal state/future state)

3. SIPOC (Supplier/Input/Process/Output/Customer)
4. SWOT (Strengths/Weaknesses/Opportunities/Threats)
5. VOC (Voice of the Customer)
6. Systems Flowchart/Information Flow Diagrams
    a. Database perspective
    b. User perspective
    c. Software execution perspective
7. Gemba Walk (Go and See Analysis)
8. B-SMART Targets
    a. B = Balanced
    b. S = Specific
    c. M = Measurable
    d. A = Attainable
    e. R = Results Oriented
    f. T = Time Based
9. JIT (Just-In-Time)/Kanban/Cells
10. Spaghetti Chart
11. Lean Events/RIE (Rapid Improvement Events)/Kaizen Events
12. Improvement Project
13. Just-Do-It
14. 5S
15. Poka-Yoke
16. Six Sigma/DMAIC
17. TPM (Total Product Maintenance)
18. Standard Work
19. 5 Whys
20. Brainstorming
21. Fishbone Charts
22. Pareto Charts
23. Affinity Diagrams
24. Control Charts
25. PICK (Possible, Implement, Challenge, Kill) Chart/Impact/Effort Matrix
26. Theory of Constraints (TOC)/Bottleneck Analysis
27. Project Charter

With this foundation of Lean tools, we can move forward with the IT improvement process.

ACCEPTANCE TOOLS

This chapter will now give a brief discussion of each of the acceptance tools. These can be more important than filling out the A3 if you are working in a highly resistive organization. Often these are glossed over because of their "warm and fuzzy" nature, but have been the key to the success and failure of numerous Lean implementations. These tools are:

1. Breakthrough Thinking/Concept Management/Purpose Expansion
2. Team Effectiveness Surveys
3. Change Readiness Surveys
4. Myers–Briggs Assessments
5. JoHari Window

Acceptance Tool #1—Breakthrough Thinking/ Concept Management/Purpose Expansion

Breakthrough Thinking and Concept Management are tools that developed sequentially. These tools can be utilized as a change model which focuses on (1) innovation and creativity and (2) making sure we are "doing the right things." These tools focus on asking "Why are we doing this?" using the "purpose expansions" before asking, "Are we doing this right?" which tends to be the focus of the "root cause analysis." The purpose expansion has become quite popular in Japan, especially amongst the users of the Toyota Production System (TPS). The following discussion offers a brief introduction of all three of these concepts (Breakthrough Thinking/Concept Management/Purpose Expansion).

To solve difficult problems and analyze new opportunities hoping to find creative solutions, our present thinking paradigm must change. Gerald Nadler and Shozo Hibino published *Breakthrough Thinking: The Seve Principles of Creative Problem Solving* in 1990 and *Creative Solution Finding* in 1993. In these two books they defined a Japanese-developed paradigm shift in thinking. They called this new thinking paradigm "Breakthrough Thinking." From a historical viewpoint, our thinking paradigms have been continuously shifting over time. Our conventional thinking paradigm (Descartes Thinking), is out of date with a rapidly changing world and needs to shift again to a new thinking paradigm. In the twenty-first century, we have to be Multi-Thinkers who are able to use three thinking paradigms; God Thinking, Conventional (Descartes) Thinking, and Breakthrough Thinking (BT).

God Thinking focuses on making decisions based on God's will. For some decisions, there is no need for analysis. Behavior is firmly dictated by God's will, our values systems, and our life philosophies. For example, morality or ethical issues are decided and are not open for discussion. Conventional Thinking starts with an analysis process that focuses on fact or truth finding. When we make a decision, our behavior is based on the facts or on scientific truth. We need the facts in order to make our decisions. Breakthrough Thinking starts with the ideal or ultimate objective. When we make a decision, we base our behavior on this objective.

The three thinking paradigms are completely different, and each has a different approach. We have to select and utilize each of these paradigms on a case-by-case basis. Someone who uses and interchanges these thinking paradigms is referred to as a "Multi-Thinker."

Since there is no future which continues along the same lines as our past and present (because of the drastic changes going on in the world), we cannot find futuristic solutions based on past and present facts. Our thinking base should be changed away from facts and refocus on the substance, essence, or ideal.

To identify the substance of things is not easy. We have to transform ourselves from having a conventional machine view to a systems-oriented view. The traditional perspective of conventional thinking is to view things as a reductionistic machine, breaking everything down into elemental parts, and neglecting the "whole" organic view.

Breakthrough Thinking suggests that "everything is a system," which focuses BT on a "holonic view." If we define everything as a system, then everything is a "Chinese box," which means that a bigger box (system) includes a series of smaller boxes (systems). A small box (system) contains still smaller boxes (systems) and so on. Each box (system) has its purpose(s). If you repeatedly ask, "What is the purpose?" and then "What is the purpose of that purpose?" and then "What is the purpose of that purpose of that purpose?" etc., you can reach the biggest box, which is "wholeness." You can view everything from the perspective of this wholeness. BT calls this search the "Purpose Expansion."

Breakthrough Thinking consists of a thinking paradigm and thinking process. The thinking paradigm of Breakthrough Thinking is the opposite of the paradigm of conventional thinking. Its main points are expressed as seven principles.

A. Uniqueness principle—Always assume that the problem, opportunity, or issue is different. Do not copy a solution or use a technique from elsewhere just because the situation may appear to be similar. In using this principle, we have to think about the locus or solution space of the problem. This locus is defined using three points:
   1. Who are the major stakeholders? Whose viewpoint is most important?
   2. What is the location?
   3. When (what is the timing)?
B. Purposes principle—Explore and expand purposes in order to understand what really needs to be accomplished and to identify the substance of things. You can tackle any problem, opportunity, or issue by expanding purposes, if you change your epistemology to a systems view. Understanding the context of purposes provides the following strategic advantages:
   1. Pursue the substance of things—We can identify the most essential focus purpose or the greater purpose, often referred to as the substance (core element) of things by expanding purposes.
   2. Work on the right problem or purpose—Focusing on the right purposes helps strip away nonessential aspects to avoid working on just the visible problem or symptom.
   3. Improve the ability to redefine—Redefining is usually very difficult. Once you have redefined, you can have different viewpoints, each of which enables you to solve problems from different directions.
   4. Eliminate purpose/function(s)—From systems theory we learn that a bigger purpose may eliminate a smaller purpose. By focusing on the bigger purpose, you can eliminate unnecessary work/systems/parts, which means that you can get more effective solutions.
   5. More options, more creative—If you have a purpose hierarchy, you have a lot of alternative solutions.
   6. Holonic view—Take a "big picture" perspective.
C. Solution-after-next (SAN) principle—Think and design futuristic solutions for the focus purpose, and then work backward. Consider the solution you would recommend if in three years you had to start all over. Make changes today based on what might be the solution of the future. Learn from the futuristic ideal solution for the focus purpose, and do not try learning from the past and present situation.

D. Systems principle—Everything we seek to create and restructure is a system. Think of solutions and ideas as a system. When you see everything is a system, you have to consider the eight elements of a system in order to identify the solution.
   1. Purpose—mission, aim, need
   2. Input—people, things, information
   3. Output—people, things, information
   4. Operating steps—process and conversion tasks
   5. Environment—physical and organizational
   6. Human enablers—people, responsibilities, skills, to help in the operating steps
   7. Physical enablers—equipment, facilities, materials to use in the operating steps
   8. Information enablers—knowledge, instructions
E. Needed information collection principle—Collect only the information that is necessary to continue the solution-finding process. Know your purposes for collecting data and/or information. Study the solutions, not the problems.
F. People design principle—Give everyone who will be affected by the solution or idea the opportunity to participate throughout the process of its development. A solution will work only if people know about it and help to develop and improve it.
G. Betterment timeline principle—Install changes with built-in seeds of future change. Know when to fix it before it breaks. Know when to change it.

The Breakthrough Thinking (BT) process is an approach of reasoning toward a situation specific solution and a design approach. It is an iterative, simultaneous process of mental responses based on the Purpose-Target-Results Approach (PTR Approach). PTR's three Phases are:

1. Purpose—Identifying the right solution by finding focus purposes, values, measures
2. Target—Targeting the solution of tomorrow—ideal SAN vision and target solution
3. Result—Getting and maintaining results toward implementation and systematization

For a more detailed discussion, please read *Breakthrough Thinking*. It will offer you extensive detail on the Breakthrough Thinking process.

Concept Management (CM) is a Japanese movement which integrates Breakthrough Thinking (BT), World Class Management (WCM), and Total Quality Management (TQM). BT is the technique utilized to develop ideas. It moves away from the slowness and costliness of traditional root cause analysis commonly used in the United States and Europe. WCM offers the formal structure around which the ideas are turned into goals and a measurement/motivation system. TQM is the process for team-based idea/change implementation. CM is an idea generation and implementation process used by companies like Toyota and Sony that breaks us out of the traditional, analytical thinking common to companies such as the Ford Motor Company, which uses the TOPS program, or the Russian TRIZ program. Instead, it focuses on forming a purpose hierarchy through a series of steps.

Concept Management uses the term "concept" to mean innovative purpose-driven change creation, and "management" to mean leadership. Therefore concept management is "innovative, change-oriented, purpose-driven (goal focused), creative leadership." This leadership occurs through the integration of ideas, primarily the ideas expressed in two leading-edge philosophies: Breakthrough Thinking and World Class Management.

Nadler and Hibino described a "Paradigm Shift in Thinking" called "Breakthrough Thinking." Thinking paradigms have shifted over our history, for example, Primitive, Early Greek, Classical Greek, God Thinking, Descartes, etc. From the historical viewpoints, our thinking paradigms have been continuously shifting over time. Our conventional thinking paradigm (Descartes Thinking) is out of date with a rapidly changing world and needs to shift again to a new thinking paradigm, Breakthrough Thinking. In the twenty-first century, we have to be Multi-Thinkers who are able to use all three thinking paradigms; God Thinking, Conventional (Descartes) Thinking, and Breakthrough Thinking.

The three thinking paradigms are completely different, and each has a different approach. We cannot neglect any of these three thinking paradigms because each has an influence in the decision making process. We have to select and utilize each of these paradigms on a case-by-case basis. Someone who uses and interchanges these thinking paradigms is referred to as a "Multi-Thinker."

World Class Management is broad in its application, and numerous publications discuss the subject in detail (see the author's book *eManager: Value Chain Management in an eCommerce World* or *Making Innovation Happen: Concept Management through Integration*). However, in order to get a clear understanding of how World Class Managers manage change, the focus would be on:

1. People—Employees and stakeholders are the source of change opportunities. They need to be motivated properly through an appropriate measurement system in order to drive change.
2. Customers—Customers are the reason for change. In order to be competitive we need to give our customers a clear reason why they should not buy from anyone else but us.
3. Performance—Performance requires focus on a goal, whether it is financial or quality or some other focus. Then we need to measure, monitor, and offer feedback information about our performance.
4. Competitors—Competition creates fear, but it also creates opportunity. Competitors need to be analyzed and understood in order to be defeated.
5. Future—The future is coming whether we are ready for it or not. If we are not ready for it, it will pass us by, along with our customers and competitors.
6. Integration—Through integration everyone and everything work together. Managers are not merely bosses; they are leaders and facilitators by example. They work side by side with the employee.

World Class Management is not a system or a procedure, it is a culture. It is a continually molding process of change and improvement. It is a competitive strategy for success.

In the United States, TQM has fallen into disfavor because of its analytical approach to change. The analysis process is deemed too slow to be competitive. But that is primarily because TQM utilized root cause analysis. With Breakthrough Thinking we can revisit our use of TQM.

There are two major aspects to TQM: a philosophical, and an operational. From the philosophical we get guidelines, and from the operational we get techniques. Traditionally, the philosophy of TQM could be stated as "Make sure you are doing the right things before your worry about doing things right." Total Quality Management focuses on careful, thoughtful analysis. However, the analysis should be creative, innovative, and innoveering oriented. It wants to make sure that we are implementing positive, goal-focused changes before we move a muscle.

TQM is an enterprise-wide change model. Some people define TQM as making the "entire organization responsible for product or service quality." To some, TQM is a behavior-based philosophy of motivation and measurement. TQM does, in fact, require a cultural shift for all members of an organization in that it uses an entire philosophy about how businesses should be run. TQM is filled with ideas and attitudes:

- Attitude of Desiring and Searching Out Change
- Think Culture—Move from Copying to Innovating
- Focus on the Goal
- Measurement/Motivation Planning
- Top-to-Bottom Corporate Strategy
- Companywide Involvement
- Clear Definition and Implementation of Quality
- Education, Training, and Cross-Training
- Integration and Coordination
- Small, Step-by-Step Improvements

TQM implementation starts with a coordinating team, often referred to as a quality council. This is a team composed of high-level corporate leaders from all the functional areas, usually at the vice-president level. This team is appointed by the CEO and operates under his/her direction. The CEO actively directs the endeavors of the team, and is often an active team member. This quality council is then responsible for organizing, chartering, and measuring the performance of the other TQM teams within the organization. It oversees the installation, training, performance, and measurement of the other teams. This team aims to keep all teams focused on the corporate goal and vision.

Concept Management works in a series of stages. The stages are:

1. Concept Creation—The development and creation of new ideas through the use of Breakthrough Thinking's innovative methods of creativity.
2. Concept Focus—The development of a target which includes keeping your organization focused on core values and a core competency. Then, utilizing the creativity generated by Concept Creation, a set of

targets are established using World Class Management, and a road map is developed, helping us to achieve the targets.

3. Concept Engineering—This is the engineering of the ideas, converting the fuzzy concepts into usable, consumer-oriented, ideas. TQM through the use of a focused, chartered team and through a managed SPS process helps us to manage the concept from idea to product.

4. Concept In—This is the process of creating a market for the new concept. We transform the concept into a product, service, or system, using World Class Management techniques. We may utilize Breakthrough Thinking to help us develop a meaningful and effective market strategy.

5. Concept Management—Both the management of the new concepts and a change in the management approach (management style) are effected by the new concept. Concept Management is the integration of the first four stages of the Concept Management process (Creation, Focus, Engineering, and In).

For more detail on the concept management process, please read *Making Innovation Happen.*

Acceptance Tool #2—Team Effectiveness Surveys

Team dynamics are critical to successful Lean implementations. Everything is accomplished as a team, and a good Lean facilitator will understand team dynamics and team member relationships. To help in this understanding, a Team Effectiveness Survey is useful. The types of questions that would be asked in this survey include (taken from the MainStream Management teaming effectiveness survey):

Goals and Objectives

1. Clear on team's objectives.
2. All pull in same direction.
3. Doing what's needed for company's success.
4. Have numerical goals and chart progress.
5. Meet our objectives in the 90% range.

Roles and Responsibilities

   6. Expectations are clear.
   7. Comfort level with role.
   8. Understanding of my role by my management.
   9. Awareness of each other's roles.
  10. See how our roles fit in the big picture.

Enthusiasm and Motivation

 11. Work is fun and rewarding.
 12. Team is optimistic.
 13. Self satisfaction derived from achievements.
 14. Caring is prevalent in our team.
 15. Enjoy challenges.

Trust and Openness

 16. Trust is a part of the team.
 17. Sensitive matters are kept confidential.
 18. Team members assist each other.
 19. No fear of reprisals bringing up concerns.
 20. Respect.

Leadership and Direction

 21. Decision making is encouraged.
 22. Input into decision making.
 23. Shared leadership.
 24. Lead by example.
 25. Acceptance of decisions.

Information and Communication

 26. Information is shared readily.
 27. No surprises—effective communication.
 28. Information is readily at hand.
 29. Performance data is available.
 30. Proactive communication vs. grapevine method.

Acceptance Tool #3—Change Readiness Surveys

A second useful survey is the change readiness assessment which includes questions about the change process under consideration. It evaluates an organization's "readiness" for change at various levels within the organization (taken from the MainStream Management change readiness survey):

For management (If management is doing the survey they would answer the questions about how they perceive themselves. If staff is answering the question they would answer based on how they perceive management to be.):
- Give personal time for Lean.
- Drive policy changes to support Lean.
- Communicate everything about Lean.
- Honest about negative issues with Lean.
- Make long-term commitment to Lean.
- Stick it out in tough times getting to Lean.
- Provide training to employees to work in Lean.
- Ask employees for their ideas about Lean.
- Provide time, money, and people for Lean.
- Try out ideas generated by employees.

For implementation team (IT) members (If management is doing the survey they would answer the questions about how they perceive the staff doing the work. If staff is answering the question they would answer based on how they perceive themselves to be.):
- Try new way of doing work.
- Work with management to develop Lean ideas.
- Provide honest feedback.
- Improve on work methods.
- Participate on committees or implementation teams.
- Cooperate with each other during Lean implementation.
- Willingness to refine ideas getting to Lean.
- Deal with confusion while trying out Lean ideas.
- Take risks trying out new ideas.
- Learn new skills.

Policies and procedures
- Allow employees and managers to do work in new and innovative Lean ways.

- Recommendations can be implemented painlessly.
- Allow employees to move to where the work is.
- Team and individual accomplishments are rewarded.
- Motivate people to change to Lean.
- Allow employee time to participate in Lean activities.
- Communication channels inform on Lean changes.
- Encourage employee feedback.
- Change to Lean can be monitored.
- New ideas are recognized at Headquarters.

These surveys are invaluable and generate information like:

- Staff perceived management to be disconnected and uninterested in their process.
- Staff felt that management did not care about their ideas.
- Staff had confidence in their direct line supervisors, but not with anyone above that level.
- Staff felt that the reward system did not motivate them to facilitate changes.
- Management felt that staff was resistive to change, in that they already feel that they know how to do things in the best way possible.
- Management felt that staff would be unwilling to take time from their workload to facilitate the change process.

All this information was invaluable in preparing the organization for change, designing the training, and facilitating in team building.

Acceptance Tool #4—Myers–Briggs

If the surveys identified teaming challenges that seem significant, the Lean facilitator may want to look deeper into the personalities of the team members that he or she will be confronted with. A good tool for this evaluation is the Myers–Briggs Assessment. This tool was developed in the 1950s and has proven itself as an excellent tool for helping people understand themselves. It ranks everyone by:

- How we energize ourselves (in the range from E to I)
  - Extravert (E)
    - Attention seems to flow out to objects and people in the environment
    - Desire to act on the environment

- – Takes action
- – Impulsive—frank
- – Communicates easily
- – Sociable
- • Introvert (I)
  - – Attention to the inner world of concepts and ideas
  - – Reliance on enduring concepts vs. transitory external events
  - – Thoughtful contemplative detachment
  - – Enjoyment of solitude and privacy
- • What we pay attention to (in the range from S to N)
  - • Sensing (S)
    - – Focus on here and now—immediate situation
    - – Enjoys the present moment
    - – Realistic
    - – Acute powers of observation
    - – Memory for details
  - • Practical Intuition (N)
    - – Tie seemingly unrelated events together
    - – Creative discovery
    - – Perceive beyond the here and now
    - – May overlook current facts
    - – Theoretical—abstract
    - – Future oriented
- • How we make decisions (in the range from T to F)
  - • Thinking (T)
    - – Tough minded
    - – Makes logical connections
    - – Principles of cause and effect
    - – Tends to be impersonal
    - – Analytical—objective
    - – Concern for justice
    - – Desires a connection from the past to present to the future
  - • Feeling (F)
    - – Tender minded
    - – Weighs the relative merits of the issues
    - – Applies personal and group values subjectively
    - – Attends to what matters to others
    - – Concern for the human as opposed to the technical aspects of the problem

- How we are oriented to the world (in the range from P to J)
  - Perceptive (P)
    - Open to incoming information
    - Curious and interested
    - Spontaneous and curious
    - Adaptable
    - Open to new events and changes
  - Willing to take in more information before making a decision-Judging (J)
    - Seeks closure
    - Organizes events
    - Plans operations
    - Shuts off perceptions as soon as they have observed enough to make a decision
    - Organized
    - Purposeful
    - Decisive

This analysis can be invaluable in team creation because what you need on your team is a balance. Too many of any one personality type can disrupt the decision making process. For example, in Figure 6.5 we can see all the

ISTJ	ISFJ	INFJ	INTJ
Analytical MANAGERS of FACTS/DETAIL	Sympathetic MANAGERS of FACTS/DETAIL	People-oriented INNOVATORS	Logical, critical, decisive INNOVATORS
ISTP	**ISFP**	**INFP**	**INTP**
Practical ANALYZER	Observant, loyal HELPER	Imaginative, independent HELPER	Inquisitive ANALYZER
ESTP	**ESFP**	**ENFP**	**ENTP**
REALISTIC ADAPTERS material world	REALISTIC ADAPTERS human relations	Warm, enthusiastic PLANNERS of CHANGE	Analytical PLANNERS of CHANGE
ESTJ	**ESFJ**	**ENFJ**	**ENTJ**
Fact-minded practical ORGANIZER	Practical HARMONIZER	Imaginative HARMONIZER	Intuitive, innovative ORGANIZER

FIGURE 6.5
Myers–Briggs type indicator.

different categories where individuals can fall. If, for example, we had a lot if Is and few or no Es on the team, we would have limited and poor discussions in our teams.

Digging a little deeper, we can learn conditional information about a Myers–Briggs Assessment. For example, people with a specific management style have the following characteristics:

SJ Management Style

Leadership style:	Traditionalist, stabilizer, consolidator
Work style:	Works from a sense of loyalty, responsibility, and industry
Learning style:	Learns in a step-by-step way with preparation for current and future utility
Acknowledged for contributing:	Timely output
Values:	ORDER

SP Management Style:

Leadership style	Troubleshooter, negotiator, firefighter
Work style:	Works via action with cleverness and timeliness
Learning style:	Learns through active involvement to meet current needs
Acknowledged for contributing:	Expeditious handling of the out of the ordinary and unexpected
Values:	FREEDOM

NF Management Style

Leadership style:	Catalyst, spokesperson, energizer
Work style:	Works by interacting with people about values and inspirations
Learning style:	Learns for self-awareness through personalized and imaginative ways
Acknowledged for contributing:	Something personal or a special vision of possibilities
Values:	HARMONY

NT Management Style

Leadership style:	Visionary, architect of systems, builder
Work style:	Works on ideas with ingenuity and logic
Learning style:	Learns by an impersonal and analytical process for personal mastery
Acknowledged for contributing:	Strategies and analyses
Values:	COMPETENCE

Or digging further we find the following personality characteristics:

IS
- THOUGHTFUL REALIST
- Leads through attention to what needs doing
- Individual focus: Practical considerations
- Organizational focus: Continuity
- "Let's keep it!"

IN
- THOUGHTFUL INNOVATOR
- Leads through ideas to what needs doing
- Individual focus: Intangible thoughts and ideals
- Organizational focus: Vision
- "Let's think about it differently!"

ES
- ACTION ORIENTED REALIST
- Leads through action, doing
- Individual focus: Practical action
- Organizational focus: Results
- "Let's do it!"

EN
- ACTION ORIENTED INNOVATOR
- Leads through enthusiasm
- Individual focus: Systems and relationships
- Organizational focus: Change
- "Let's change it!

NF
- Warm
- Trusting
- Spiritual
- Idealistic
- Unselfish
- Romantic
- Affirming
- Caretaker
- Empathic
- Sympathetic
- Compassionate
- Wanting harmony
- Great communicator
- Likes to please people
- Promoting growth, well-being
- Relates current experience to past experiences

SJ
- Firm
- Stable
- Efficient
- Realistic
- Decisive
- Punctual
- Dependable
- Orderly, neat
- Seeks closure
- Good planner
- Goal oriented
- Executive type
- Organized person
- Providing security
- Always has a view
- Good at sorting/weeding out

NT
- Creative
- Original
- Rational
- Powerful
- Visionary
- Objective
- 98% right
- Firm minded
- Under control
- Seeking judgment
- Superior intellect
- Able to find flaws
- Able to reprimand
- Calm, not emotional
- Precise, not repetitive
- Eminently responsible

SP
- Eclectic
- Carefree
- Practical
- Spontaneous
- Problem solver
- Good negotiator

- Hands-on person
- Flexible, adaptable
- Proficient, capable
- Do many tings at once
- Curious, welcomes new ideas
- Can deal with chaos
- Fun loving, enjoys life
- Superior ability to discriminate among options, sees shades of gray

In the end, Myers–Briggs Assessments help both the facilitator and the team members. This tool:

- Helps individuals to know themselves
- Gives a tool to "be with" others
- Gives a base line from which to develop adaptive behaviors
- Helps the team learn how to better communicate by understanding and by talking others' "language"
- Develops better facilitation methods
- Develops more effective exercises
- Appreciates the differences in others
- Teaches us the value of type diversity
- Learns to accept others for who they are
- Leverages each person's type by identifying their role in a team environment
- Conducts more effective meetings
- Helps understand how previously annoying behavior can be seen as amusing, interesting, and as a strength

The websites for the Myers–Briggs Assessments are http://www.human-metrics.com/cgi-win/jungtype.htm or http://www.myersbriggs.org/my-mbti-personality-type/, which introduces you to the Myers–Briggs test. These lead you to the website http://www.humanmetrics.com/cgi-win/JTypes1.htm, where you can actually take the test and get your score. Additionally, MainStream Management, the source of a lot of the Myers–Briggs information, can give the reader even more depth on the usefulness of this tool.

Myers–Briggs is just one of many personality analysis tools that are available. However, since the author has found this tool to be one of the most useful, he has spent more time using it than any of the other tools.

Acceptance Tool #5—JoHari Window

The JoHari Window is a tool for gaining insight into how we see ourselves and how others see us. It is an invaluable tool when we are trying to investigate the openness of team members. It helps us understand their willingness to communicate. To accomplish this, the JoHari Window uses "disclosure" (or telling) and "feedback" (or asking) to determine our individual openness. As with the Myers–Briggs Assessment, in the JoHari Window we take a survey and then plot the results of this survey on a graph. The graph divides us into four segments, as seen on Figure 6.6.

The JoHari Window is a conceptual model for describing, evaluating, and predicting aspects of interpersonal communication. The window-panes show us how we present and receive information about others and ourselves. The model allows us to see movement from one pane to another as trust ebbs and flows and actors exchange feedback. The size and shape of the panes will change over time.

The literature on human behavior is filled with other, similar two-dimensional models, like the Blake Grid and Kilman Conflict model. But the author has found the JoHari Window offers the most significant insights in facilitating Lean acceptance and understanding.

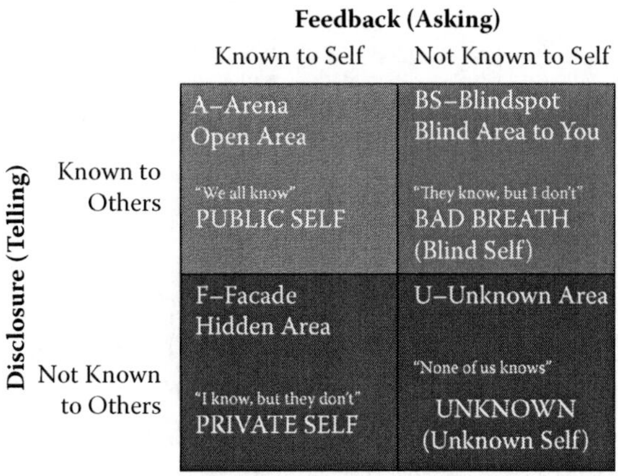

Feedback (Asking)

	Known to Self	Not Known to Self
Known to Others	A–Arena Open Area "We all know" PUBLIC SELF	BS–Blindspot Blind Area to You "They know, but I don't" BAD BREATH (Blind Self)
Not Known to Others	F–Facade Hidden Area "I know, but they don't" PRIVATE SELF	U–Unknown Area "None of us knows" UNKNOWN (Unknown Self)

Disclosure (Telling)

FIGURE 6.6
JoHari Window.

Using the JoHari segments we identify each of these segments as:

- A—arena—this represents the part of yourself that is known by you and also known by others. This windowpane represents free and open exchange of information between others and me. This is public behavior information, which is available to everyone. The pane increases in size as the level of trust increases between others and me. As more information, particularly personally relevant information, is shared, this trust increases. This represents a manager with a capacity for open relationships.

  In this window the glass is two-way. There is open exchange of facts, feelings and opinions between the people communicating through this pane.

- BS—blind spot—this represents what others know about you, but which you do not realize about yourself. As "you" work with others, you communicate all kinds of information of which you may be unaware, but which others pick up. This occurs through the use of verbal cues, mannerisms, the way you say things, or the style in which you relate to others. The extent to which you are insensitive to much of your own behavior and what it may communicate to others can be surprising and disconcerting. For example, we see it in a manager's tendency to press too hard in trying to speed up relevant discussion at a meeting to the detriment of what others may feel is needed, like open discussions. Many of us know and realize that others find things we do or say difficult or puzzling. "Blind spotting" demands considerable self-awareness and self-control. When you look in the mirror, you see yourself as you would "like to see yourself." You may not like certain personal traits that are in the blind spots, but you are just not able to address these areas and change them because you are unaware of them.

- F—façade—this represents what is known by you about yourself, but is hidden from others. For one reason or another, you keep information hidden. You fear risking too much. One reason for "my facade" could be that I do not feel supported at home or in my work situation. Perhaps you want to protect yourself from being criticized. You may keep certain kinds of information secret to support and protect others. Your reasons may be selfish in that you wish to control the situation, and nondisclosure could be tactically helpful. Another rea-

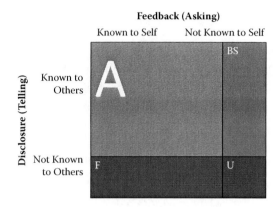

FIGURE 6.7
JoHari Window increases openness.

son may be for tact or diplomacy, deflecting potential resentment. "Privacy" may protect you and others. The private self is controlled.

- U—unknown—this is that part of you which is unknown by others as well as unknown by yourself. What affects you may be below the surface of awareness of both parties. For example, early childhood experiences may give rise to aversions learned through experience. We may have unrecognized resources and traits.[2]

The goal of a good communicator is to enlarge the arena window as much as possible in a balanced fashion. To accomplish this we attempt to reduce the "unknown" regions. We attempt to reduce what we do not know about ourselves, and what others do not know about us. The result is shown in Figure 6.7.

We increase disclosure because we increase trust. We are more willing to give out information about ourselves. We share more of what we think and how we feel. We share, but we do not become the "chatterbox" that rambles incessantly. What we share is meaningful disclosure. We become more open and honest in answering questions and in sharing information

---

[2] Many of the comments in this section are the result of the work of Chris Jarvis, and he cites the following references:

Luft, J., and Ingham, H., "The JoHari Window: A graphic model for interpersonal relations," Univ. Calif. Western Training Lab, 1955.

Berne, E., *The Games People Play,* Grove Press, NY, 1964.

Goffman, I., *The Presentation of Self in Everyday Life,* Penguin.

Shannon, C., and Weaver, W., *The Mathematical Theory of Communication,* Illinois Univ. Press, 1968.

as needed. We share our thoughts and feelings while still making others feel important.

We increase feedback by being willing to listen. Asking meaningful questions triggers this. We must be truly interested in how others perceive us. We want to know their honest opinions about the actions that we take. This helps us improve our relationship and decreases the size of the blind box.

As we take the test we will find ourselves in one of four types of configurations. These are shown in Figure 6.8.

Type A is like the children who are just learning about life and about how to express themselves. The arena is very small, and the unknown is by far the largest.

In type B we have a huge façade and a mid-sized unknown. This is a person who knows how to ask questions and how to listen, but is not very good at opening up and disclosing his or her own feelings.

In type C we have a huge blind spot and a small façade. This is "Chatty Charlie," always talking and mostly about himself. He always supplies far more information than anyone is interested in. This individual is a poor listener and is fearful of what may be disclosed in any feedback process.

Type D is well rounded and a good communicator. This person is balanced in their ability to tell and ask.

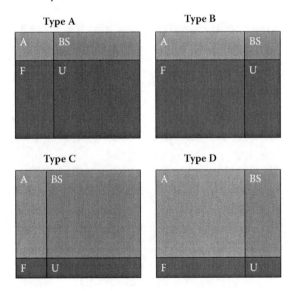

FIGURE 6.8
JoHari Window types.

It would not be good to be too extreme in our sharing and asking. There are areas of intimacy and privacy where we can learn "more than we really want to know." Additionally, there are areas of our lives that are as yet undiscovered. There will always be some unknown territory.

In order to be a good facilitator, you would need to be a strong type D personality. Appendix 6A contains one version of the JoHari test. There are many other versions as well, and these can be found on the Internet if desired.

TECHNICAL TOOLS

This chapter will now give a brief discussion of each of the Lean technical tools. These are the tools that are used in the creation of the 9-Step A3. You will not use all of these tools on any one A3. You may not even use half of these tools. The trick is to use the right set of tools that will make your A3 meaningful and complete. These tools are:

1. 7 Wastes
2. Value Stream Mapping (current state/ideal state/future state)
3. SIPOC (Supplier/Input/Process/Output/Customer)
4. SWOT (Strengths/Weaknesses/Opportunities/Threats)
5. VOC (Voice of the Customer)
6. Systems Flowchart/Information Flow Diagrams
7. Gemba Walk (Go and See Analysis)
8. B-SMART Targets
9. JIT (Just-In-Time)/Kanban/Cells
10. Spaghetti Chart
11. Lean Events/RIE (Rapid Improvement Events)/Kaizen Events
12. Improvement Project
13. Just-Do-It
14. 5S
15. Poka-Yoke
16. Six Sigma/DMAIC
17. TPM (Total Product Maintenance)
18. Standard Work
19. 5 Whys
20. Brainstorming
21. Fishbone Charts

22. Pareto Charts
23. Affinity Diagrams
24. Control Charts
25. PICK (Possible, Implement, Challenge, Kill) Chart/Impact/Effort Matrix
26. Theory of Constraints (TOC)/Bottleneck Analysis
27. Project Charter

Technical Tool #1—7 Wastes

Taiichi Ohno developed the original catalog of the wastes and made them part of the Toyota Production System (TPS). These have become the foundation of the Lean process. Whenever a process is investigated because of poor quality, poor cycle time, or poor cost performance, the seven wastes are used to drill down and identify process deficiencies. These seven wastes are used to differentiate between "value-added" and the "non-value-added" activities that we are trying to eliminate. These seven categories of waste are:

1. Overproduction ahead of demand
2. Waiting
3. Unnecessary transportation
4. Overprocessing due to poor product or process design
5. Inventories beyond the absolute minimum
6. Unnecessary movement by employees during the course of their work
7. Production of defective parts

Many organizations have added an eighth waste, which is extremely appropriate for IT. We will include it in our discussion of the 7 Wastes. This eighth waste is:

8. Underused employee abilities or creativity.

Overproduction

Definition—Producing more, sooner, or faster than the "receiving" process or customer needs. Producing product for "anticipated" demand for which there are currently no orders. Producing higher-quality or more complex products than necessary. Any activity that increases storage space (inventory), transportation, damage (rework), delays, and overstaffing costs.

Results—Excess product that ends up getting stored or discarded. Products produced ahead of customer demand which end up being stored (another waste) and often discarded.

IT Application/Examples—Overproduction of information or excessive data collection beyond what is required. Developing excessively complex solutions to simple problems. Developing complex solutions to nonrepetitive problems. Dealing with all the "exceptions" by building an excessively complex product. Often considered to be the worst type of waste, overproduction of software is considered a plague within the IT industry. For example, numerous computer stores have overstocked inventory, anticipating a market that never develops. This inventory rapidly loses value and within one year may only be worth half of what it was purchased for, thereby generating enormous costs and losses. Similarly, manufacturers and software developers overproduce and overdevelop in a product market which has high price (value) deterioration.

Waiting

Definition—Time delays (people waiting or queuing), process idle time, time on hand that impedes or stops work flow. Delays caused by shortages, downtime, or unnecessary (redundant) approval cycles.

IT Application/Examples—Poorly developed reports or queries. People waiting for hard copy reports instead of using electronic reports. People waiting on input data. Poor computer response times. Poor utilization of resources, including people and systems resources. Waiting to get the "final" requirements for a project often results in a software developer working on other projects which are not "value-added" or possibly result in overproduction.

Unnecessary Transportation

Definition—Unnecessary transportation, multihandling, temporarily storing and moving materials, people, or information from one storage location to another. Movements that cause damage, missing items, or becoming an obstruction. This waste generates increased and unnecessary processing cycle time.

IT Application/Examples—Transferring data files, especially when it is between incompatible computer systems, software packages, or databases. Delivery of paper reports that could be electronic.

Overprocessing

Definition—Unnecessary, incorrect, or redundant processing of a task. Processing higher quality products than necessary. Adding more value to the product or service than the customer is willing to pay for. Processing with poor tools or improper product design.

IT Application/Examples—Excessive or redundant reconciling because of different systems. Having to enter the same information or orders in two or three systems. Overuse of technology when simplicity will do. For example, having to go back to the customer to get information about product or software requirements because the specifications were not fully developed the first time around is overprocessing. We need some form of standard work which would assure that the specifications are complete the first time around.

Excess Inventory

Definition—Material, product, or information waiting to be processed. Producing, holding, or purchasing unnecessary inventory, caused by wastes 1 and 4 which can take up space, impact safety, and become damaged or obsolete. Any resource that is stored and is not directly required to satisfy current customer orders.

IT Application/Examples—Storing computers, computer parts, outdated or obsolete information in databases. Too much data in transactional databases slowing down response time. Software development that goes beyond what the customer ordered, causing the process to run slower or to be excessively complex.

Unnecessary Movement by Employees

Definition—Excess activity (movement) or unnecessarily repeated activity. Handling unnecessary steps which could/should be automated. Poor layout (causing delays) or nonergonomic motion (causing possible injury). This includes any extra steps taken to accommodate inefficient processes, repair defects, or compensate for poor scheduling of other project activities.

IT Application/Examples—Excessive/unnecessary keystrokes. Repetition in a process. Poor process design requiring combination of mouse and keyboard activity. Poor process design requiring reentry of data instead of reuse of data. Difficulty in understanding codes or titles for information. Inefficient sequence of data input (illogical considering the input sources). Not properly considering input sources when designing input screens. Building "exception" functionality into a process so that every execution of the process is required to bypass some features which may only be required 5% or less of the time.

Production of Defective Parts

Definition—Rework. Products or services that do not conform to customer expectations. Correction of errors. Quality and equipment problems causing rework, replacement production, and scrap.

IT Application/Examples—Out-of-date information. Unused reports. Hard copy instead of electronic copy. Fixing data late in the process stream versus collecting data correctly in the beginning. Excessive verification of the data "after the fact." Implementation of a software product that is not fully tested and ready for implementation, causing rework.

Underused Employee Abilities or Creativity

Definition—Unused or underutilized people talents. Lost time, ideas, skills, and improvements resulting from not empowering employees or tapping their creativity and talents to solve problems.

IT Application/Examples—Inadequate or unavailable computer hardware/software for employees. No channel to capture employee ideas or questions. Lack of schedule of when IS improvement resources will be available. Dictatorial development style rather than team participation in the design and development process.

The 7 Wastes are the first Technical Tool discussed, not because it is the first step in a Lean process, but because it is one of the most important steps. The actual flow of a Lean process should follow the 9-Step A3 format discussed in an earlier chapter. And the 7 (now 8) Wastes are brought in as appropriate to analyze the current state process. Each step in the current state process should be challenged against the 7 Wastes to assure that it is value added.

Technical Tool #2—Value Stream Mapping (Current State/Ideal State/Future State)

A good analytical tool developed by Toyota and used in Lean activities to assist teams in understanding a process is the Value Stream Mapping (VSM) exercise. But before we discuss this tool, we need to understand what a value stream is. We start by defining value as the amount that a customer is willing to pay for a product or service. It is the amount required to fulfill a customer need or desire. Components of value include items like:

- Durability
- Quality
- Utility
- Price
- Capacity
- Functionality
- Timeliness
- Aesthetics
- Availability

The value stream incorporates all the events and activities in a product or process' supply chain that would affect those items to which the customer gives "value," which brings us to the point where we need to differentiate between value-added and non-value-added activities.

- Value-added activity—anything that directly increases the value of the product or service being performed (from a customer's perspective).
- Non-value-added activity—any support activity that does not directly add value to the product or service. Activities that add cost or time to the process, such as control systems, are non-value-added.

For example, drilling a hole is value added. But positioning the item to be drilled, changing the drill bit, cleaning the work station, moving the item to inventory, etc. are all non-value-added steps. In a service environment, value added is the performing of the service. Non-value added includes all the support functions that occur and which prepare the environment to perform the service. In Value Stream Mapping (VSM) we differentiate between value-added and non-value added activities.

Mapping the Process

Value Stream Mapping (VSM) is a waste identification tool that is used to identify Lean improvement opportunities by focusing on the non-value-added processes that get identified. It does not focus on working harder; it focuses on working smarter.

VSM creates a visual description of the value stream by looking at the entire system including all inputs, the process, and all outputs. VSM shows the linkages that exist throughout the system and challenges the current state of all activities. It identifies the sources of non-value-added waste that is identified in the value stream.

In the end, VSM becomes the foundation for the development of an improvement plan by presenting a complete picture of the current state of the processes involved. Using this information, VSM can then be used to establish a vision of what the desired future state condition should look like. This future state becomes the vision for the improvement plan, and from this we develop a collection of improvement actions, often referred to as "events." [3]

The VSM process has four phases (refer to the 9-Step A3 discussion in an earlier chapter to see how these flow in the overall Lean improvement process):

- Preparation
- Current state map
- Future state map
- Improvement plan

---

[3] Major pieces of this section are taken from MainStream Management training materials.

Preparation

In the preparation phase we focus on identifying the limits and ranges of the system under consideration. If we are dealing with a manufactured product, we identify the interactions involved in developing that product or the related product family. The product family is a group of products that go through a similar processing sequence and that use common equipment and resources. If we are dealing with an IT service, we look at the customer, the service performed, and the sources of materials or information that are required pieces of that service. For example, a new account or new product setup is a repetitive process that can have numerous steps. We need to map out that process in order to identify all the wastes that may exist in the process.

Product or process selection needs to be done carefully. We start by looking at those processes that have the largest impact on the business. The product or service selected for mapping should be one that has established a history of problems, like delivery problems, quality failures, cost overruns, etc. The VSM should focus on a product that has an urgent need for improvement.

Then we define the "scope" of the analysis, where we set arbitrary boundaries for the beginning and the end of the process. If the VSM limits are set too narrow, we may miss some big improvement opportunities. If the limits are set too large, we spend a lot of time going way beyond anything that will help the process under consideration. We end up trying to solve world hunger.

Once the product or process has been selected, the team needs to bring in the resident "gurus" on that item. The team also needs to include a customer and supplier to the process (see the SIPOC discussion—Technical Tool #3). The team also needs a facilitator who is often referred to as the Value Stream Focal. This individual makes sure that the VSM analysis process stays on track, and he or she reports the progress of the VSM mapping team to the project champion. The facilitator is the leader in the VSM discussion and implementation efforts. This individual becomes the scheduler, negotiator, and arranger, making sure the VSM team has the resources they need in order to stay on track.

Mapping Process

Before the actual mapping process can begin, the facilitator needs to make sure that the team has been properly formed to include all relevant stakeholders and product authorities. In a manufacturing environment this would include experts from the customer and supplier locations as well as internal experts from production, engineering, maintenance, quality, scheduling, shipping and receiving, transportation, etc. In an IT environment this would include experts from the customer (user) and supplier (data sources and data input) as well as internal experts from database management and software development. The team should include at least one process expert for every step in the product's value stream.

With the team in place, the facilitator organizes training on the VSM tools that will be used for the mapping exercise. Then the team goes on to define "value" from the perspective of the customer. What is it that the customer wants, and what is the customer currently settling for? We need to look at the product "what, when, where, how, why, and how much" from the customer perspective. This needs to be documented and displayed for the team and kept at the forefront of their VSM effort. This information should become the improvement goal of the VSM and later the Lean effort.

With the customer information documented, the team needs to review the key performance indicators (metrics) that are in place and then needs to challenge whether they are the correct performance indicators. These should include indicators like demand (time and quantity), quality, cost, capacity, backlog, delivery, bottlenecks, etc. (there is a more thorough discussion about Lean metrics or measures later in this book). The team needs to select and focus on just a few key measures. These measures need to focus on the customer while at the same time balancing between the needs of the other stakeholders and the members of the organization.

At this point the team should be in place and the goals established. Now the team is ready to observe the process and to gather data on the process. This requires a detailed walk through every step of the value stream. The team takes detailed notes on the flow of the materials, information, and people as they move through this flow (see Technical Tool #7—Gemba Walk or Go and See Analysis). They have a basic set of data that they need to take for each step, which would include information like:

- What triggers the process to begin at this step?
- How do we define the completion of this step?
- What is the total flow time through this process?
- What is the amount of time where value is actually added to the product or process?
- How many people are involved in the process?

- How much time is the equipment actually used? How much of this equipment time is value-added? How does machine value-added time affect worker value-added time?
- Are there any specific quality issues?
- Who is the customer of this step?

After the interview process the team is now ready to create the Value Stream Map. A table is created for each step in the process, which has all the relevant information that will be needed to analyze the value stream. In Figure 6.9 this table is referred to as the "Process Baseline Data."

In order to draw the map, there are some specific icons that are used. Consistency is important throughout the organization so that everyone can look at someone else's Value Stream Map and immediately understand the message that is being projected. A basic set of icons that are used can be found in Figure 6.9.[4]

With these icons and the foundational data we are ready to map out the process that we are studying. An example of a very short process map is shown in Figure 6.10. Most maps will be much larger because the number of steps in a process can be quite extensive. Often we hang butcher paper

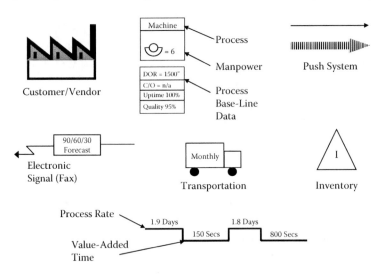

FIGURE 6.9
Value Stream Mapping (VSM) icons.

---

[4] Most of the slides from this chapter are taken with permission from the MainStream Management Consultants training program, and the author was graciously allowed to use this material in this book. These graphics help to make the concepts more understandable.

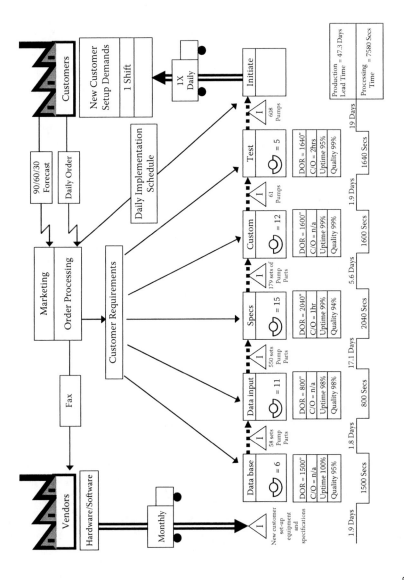

FIGURE 6.10
Sample Value Stream Map (VSM).

across the wall of a conference room. The paper is about three feet wide and as much as 20 feet long and is used to graph out the complete value stream. We post the paper on a wall and tape the value stream icons and Process Baseline tables on the paper, and then draw the appropriate connecting lines.

Figure 6.10 is the VSM of a new customer setup process. In it we see vendors providing equipment input into the system and customers receiving the needed services and equipment to initiate the order processing environment. We also see the customer's input into the information system after being processed by the IT setup process. In the process itself we see each of the setup steps, starting with Database Setup and ending with Test. For each of these steps we see the number of employees assigned and some other relevant data that we deemed critical for measuring this production process. The VSM also shows us the total production lead time (47.3 days or 1,362,240 sec. [47.3 days × 8 hr./day × 60 min./hr. × 60 sec./min.]) and the actual processing time (7, 580 sec.). This information will be used to identify the total value-added and non-value-added time. For this example the value-added time is 0.56% of the total time, and the non-value-added time is 99.44% of the total time. In this case there is tremendous room for improvement. Before you think this example is unrealistic, you should do a VSM on your organization. Less than 5% value-added is the norm, not the exception.

The value of the VSM process can now be seen in the diagram. We now review the VSM, attempting to find the sources of waste (the high non-value-added times). We look for the eight types of waste (see Technical Tool #1—7 Wastes). For the new customer setup example we see an enormous delay between Data Input and Specs. This delay of 17.1 days also results in a large interim inventory of work, assuming that people are not just sitting around for the 17 days.

Another area of significant concern is the average 19-day delay between testing and initiation of the process at the customer site. The result is an enormously large finished goods inventory of projects that are just sitting around and waiting to be implemented. Similarly, all the delays and all the inventories in the process need to be challenged. This organization needs to get its production process to where it adds value more than just one half a percent of the time. And implementing these improvements will require some major revamping of the current system. The process for identifying improvements has the following steps (these are all pieces of the overall 9-Step A3 problem solving process):

- Create an ideal state value stream map.
- Use the Ideal State VSM to create a realistic future state value stream map.
- Develop an action item list of improvement opportunities.
- Classify/prioritize the action item list.
- Select improvement events based on the highest priority areas of improvement.

Ideal State Value Stream Map/Future State Value Stream Map

The objective behind developing a future state value stream map (FS-VSM) is that we need to identify a target goal for our improvement effort. We start by throwing away the current state VSM, and we redraw an ideal VSM (IS-VSM). How would the perfect system operate? Next, using the ideal VSM, we come down to reality, realizing that we have limited resources. This is an important thought process. The author can remember two instances where the team, working on the IS-VSM, decided that the ideal state would be the elimination of the entire system—the entire system was a "waste." Other, more realistic examples could be where the IS-VSM may require a new building, but the FS-VSM requires us to remodel and renovate the existing location. We use our IS-VSM as the long-term goal when we create our FS-VSM. From this we can take our CS-VSM and identify changes that will need to be made in order to bring out current operating state to the desired future state. If we look at Figure 6.11 (taken from MainStream Management's training program) we see three versions of any value stream:

- What we think it is.
- What it actually is (which is the current state value stream [CS-VSM] that we develop during the VSM process).
- What is achievable (which is the FS-VSM).

Using the CS-VSM of Figure 6.10, we develop an IS-VSM, and from that a FS-VSM, which can be seen in Figure 6.12. The differences between Figure 6.10 and Figure 6.12 define the improvement gaps. These are the opportunities for improvement, and the process of identifying these gaps is often referred to as the gap analysis.

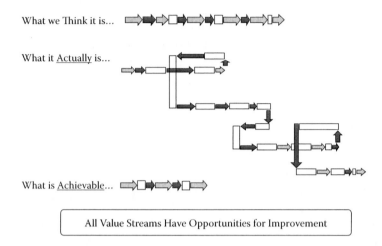

What we Think it is...

What it Actually is...

What is Achievable...

All Value Streams Have Opportunities for Improvement

FIGURE 6.11
The three versions of any value stream.

Develop an Action Item List of Improvement Opportunities

Using Figure 6.10 as the current state and Figure 6.12 as the future state (FS-VSM), we can now generate an action item list of improvements. In some Lean activities, this list is referred to as the Lean Newspaper. These improvements are highlighted in Figure 6.13, where we see the specific areas that are targeted for change. Refer to the discussion of the 9-Step A3 process to see how each of these steps fit into the overall Lean exercise.

Classify the Action Item List

We should now have an action item list of improvements. Next we will need to classify each item on the list by assigning it a priority based on issues like:

- How hard is this change to implement?
- What is the overall impact that this change will have to the process?
- What is the cost?
- What is the time span for implementation?
- How does this relate to the champion's priorities for this Lean activity?

We use these priorities to rank each of the change items. Then we use this ranking to identify Lean "events" around each of these areas of change.

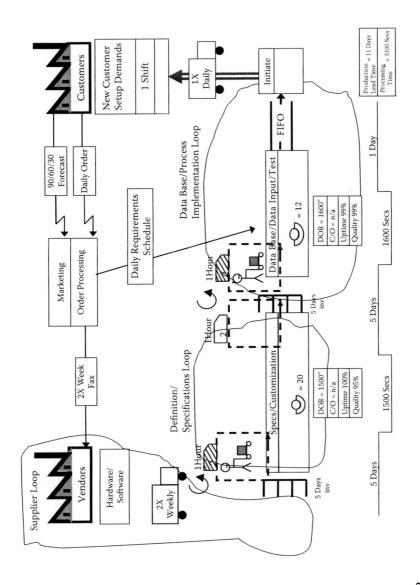

FIGURE 6.12
FS–VSM.

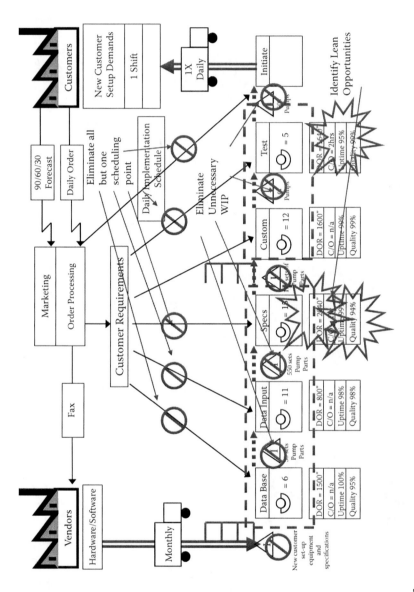

FIGURE 6.13
VSM improvements.

These recommendations are brought before the process improvement champion for approval or modification. Using this approval, the facilitator moves forward with the planning process for the improvement events.

An excellent tool the author likes to use for this prioritization process is the PICK (Possible, Implement, Challenge, Kill) Chart/Impact/Effort Matrix which is listed as Technical Tool #25 in this chapter.

Select Improvement Events Based on the Highest Priority Areas of Improvement

An improvement event goes through a process very similar to the organizing of any team activity. Ideally, each improvement event should have its own 9-Step A3 analysis before starting the improvement process. The A3 is a tool that is used at high-level assessments as well as at the "in-the-dirt" type of assessments that may be generated by the task list generated by a VSM exercise. Later in this book an entire chapter is dedicated to the execution of a Lean event, often referred to as an RIE (rapid improvement event) or a Kaizen Event.

Technical Tool #3—SIPOC (Supplier/Input/Process/Output/Customer)

The SIPOC tool is an excellent tool used in the analysis of a process' current situation. When accomplishing a 9-Step A3 analysis or an RIE, one of the main factors for success is the set of boundaries that are established for the process being analyzed. The boundaries are established by the process owner or champion, but are reconfirmed during the team event using a SIPOC. SIPOC is an acronym for Suppliers, Inputs, Processes, Outputs, and Customers. Each term is defined as follows:

- Supplier(s)—Who submits anything to the process? Those organizations or individuals who supply materials, equipment, people (expertise), requirements specifications, or data, including work in process or entire subsystems to create the value which the customer desires. Suppliers can supply materials, equipment, data, information, or expertise. Every element except the customer in the value stream is a supplier for either the customer or for the following process. Delivering value to the end customer requires the suppliers to deliver value at each step.

- Inputs—What are the inputs that are needed for the successful execution of the process? This is a description of where all the inputs to the process come from and what they are. It is the physical or information inputs defined. It is a clear description of exactly what the suppliers supply.
- Processes—What are the major process areas? This includes the steps that deliver value as well as all the non-value-added steps used to accomplish this process. The process may be broken down into subprocesses if they are important to the discussion of where value comes from. This discussion leads to a current state value stream mapping exercise, discussed in Technical Tool #2.
- Outputs—What does the process generate, both intended and unintended? This includes all the products that are delivered from the value stream even if they do not go directly to the customer. These outputs help define the delivery of value.
- Customer(s)—Who receives the output that is created by this process? Most important is the person or organization that receives value from the processes and outputs. Customers define value and determine if it has been delivered. Defining customers is a critical element of delivery value. This is usually defined by the person or organization that puts the outputs to use. (Also look at Technical Tool #5—Voice of the Customer [VOC].)

The author prefers to perform this assessment using flip charts and in reverse order, starting with a review of the customers of this process, then going to the expected outputs, etc.

Technical Tool #4—SWOT (Strengths/ Weaknesses/Opportunities/Threats)

SWOT analysis provides a strategic perspective of the organization in its current state. It is used to create a list of political, environmental, technical, managerial, or programmatic issues in an orderly format during strategic planning sessions. SWOT analysis provides input to strategic planning and forces discussion and assessment of internal (Strengths, Weaknesses) and external (Opportunities, Threats) issues that are affecting the organization. It also forces the team to prioritize the issues within each category and drives toward consensus.

SWOT analysis is generally a flip chart exercise where the facilitator draws ideas out of the team. Four flip charts are used, labeled: Strengths (areas to build upon), Weaknesses (issues to overcome), Opportunities (areas of competitive advantage that we should exploit), and Threats (concerns that we need to mitigate). Strengths and Weaknesses require an internal perspective of the organization, and Opportunities and Threats require a look beyond the organization to external aspects or effects on the organization.

For prioritization, give each team member one or two votes, and have the team vote on each item. The items with the most votes become the strategic drivers. The SWOT exercise provides an understanding of internal and external factors that are barriers or enablers to achieving strategic objectives. This list is then used to define the strategic priorities and goals for the organization.

Technical Tool #5—VOC (Voice of the Customer)

Voice of the Customer (VOC) is a tool which gives the user the customer's perspective as to what is important and what is not. The customer defines what is value added and what is waste. The first step in improving a process is to understand the customer's needs. Gathering the VOC has two parts, (1) identifying the customer and (2) documenting the VOC.

Identifying your customer may be more difficult than it seems on the surface. Consider each of these prospective customers when defining the customer:

- Immediate vs. ultimate customers
- Internal vs. external customers
- Current happy and unhappy customers (consider the extremes)
- Heavy vs. Light customers with respect to demand on the organization's resources (the Pareto principal predicts that 20% of your customers consume 80% of your IT resource.)
- Lost customers
- Potential future customers who would be your customer "if only"

Similarly, there are many ways to gather VOC data. Consider the following as options:

- Surveys—online, mail, etc.
- Interviews

- Focus Groups
- Complaint departments or systems
- Market research
- Customer databases
- Observation
- Customer contracts or specifications

In gathering the VOC data, caution must be exercised to ensure an unbiased sample of the most appropriate customer groups.

To better serve your customer, you must determine your customer's needs. For example, what are your customer's critical to quality (CTQ) issues? CTQs are those basic stated requirements that "must" be met in order to satisfy the customer. Your customer may also have unstated or implied needs that they take for granted and do not feel they need to specify, but which you need to keep incorporated within your IT specifications. Once the VOC is established, there are three major areas where this information can be used to guide the continuous improvement process (CIP) in your IT organization.

- Self evaluation—How does your service or product measure up against the VOC? Where are you coming short? Where are you being unnecessarily excessive (wasteful)? This can also provide a road map for prioritizing future improvement efforts. The VOC is further defined in gap analysis, which is part of Technical Tool #2—Value Stream Mapping. Ultimately, only your customer can determine whether a process step is value added.
- Measures—A measurement (metrics) system should be designed around a system of key process indicators (KPI) that reflect customer expectations (see Chapter 9). This measures your ability to effectively meet your customer's CTQs. Chapter 9 is on metrics later in this book.
- Plan for the future—What will your customer need in the future? How will you adapt to provide that future need? How will this affect the strategic perspective for your organization?

Technical Tool #6—Systems Flowchart/ Information Flow Diagrams

The VSM (Technical Tool #2) has given the team an excellent tool for understanding the paper and information flow of an IT process. Sometimes,

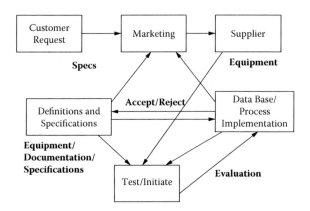

FIGURE 6.14
Detailed information flow.

however, this is not sufficient for environments where the background (within the system) information flow is very complex. In these cases it would be valuable to create a systems flowchart so that more of the information process can be detailed out and understood. A simplistic example is included in Figure 6.14.

Systems flowcharts may be needed for several "systems perspectives." These include:

Database perspective
User perspective
Software execution perspective

The actual flowchart can have dozens of information flow lines. It is not unusual to find out that only about one third of these lines are for control purposes or for error recovery purposes, both of which are system "wastes." It should become the goal of the Lean process to eliminate all the "non-value-added" information flow lines that exist.

Technical Tool #7—Gemba Walk (Go and See Analysis)

The Gemba Walk is a critical tool when developing the 9-Step A3 or when doing a VSM (see Technical Tool #2). After the goals of the process improvement activity have been established and the SIPOC has been performed defining the scope of the improvement effort, it now becomes important to physically go out and observe the process that needs to be improved. Now the team is ready to observe the process and to gather data on the process. This requires a detailed walk through every step of the value stream. The team takes detailed notes on the flow of the data, paper, materials, information, and people as they move through this flow. They have a basic set of data that they need to collect for each step, which would include information like:

- What is the performance measure for this step, and how does it tie to the system measurement goal for the entire process?
- What triggers the process to begin at this step?
- How do we define the completion of this step?
- What is the total flow time through this process?
- What is the amount of time where value is actually added to the product or process?
- How many people are involved in the process?
- What is the inventory level (for IT this would be in terms of hours of work) before and after this process? What is the backlog? Is this step a bottleneck? (Is there an excessive amount of inventory on the front end of this process?)
- How much time is the equipment actually used? How much of this equipment time is value-added? How does machine value-added time affect worker value-added time? This can be tricky because "just because you are typing does not mean you are adding value." Is the "system" forcing steps that are redundant or unnecessary? Is the system forcing waste?
- What is the batch size?
- What are the changeover times (change time between activities—system startup times)?
- What is the yield/average throughput?
- Are there any specific quality issues (areas of repeated errors)?
- Who supplies data/paper/etc. to this step?
- Who is the customer of this step?

After the interview process the team is now ready to create the Value Stream Map (Technical Tool #2). A table is created on the VSM for each step in the process, which has all the relevant information that will be needed to analyze the value stream. In Figure 6.9 this table is referred to as the "Process Baseline Data."

Technical Tool #8—B-SMART Targets

B-SMART is an acronym for the characteristics of good goals and valid metrics. Goals and metrics are set both strategically, and during the 9-Step A3 Process. B-SMART is a guide for creating metrics that are aligned with a value stream and are used to encourage Lean behaviors.

The acronym stands for:

- B = Balanced—This refers to multiple goals. It ensures that goals are balanced across the multiple fronts of organizational output. Are the goals balanced in such a way that they do not contradict or conflict? Are all the goals achievable?
- S = Specific—Is the goal specific enough so that you know if it has been achieved? The goal is to have desirable outputs that are based on subject matter expert knowledge and experience and are applicable to the process improvement activity. Vague goals that allow multiple definitions are not specific enough.
- M = Measurable—Is the measurement system in place? This includes time frames and should include data that is obtainable from specific sources.
- A = Attainable—Is it realistic? It should be a stretch, but not so far out that it is unattainable. Resources are available. Success may have some risk, but it is possible.
- R = Results oriented—Does the goal or metric motivate change? Will it drive people toward results? Metrics and goals should link to the mission, vision, and goals and be meaningful to the user.
- T = Time based—Is there a time limit for achievement? This provides step-by-step views versus giant leaps, and goals are measurable at interim milestones.

Facilitators who use B-SMART should work to identify what type of metrics (financial, behavioral, core-process) are appropriate to the process improvement activity. Additionally, the team needs to define the purpose for collecting data. Define what the team needs to know from the data being collected and whether the team can take action on the data collected. Then the team needs to create a standard definition for the metric to include the type of metric, reason for its selection, data source and method of collection, formula, and periodicity.

Then the team needs to create a data collection process that includes who will be collecting data and how the data will be used. The data collection process should be as simple as possible and be automatic. The least amount of effort exerted by personnel to collect data minimizes the errors associated with the data.

Using B-SMART should help the team establish and use balanced measures that ensure overarching goals are achieved and timely leadership/management action is taken. It offers the means in place to ensure the attainment of one metric and goal is achieved without harm to other areas of importance, for example, achieving the due date without sacrificing quality.

Technical Tool #9—JIT (Just-In-Time)/Kanban/Cells

Just-In-Time (JIT) systems have the fundamental objective of bringing in only what is needed when it is needed and in the amount it is needed. JIT does not believe in stockpiling anything. It attempts to minimize materials, equipment, labor, and space. In any process, JIT wants employees to only have the one piece they are working on, nothing else before their process or after it (no backlog of work—this is inventory). JIT utilizes the Pull System where nothing is introduced into the process until it is requested. For example, we produce nothing until the customer requests it (no overproduction), and we buy nothing until the production process begins and materials get requested from the vendor. Therefore, materials are "pulled" from their source, and never "pushed" into the process because some schedule anticipates that they should be there. The pull system works on feedback from the user/customer before work is introduced into the process. Work is not automatically generated just because we have spare time on our hands.

A typical JIT company will utilize small, inexpensive machines in the process, not large, multifunction ones. It will have one-piece project flow, not batches of projects. It will have standing operators that move around between functional steps in the process. It will be intolerant of abnormalities in the process. It will continually look for waste reduction opportunities in the process.

In order to cover JIT adequately it would require several books. There are literally hundreds of books available on this subject. The author will leave it to the reader to choose from these sources for further in-depth reading and understanding.

Technical Tool #10—Spaghetti Chart

Another mapping tool is valuable in showing travel time for reports/materials and/or the people involved in the process. The tool for this analysis is referred to as the spaghetti diagram. This is simply a floor plan of the area under consideration with lines showing the people movement or the materials movement for a particular process. With this diagram we can calculate travel time and travel distance, and excess travel is an enormous "waste." We should look at ways to reduce this travel time.

Figure 6.15 shows an actual example of staff travel time that was analyzed using spaghetti charting. It shows travel time and travel distance to get supplies, make copies, deliver reports, etc. for a particular process. By rearranging the layout and changing the sequence of the process steps, the total travel time and distance was reduced by 75%.

The spaghetti chart is created by simple observation. The facilitator of the Lean activity sits and watches the activities of someone engaged in the process under study. This occurs several times, and an average travel time/distance is recorded. Then, this spaghetti chart is used during the Lean

FIGURE 6.15
Spaghetti chart example.

event to highlight "wasted" travel, and the team is encouraged to consider alternative layouts that may reduce travel.

Technical Tool #11—Lean Events/RIE (Rapid Improvement Events)/Kaizen Events

The task list generated during Step 6 of the development of the 9-Step A3 results in three major types of tasks:

1. Just-do-its (see Technical Tool #13)
2. Improvement projects (see Technical Tool #12)
3. Improvement events (RIEs or Kaizen events)

The Lean event, also referred to as an RIE (rapid improvement event) or Kaizen event, is a structured process for identifying waste and developing a plan for implementing change. The foundation tool of the Lean event is the 9-Step A3 tool which is outlined in Chapter 3. It gives structure to the change process. The typical Lean event follows this sequence of steps (however there is no "typical Lean event." Every event gets customized by the Lean facilitator to maximize a particular improvement process. The typical event steps are:

- Develop a 9-Step A3 (Steps 1 through 7—see Chapter 3).
- Prioritize the task list (Steps 6 and 7—of the 9-Step A3).
- Select the first task that requires a Lean event.
- Develop a separate 9-Step A3 for the selected improvement task (Steps 1 through 3—these will be reworked during the actual event).
- Define the team charter (see Technical Tool #27)—from this we will identify the team that will be used for the event.
- Perform team readiness and change readiness assessment (see Acceptance Tools #2 through #5) to make sure you have a balanced team.
- Schedule the event (usually about one concentrated week when everyone focuses on the improvement process).
- During the actual one week event, we typically do the following:
  - Lean training, which at a minimum should include:
    – Explanation of what Lean is (definition)
    – Discussion of the 7 Wastes (Technical Tool #1)
    – Explanation of the SIPOC and SWAT tools (see Technical Tools #3 and 4)

- – Explanation of the VSM process (see Technical Tool #2)
- – Review of the 9-Step A3 document and how it is the guideline for the Lean event (see Chapter 3)
- Review/perform a SWOT (see Technical Tool #4)
- Review/perform a SIPOC (see Technical Tool #3)
- Current state VSM (see Technical Tool #2)
- Ideal state VSM (see Technical Tool #2)
- Future state VSM (see Technical Tool #2)
- Improvement task list (work through Steps 1 through 6 of the A3 that is specific to this improvement process—see Chapter 3)
- Execution plan for the task list (Work through Step 7 of the A3 that is specific to this improvement process)
- Plan a "governance process," which is where the team meets regularly to do a status check on the improvement process (work through Step 8 of the A3 that is specific to this improvement process)
- Report-out to the champion of this improvement process
- Hold regular follow-up status (governance) meetings

An example of a Lean event can be found in Chapter 8.

Technical Tool #12—Improvement Project

The task list generated during Step 6 of the development of the 9-Step A3 results in three major types of tasks:

1. Just-do-its (see Technical Tool #13)
2. Improvement projects
3. Improvement events (see Technical Tool #11)

An improvement project is a one-time activity, like the construction of a new building or a remodel. Projects are monitored just like a process improvement project, but because they are not a repetitive process, we do not look for repetitive process waste. However, we should consider the 7 Wastes (Technical Tool #1) as we proceed with the project activity.

Technical Tool #13—Just-Do-It

The task list generated during Step 6 of the development of the 9-Step A3 results in three major types of tasks:

1. Just-do-its
2. Improvement projects (see Technical Tool #12)
3. Improvement events (see Technical Tool #11)

A Just-do-it is generally something that is so simple that performing it as a project or as an event would be excessive. For example, a Just-do-it would be writing a letter, or signing an approval document, or moving a file cabinet. You would "just do it" and declare that task as completed.

Technical Tool #14—5S

The objective of a 5S activity is to create an organized, safe, and productive work environment. This requires some reorganization of the physical workplace layout. It requires a change in how we move and manage our physical work environment. It changes how current activities are performed. The 5Ss are:

- Sort—separate the needed from the unneeded items
- Set in order (straighten)—physically rearrange the layout—organize the work area
- Shine—clean and remove reasons for contaminants
- Standardize—implement procedures and signaling systems that ensure worker understanding of the process
- Sustain—set up systems to ensure open and complete communication

The 5S process begins with a scan of the current workplace. The objective of the scan is to document current operating conditions. We start by clearly defining the target area that is under consideration. Then we try to define the purpose and function of the targeted areas. We use our maps (VSM, spaghetti chart, and system flowchart) to show the physical flow between equipment and people. We look for problem areas, like inconsistent or intermittent flow, quality failures, or bottlenecks. We record current problems on a checklist. We photograph and document these problem areas and put them on a display board so the entire team can review and evaluate these areas. The team then searches for alternative solutions to these problems. For example, is the copy machine or the printer too far away from the workplace, resulting in excessive travel time "waste?" Sometimes we "centralize" equipment of this type so that it is easier to control the equipment, but the result is that we cause our employees to "waste" hundreds of hours in travel time going back and forth to these central locations.

Once the scan has been finished, the team goes on to complete the Workplace Scan Diagnostic Checklist (shown below). Each 5S step is then analyzed using questions similar to the ones on the checklist.

Sort

For the Sort phase we start by identifying a reject area where we will place all the "tagged" items. Then we go through and question every physical item in the target area including all equipment, inventory (piles of documents/paper/manuals), tools, etc. We "red tag" (see Figure 6.16) all tools or equipment that have not been used in the production process for more than one year, and we question all inventory items that have been in inventory for more than three months (these time periods are general and need to be adapted to the specific work environment). We need to question the existence and purpose of everything in the target area. We look for all items that are currently not in use or which simply do not belong in the target area. We also look for potential safety hazards. The slogan for this phase of 5S is, "When in doubt, move it out." The list of areas to inspect includes:

Search
- Floors
- Aisles
- Operation areas
- Workstations
- Corners, under equipment
- Small rooms
- Offices
- Loading docks
- Inside cabinets

Look for unneeded equipment
- Machines, small tools

Workplace Scan Diagnostic Checklist			# Problems	Rating			
			5 or more	Level 0			
			3 - 4	Level 1			
			2	Level 2			
			1	Level 3			
			None	Level 4			
Step	Item	Date:					
Sort	**Determine what is and is not needed**						
	Unneeded equipment, tools, etc. … are present						
	Unneeded items are on walls (bulletin boards etc.)						
	Items are present in aisleways, stairways, corners, etc.						
	Unneeded inventory, supplies, parts, materials are present						
	Safety hazards (water, oil, chemicals) exist						
Straighten	**A place for everything …**						
	Correct places for items are not obvious						
	Items are not in their correct places						
	Aisleways and equipment locations are not identified						
	Items are not put away immediately after use						
	Height and quantity limits are not obvious						
Shine	**Cleaning and looking for ways to keep it clean**						
	Floors, surfaces, and walls are not free from dirt						
	Equipment is not kept free from dirt, oil, and grease						
	Cleaning materials are not easily accessible						
	Lines, labels, and signs are not clean						
	Other cleaning problems are present						
Standardize	**Maintain and monitor the first three categories**						
	Necessary information is not visible						
	All standards are not known and visible						
	Checklists don't exist for all cleaning and maintenance jobs						
	All quantities and limits are not easily recognizable						
	How many items can't be located in 30 seconds or less						
Sustain	**Stick to the rules**						
	How many workers have not had 5-S training						
	How many times last week was daily 5-S not performed						
	Number of times that personal belongings were not stored						
	Number of times job aids are not available or up to date						
	Number of times last week 5-S inspections were not done						
		Total					

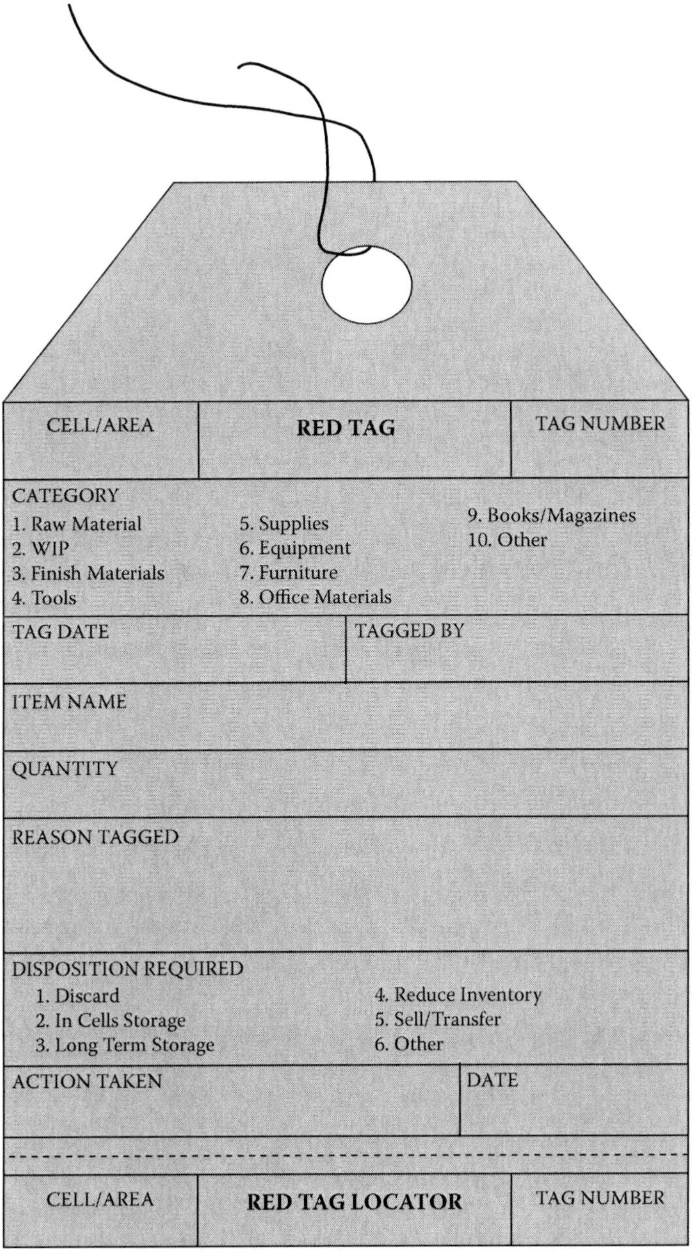

CELL/AREA	**RED TAG**	TAG NUMBER

CATEGORY

1. Raw Material	5. Supplies	9. Books/Magazines
2. WIP	6. Equipment	10. Other
3. Finish Materials	7. Furniture	
4. Tools	8. Office Materials	

TAG DATE	TAGGED BY

ITEM NAME

QUANTITY

REASON TAGGED

DISPOSITION REQUIRED

1. Discard	4. Reduce Inventory
2. In Cells Storage	5. Sell/Transfer
3. Long Term Storage	6. Other

ACTION TAKEN	DATE

- -

CELL/AREA	**RED TAG LOCATOR**	TAG NUMBER

FIGURE 6.16
Red tags.

- Dies, jigs, bits
- Conveyance equipment
- Plumbing, electrical parts

Look for unneeded furniture

- Cabinets
- Benches, tables
- Chairs
- Carts

Search these storage places

- Shelves
- Racks
- Closets
- Sheds

Search the walls

- Items hung up
- Old bulletin boards
- Signs

Look for unneeded materials

- Raw material
- Supplies
- Parts
- Work in process
- Finished goods
- Shipping materials

Look for other unneeded items

- Work clothes
- Helmets
- Work shoes
- Trash cans

As we identify items that need to be tagged, we "red tag" them (see Figure 6.16) and log them on the unneeded items log (see Figure 6.17). The tagged items are then removed to a "5S reject/removal area," where each of the items is evaluated and a disposition decision is made. The disposition of each item is then recorded using the item disposition list (see Figure 6.18), and the item is no longer a distraction to the current targeted process.

Needless Items (describe)	# of Items	Date	Reason for Tagging	Notes / Disposition

FIGURE 6.17
Unneeded items log.

Set in Order (Straighten)

The motto for the straighten phase is "A place for everything and everything in its place!" The process requires that we decide where we are going to keep items and then organize ourselves so that we keep these items in their appropriate locations. We need to organize not only a location, but also a methodology or a "how" we are going to keep them there. We use visual techniques for the proper identification of each work area. Once we have made these decisions, we then focus on the implementation of the changes that will make this process effective. As we proceed with the change process we need to evaluate and document the "before and after" effects of the changes we are making.

For the straighten phase we work to identify specific locations for each item that is used in a process. We accomplish this by:

Use this list to help determine the disposition of each red tagged item, then transfer the information onto both the red tag and the Needless Item Log.

Category	Action
Obsolete	• Sell • Hold for depreciation • Give away • Throw away
Defective	• Return to supplier • Throw away
Used about once per week	• Store in area
Used less than once per month	• Store where accessible in plant
Seldom used	• Store offsite (or in distant place) • Sell • Give or throw away
Use unknown	• Store until information is found

FIGURE 6.18
Item disposition list.

Making it obvious where things belong
Drawing lines
  − Divider lines
    − Aisle ways
    − Operations areas
  − Marker lines
    − Position of equipment
    − Inventory
    − WIP
    − Finished product area
  − Range lines
    − Range of motion for doors
    − Range of motion for equipment
  − Tiger lines—safety
  − Outlines or shadows
    − Tool or equipment placement
  − Arrows—direction
Making labels
  − Color coding
  − Item location (tools, parts)
    − Storage location of tools
    − Storage location of parts/inventory

Creating signs
- Equipment related information
- Indicate location of areas
- Visualizes processes and functions
- Show location, type, and quantity of inventory
- Scrap or trash area
- Provides direction in the factory

For the straighten process we look at:

Equipment
- Machines
- Small tools
- Dies
- Jigs
- Bits
- Conveyance equipment
- Cleaning equipment

Furniture
- Cabinets
- Benches, tables
- Chairs
- Carts
- Shelves
- Racks

Materials
- Raw material
- Supplies
- Parts
- Work-in-process
- Finished goods
- Shipping materials
- Cleaning supplies

Other items
- Charts, graphs, bulletin boards
- Books, paperwork
- Pens, pencils
- Work clothes
- Trash cans

Task	Location	Who	When	Materials/ Tools Needed

FIGURE 6.19
Shine cleaning plan.

Shine

In the Shine phase we focus on preventing dirt and contamination from occurring. The objective is to create pride in the workplace, to create a safer environment, to set an environment for fewer breakdowns, and to promote a higher level of product quality.

The implementation of the shine phase starts, as always, by analyzing the current situation. We develop a shine cleaning plan (see Figure 6.19), where we list all the areas that need cleaning. Once the team has identified the areas that need cleaning they will:

- Identify all needed cleaning materials
- Build a cleaning cart
- Clean everything, inside and out
- Inspect the thoroughness of the cleaning process
- Replace worn wires, hoses, tubing, filters, etc.
- Compare "before and after" results

During the shine process we look at everything. For example, our inspection list should include:

- Ceilings
- Aisles
- Workstations
- Corners, under equipment
- Loading docks
- Walls

- Doors
- Pillars, posts
- Floors
- Machines
- Conveyance equipment
- Plumbing, sinks
- Cabinets, shelves, racks
- Carts, racks
- Drawers, storage bins
- Fixtures, power boxes

Standardize

In the Standardize phase we focus on documenting all the 5S standards and making them visible to everyone involved in the process. We also make sure that a system exists which will maintain and monitor the work conditions to make sure that 5S standardization is continually maintained. This would include systems like the following for each of the 5S phases:

- Sort
  - Amount of inventory
  - Tools that belong in the area
  - How often to remove scrap
- Set in order
  - Location of pathways
  - Location of tools, equipment
- Shine
- Cleaning schedule
- Maintenance tasks
- Checklist of what to look for as cleaning is performed

With the systems in place to monitor the performance of each of these items, we can develop workplace display boards that are updated regularly with photos, maps like spaghetti charts, data, and graphs. This would give everyone in the workplace a visual representation of the 5S performance improvements as they occur.

Sustain

In the Sustain phase we focus on committing everyone involved in the work environment to adhere to the 5S standards. This includes everyone from production employees to top management. We want to establish a 5S culture of total employee involvement where 5S becomes a habit. We want 5S to become part of the corporate-wide communication plan. To accomplish these objectives we need organization-wide training and methods of communication. And we need to standardize these throughout the organization.

A Sixth "S"—Safety

In the United States, especially in the military and in military-related industries, a sixth "S" has been added, Safety, and they refer to this process as the 6 S process (not to be confused with Six Sigma). In the safety activity you would:

- Look for unsafe conditions
- Look for potentially unsafe acts
- Look for difficult tasks (are they ergonomic)
- Try the jobs yourself … where could you get hurt?
- List the opportunities
- Resolve them
- When performing a 6S activity at a workplace, be sure to investigate, identify, and correct possible hazards associated with the following:
- Ergonomics
- Environment
- Fire protection
- Machine and tool guarding
- Preventive maintenance
- Housekeeping
- Training

Baxter Healthcare engaged in a 5S project that focused on office supplies' cost reductions. They had initially set a goal of reducing spending by 30% by changing the ordering process and by making supplies more readily available so that individuals did not feel the need to stockpile their own set of supplies. After a 6-month effort they were able to reduce office supply spending by a surprising 60%. Additionally, on-hand supplies inventory was reduced by 50%, and space that was previously wasted on inventory storage has now been made available for other functions.

For IT, the 5S process is critical. First, try to 5S your own personal workspace. Generally, for IT personnel, their workspace is a disaster and needs organization. Next, try 5S-ing the files on your computer and organizing them into some form of standard work. Again this can be a challenging process. Here is a list of how the 5Ss can be applied to IT (but do not limit yourself to these—creatively look for other ways that the 5S principles apply):

- Sort—organize your work into:
  - High priority/low priority.
  - Large jobs/small jobs.
  - Identify interdependencies.
- Set in order
  - Start with your desk.
  - Then set in order the contents of your computer.
  - Prioritize the tasks that you "sorted."
- Shine
  - Remove non-value-added tasks.
  - Eliminate your backlog (if it has been there more than 6 months, it probably is not needed).
  - Clear out non-value-added software that complicates your processing time and bogs down your computer.
- Standardize
  - Physical storage areas.
  - Desks.
  - Computer storage areas (personal and common).
  - Standardize on the 9-Step A3 for problem analysis.
  - Standardize the design/analysis/development/testing/release/ support process.
- Sustain
  - Watch for small issues that may grow into large issues, and solve them before they become large.
  - Use teaming to brainstorm on potential problem areas and their solutions.
- Safety
  - Check the security of your work environment, both physical and electronic.
  - Ergonomics.

Technical Tool #15—Poka-Yoke

Poka-Yoke—Poka-Yoke is a Japanese term that means "mistake proof." It is a method of redesigning processes to prevent errors. It is one of the foundational quality improvement tools in any Lean process. Some everyday life examples of Poka-Yoke tools include:

- Computer disks that can only be inserted in the drive one way
- Automatic seat belts
- Auto-shut-off irons
- Automatic sinks in public restrooms
- Low clearance barriers in a parking garage

In our IT development environments there are four different levels of quality (see Figure 6.20). Unfortunately we find that in the United States we tend to fall into one of the first two levels, where inspection and quality certification occur with the customer or at some other point at the end of the development process. This is unfortunate for many reasons. With level one and two, we often find that an extensive amount of unnecessary development effort has been extended without inspection or validation. This effort may be unnecessary or wasted if there is a fault in the process. This wasted effort could have been saved if the error was caught earlier in the process. Additionally, catching the problem late

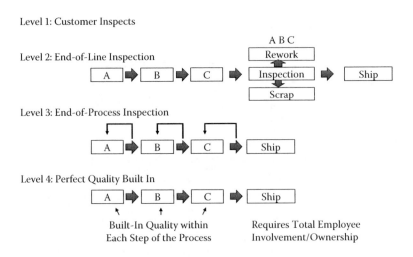

FIGURE 6.20
Four levels of quality.

often means that the cost of rework is much higher. This failure to catch the problem earlier may also cause delays causing extensive customer dissatisfaction or frustration.

The third level of quality is the basic level of quality for all JIT (Just-in-Time) systems (see Technical Tool #9), where inspection becomes part of the production process. Inspection occurs at the end of each production step.

The fourth level of quality is the level that Poka-Yoke strives for, where inspection is not a separate step. Rather, it is a wasted and eliminated step. With Poka-Yoke, redesign the production process so that it will validate and eliminate quality errors.

Once again, in order to cover Poka-Yoke or the topic of Lean quality adequately, it would require a book all by itself. The author will leave it to the reader to identify one of the abundant sources on these topics for further reading and understanding.

Technical Tool #16—Six Sigma/DMAIC

The term Six Sigma (6σ)[5] is a performance measure that was developed in order to accurately measure quality. Using Six Sigma we can set process goals in parts per million (PPM) in all areas of the production process. Since its origin, 6σ has evolved into a methodology for improving business efficiency and effectiveness by focusing on productivity, cost reduction, and enhanced quality.

Six Sigma has its roots back with the efforts of Joseph Juran and W. Edwards Deming. Their programs for Zero Defects and Total Quality Management in Japan lead to the adoption of the 6σ philosophy by Motorola. Motorola was able to achieve a 200 fold improvement in production quality and saved a reported $2.2 billion using this tool. General Electric has also become the strong proponent of 6σ. They claim extensive successes. They used it during the reign of Jack Welch, and this has generated global recognition. Jack Welch made 6σ the biggest corporate initiative in GE's history. Other users include Texas Instruments and Allied Signal. Allied took 6σ to an even higher level by incorporating it not just in production but by making it a system of leadership. Other current users include JP Morgan Chase, Sun Microsystems, American Express, and Lloyds TSB. Today 6σ has

---

[5] Some of this material was developed by the author for an article in *The Encyclopedia of Management*.

evolved to become a management methodology which utilizes measures as a foundational tool for business process reengineering.

The name Six Sigma comes from the statistical use of the sigma (σ) symbol, which denotes standard deviations. The six identifies the number of standard deviations around the mean. Hence, in Six Sigma we are saying that you have to go out beyond six standard deviations around the mean before you find failure. With a high enough number of sigmas (beyond six), you would approach the point of "zero defects." The sigma levels step changes; for example moving from 3σ (93% accuracy) to 4σ requires quantum leaps of improvement. A move from 3σ to 4σ is an 11 times improvement. From 4σ to 5σ is a 27 times level of improvement, and from 5σ to 6σ is a 69 fold change. Hence, moving from 3σ to 6σ is a 20,000 fold level of improvement.

At the Six Sigma level, the product failures (number of parts beyond the allowable limits) would be 3.4 parts per million. This equates to a 99.9997% accuracy. In today's world, 98% or 99% accuracy is considered excellent. However, 6σ has now become the universally recognized standard of quality.

A guiding principle of Six Sigma is that if you want something to happen, you better measure it. Unfortunately that also means that if you measure the wrong things, you will get the wrong results. For example, measuring throughput may speed up production, but at the cost of quality. Measuring quality may increase quality, but decrease customer service. So one of the toughest challenges in Six Sigma measurement is to identify the measurement system that will trigger the correct collection of responses.

A second key principle of measures in the Six Sigma environment is that all the measures should be openly visible. Openly displaying all measures on charts and graphs is a primary motivator toward the correct response.

And a third principle to remember is that the change curve applies (see Chapter 4). When change happens, performance will initially go down before it recovers and goes back up. This drop in performance is often scary, but a little patience will soon see its recovery.

A principle of success or failure in the Six Sigma world is the requirement for cultural change or change readiness. If the organization is not primed for change, then an environment for change must be instilled prior to starting Six Sigma, or the project is doomed to failure. This requires training, team bonding, and team-based goal setting. The resistance that exists because of a lack of understanding of what the Six Sigma process is attempting to achieve can be avoided with proper training.

Six Sigma concentrates on measuring and improving those outputs that are critical to the customer. The tools to accomplish this include a range of statistical methodologies which are focused on continuous improvement using a statistical thinking paradigm. This paradigm includes the following principles:

- Everything is a process.
- All processes have variations that are inherent within them.
- Data analysis is a key tool in understanding the variations in the process and in identifying improvement opportunities.

It is in the management methodology where the key, underlying benefits of 6σ can be found, which includes a problem solving and process optimization methodology. Six Sigma creates a leadership vision utilizing a set of metrics and goals to improve business results by using a systematic five-phased problem solving methodology. There are two common problem solving project management methodologies that are commonly associated with 6σ. The first is DMAIC (Define, Measure, Analyze, Improve, Control), and the second is DMADV (Define, Measure, Analyze, Design, Verify). We will discuss the most common, DMAIC.

Six Sigma is a measurement-based strategy that focuses on reducing variations through monitoring and measurement tools. It is based on a philosophy which holds that every process can and should be repeatedly evaluated and significantly improved, with a focus on time required, resources, quality, cost, etc. The philosophy prepares employees with the best available problem solving tools and methodologies using the five-phased DMAIC process. Explaining each of the steps in the process in more detail, we have:

- Define—At the first stages of the process we look for and identify poorly performing areas of a company. We then target the projects with the best return and develop articulated problem and objective statements that have a positive financial impact on the company. We "Define" the opportunity from both the organization and the customer perspectives.
- Measure—At this stage we are trying to tie down the process under consideration. Where does it start and end? What should we be measuring to identify the deviation? What data characteristics are repeatable and identifiable? What is the capability of the process? We

use tools like process mapping, flowcharting, and FMEA (Failure Model Effects Analysis). We develop a baseline for the targeted area and implement an appropriate measurement system. We need to understand the process and its performance.

- Analyze—Having identified the who and what of this problem, we now target the where, when, and why of the defects in the process. We use appropriate statistical analysis tools, scatter plots, SPC and SQC, Input/Output matrixes, hypothesis testing, etc. and attempt to accurately understand what is happening in the process. We need to search for the key factors that have the biggest impact on the process performance and determine the root causes.

- Improve—At this point we should have identified the critical factors that are causing failure in the process. And, through the use of experiments, we can systematically design a corrective process that should generate the desired level of improvement. This improvement will then be monitored to assure success.

- Control—In the control phase we implement process control tools that can manage and monitor the process on an ongoing basis. The DMAIC process is now in full operation, but it does not stop here. We need to develop a control plan. The continuous monitoring of the process will not only assure the success of this change process, but it will also identify future opportunities for improvement.

Some excellent and highly recommend websites include onesixsigma.com and qualitydigest.com, and they include several informative articles.

Statistical process control (SPC)[6] is a foundational statistical analysis tool for Six Sigma (6σ). Statistical process control (SPC), and its companion statistical quality control (SQC), are tools utilized by a 6σ improvement process. The original objective of SPC is to provide productivity and quality information about a production process real-time. The focus was on process control and continuous improvement. The operators become their own inspectors and control their own processes.

The SPC process should collect data and report results as the process is occurring, so that immediate action can be taken. This should help a process, and its quality measures, avoid straying beyond acceptable limits and would avoid the production of bad parts. When appropriately applied, SPC can virtually eliminate the production of defective parts. Additionally,

---

[6] Some of this material was developed by the author for an article in *The Encyclopedia of Management.*

SPC creates visibility of the cause of the failure. Since an operator is able to immediately recognize that a failure is occurring, he would be able to react to that failure and observe the cause of the failure, and then take corrective action. As Peter Drucker emphasizes, the "operators become the 'owners' of not just the process, but also the parts they produce."

Because of its success, SPC has found application in other industries, including service industries, transportation industries, and delivery services, and can even be found in fast food and baggage handling. For example, on-time delivery performance can be monitored on an SPC chart.

In the SPC data collection process, the objective is to collect the necessary data that will be needed to validate that a specific process is occurring correctly. The methodology for measurement is established at the point where the appropriate data is collected. Only the data that is required for the monitoring of the process is collected. An analysis of the specific reasons for collection of the data is important because any additional, unnecessary data collection is considered to be a waste. The accuracy of the measurement process is also confirmed.

There are several tools available for the display of SPC data. These include:

1. Graphs and charts are used to display trends or to summarize the data. These tend to be bar or line graphs that report on a specific parameter of performance.
2. Check sheets or tally sheets are used to take the raw data and reorganize it into specific categories that are being observed.
3. Histograms or frequency distribution charts are used to translate raw data into a pictorial display showing the performance of specific quality characteristics.
4. Pareto principles are used to prioritize the contribution effect of specific quality problems. This tool assists in identifying which problems have the largest impact on a specific quality problem under study.
5. Brainstorming is used to generate ideas by taking advantage of the synergistic power of a team of people.
6. Ishikawa diagrams (fishbone charts) are used to create problem and solution visibility by grouping problem causes into branches. Often this is referred to as a cause and effect diagram. Using this tool in conjunction with the Plan-Do-Check-Act (PDCA) process helps to narrow down the root cause.

7. Control charts are used to validate that the variation of measurement of a specific parameter is kept within a set of control limits.

Control charts and SPC are discussed in additional detail in section "Technical Tool #24—Control Charts." This section includes examples of control charts.

Control charts and SPC are some of the fundamental tools of Six Sigma. These tools are used to measure performance and identify normal versus abnormal variation. Analyzing this data gives the evidence supporting corrective action. Some additional tools that are used in Six Sigma include:

Flowcharts (Technical Tool #6)
Pareto diagrams (Technical Tool #22)
Cause and effect diagrams (Technical Tools #21, 23, and 25)

Technical Tool #17—TPM (Total Product Maintenance)

Total Product Maintenance (TPM) (this acronym is also used for Total Productive Maintenance and Total Preventative Maintenance) is a system focused on helping to attain and maintain competitiveness in quality, cost, and delivery. TPM focuses on strategies for creating employee ownership of the process and the equipment, thereby generating in them an urgency to eliminate system waste. TPM is utilized to alleviate system wastes associated with equipment (improving the effectiveness and longevity of machines). Examples of waste include:

- Minor, medium and major stoppages (breakdowns)
- Long setup times
- Rework, defects, abnormalities, and low yields
- Planned downtime
- Incomplete 5S application
- Overproduction by large equipment
- Equipment problems at production startup

TPM is an attempt to eliminate minor work stoppages. It focuses on zero defects. This is accomplished by:

- Understanding the current changeover process
- Clarifying the problem areas in changeover, adjustment, and test runs
- Checking the precision of the equipment and replaceable parts
- Improving your positioning methods
- Taking care of the remaining adjustments
- Carrying out product maintenance (P-M) analysis
- Create changeover standards
- Maintain and manage

Once again, in order to cover TPM adequately, it would require a book all by itself. The author will need to leave it to the reader to identify one of the abundant sources on these topics for further reading and understanding.

Technical Tool #18—Standard Work

Standard work focuses on having a process standardized so that everyone who performs that activity will perform it in the same way. Standard work is used to identify the best known way to complete a task and then teaches everyone that "standard" method. Standard work ensures that the same work will take the same amount of resources to achieve the same results every time.

Standard work is a foundational tool of continuous improvement. All team members working on a process should be searching for improvement opportunities. Once discovered and implemented, the team should standardize on this improved process across all team members so everyone will benefit from using this best practice.

If work processes are not standardized across the organization, it is impossible to effectively forecast resource utilization. Standard work facilitates experimenting and testing new ideas for improving the work process. If the current process is not standard, then it will be impossible to determine the impact of improvements upon process outputs.

The standard work for every process step will be unique. Here are some general guidelines that facilitate a standardized process:

1. Involve staff from all shifts/all work centers/all locations that do the same type of work. Typically, each location or shift will have their own method of working the process. Members from all units work-

ing the same tasks should be involved in establishing best practices for standard work.

2. Let the process workers work together to define the work and gain consensus. They know the work better than anyone else, and not involving them in the definition of the standard work is a recipe for disaster. Employees also need to understand the benefits of standard work and develop ownership of the process. The best ways to develop ownership and buy-in is to involve them in designing standard work.
3. Keep it simple. Unnecessary complexity adds opportunities for failure.
4. Document the standard work and train from the documentation. Once the "best possible method" is agreed on, it must be documented so that everyone can learn the new standard and can now measure their performance against the standard.

Standard work is unique to each process, but they all share these characteristics:

1. It should be the best, safest, easiest, most cost-effective, and productive way to complete the task.
2. It preserves the corporate knowledge for the benefit of everyone who will work the process in the future.
3. It provides the basis for measurement against a standard.
4. It provides the basis for training future team members.
5. It ensures meeting the customer critical to quality (CTQ) requirements.
6. It minimizes operator-driven variability.

Technical Tool #19—5 Whys

The "Five Whys" is a simple method to help problem solving teams drill down to the "true" root causes. The Five Whys is a tool to help identify root cause (see Step 5 of the 9-Step A3 in Chapter 3). To prevent problem reoccurrence, teams must address the root causes of the problems rather than just the symptoms. The Five Whys helps teams to drill down to the events behind a problem. Teams should not take "five" as an absolute. They may need to drill deeper than five. Rarely do they identify true root causes in fewer than five steps.

The Five Whys tool implies that every event has only one cause. However, there are often several factors that come together to "cause" an event.

Teams may drill down into items that are not part their sphere of influence. Although the teams may not be able to control the ultimate root cause, they can at least inform those who do and implement improvements as far down toward the root cause chain as they are able.

A strength of the "Five Whys" tool is its simplicity. The tool starts with a simple problem statement (the problem that you are trying to solve—see Steps 1 and 3 of the 9-Step A3 analysis tool in Chapter 3) and asks, "Why did the problem occur?" When an explanation is reached, the team asks "why" again … five times, each iteration asking "why" about the previous explanation.

A good test of the logic in the drill down is to see if the chain works in reverse. Start at the fifth why and work back to the first, but instead of asking why say "therefore…" Using this process, we can identify the true root causes which become the basis for corrective measures.

Technical Tool #20—Brainstorming

Brainstorming is a simple way for a team to generate a large number of ideas in a short amount of time. Brainstorming allows the creative juices of team members to generate ideas in a open setting. By establishing that ideas do not have ranks and there are no bad ideas, the team is freed of the fear of judgment (retribution and attribution are eliminated). Doing brainstorming in a team setting lets team members build on, and be inspired by, each other's ideas. The technique is especially useful in finding creative new approaches to difficult problems. Brainstorming will not generate solution plans. However, in conjunction with other tools, such as affinity diagrams (see Technical Tool #23) and impact vs. effort ranking (see Technical Tool #25), brainstorming can become the first step in problem solving.

Brainstorming occurs in a group or team setting, ideally between six to twelve members. Necessary materials include a large stack of sticky notes, felt tip markers, and a wall-size expanse of butcher block paper. Sticky notes facilitate sorting of the ideas and leads into affinity diagramming (Technical Tool #23). The team should throw out any idea they can think of without consideration as to how feasible or outlandish the idea may seem. Team members should build on each other's ideas.

Technical Tool #21—Fishbone Charts

A fishbone diagram (or Chart) is a method for organizing and analyzing all factors that contribute to a problem. A fishbone diagram is a predefined form of affinity diagram (see Technical Tool #23). Fishbone diagrams literally look like a fish skeleton, with six ribs branching off a central spine. A problem statement serves as the fish head, with the six ribs representing the six broad categories of causal factors: Manpower, Machine, Method, Material, Measurement, and Environment. These six factors are not rigid and may need to be modified in order to fit a specific application. For example, in solving IT problems we may want to add Database, or Information Technology, or User Interface, and drop Machine or Environment.

A fishbone diagram is an excellent way to organize factors around an unfamiliar problem. In other problem solving methodologies, the fishbone diagram is referenced by alternate names: "5M&E" diagrams, "4M" diagrams (measurement and environment are left out), "cause and effect" diagrams, and "Ishikawa" diagrams. An example of a fishbone diagram can be seen in Figure 6.21.

A fishbone diagram is most effectively completed by using a cross-functional team of process and customer experts that are the most familiar with the problem. Ideally the team size is from six to twelve members. Materials needed include sticky notes, felt tip markers, and a wall area for posting the sticky notes. The procedure is as follows:

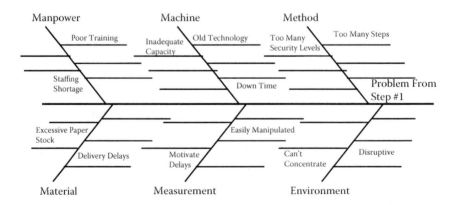

FIGURE 6.21
Fishbone chart.

- Draw the skeleton of the fish to be filled in. Identify the "problem" on the head at the right end of the spine which extends to the left. Draw three parallel ribs branching off of the spine above the spine and three more ribs below the spine. Upper ribs point from the spine towards the upper left corner and lower ribs point to the lower left.
- Label the fish skeleton. The head contains the problem statement, and the ribs are labeled Machine, Material, Measurement, Method, Manpower, and Environment.
- Have the team brainstorm ideas that could be contributing to the problem.
- Write each idea on a separate sticky note.
- Place each sticky note on the rib that most closely describes the category the idea relates to.
- After a free-flowing stream of ideas dries up, have the team concentrate on each rib, one at a time, to try and squeeze a few remaining ideas out of the team.

The resulting Fishbone Diagram gives us a type of affinity diagram (see Technical Tool #23). It helps us determine the root cause of the problem being analyzed (see Step 5 of the 9-Step A3 in Chapter 3). It works well with and supports the other root cause tools.

Technical Tool #22—Pareto Charts

The Pareto diagram is a graphical technique which separates the critical few from the trivial many. It was named after the Italian economist Vilfredo Pareto (1848–1923) who discovered that 80% of the wealth in Italy was held by 20% of the population. This 80/20 rule has later been shown to apply to almost every aspect of human endeavor. For example, 20% of customers will account for 80% of sales, 80% of sales will be generated by 20% of the sales force, 80% of our IT failures will be caused by 20% of the software or database systems, and 20% of the employees will consume 80% of a supervisor's time.

Pareto diagrams make it visually obvious which factors drive the majority of the impact. Pareto diagrams also provide a ranking order in which the factors should be addressed. Pareto diagrams are simple spreadsheet exercises. For example, if we count the number of system failures, and link them to a cause, then sort the failures from highest number of causes to lowest number of causes, we will find that 20% of the causes will have 80%

of the total number of failures (you need at least 50 data points to statistically make this work).

A Pareto diagram could be used to depict high-frequency failure areas, programming problems, customer discrepancies, complaint calls, etc. After the analysis, the prioritization is simple. You work on the cause with the highest number of failures first.

Technical Tool #23—Affinity Diagrams

Affinity diagrams are a tool offering the simple and flexible organization of ideas and information.

If the team is unfamiliar with a problem area or feels overwhelmed by a large volume of data or ideas, affinity diagrams can bring order to the chaos. Affinity diagrams simply lump ideas together. By grouping and regrouping ideas and data points, teams can begin to organize patterns of thought from incoherent information.

Affinity diagrams are often used with the brainstorming technique (see Technical Tool #20). The large volume of loosely related ideas generated by brainstorming can be organized using affinity diagramming. Fishbone diagrams (see Technical Tool #21) are a specific form of affinity diagrams.

Affinity diagrams may also be referred to as KJ diagrams after Dr. Kawatkita Jiro, an early proponent of the method.

Affinity diagrams are best developed by a team. The resources required include a wall or flip charts, sticky notes, and markers. The procedure includes the following steps:

- Create a separate sticky note for each idea or data point (similar to brainstorming—Technical Tool #20).
- Look for groups of notes that have something in common.
- Arrange the sticky notes in groups on the wall.
- Repeat this process until all the sticky notes have been grouped together, even if one of the groups is "other" or "miscellaneous."
- Some sticky notes may belong to more than one group. This is OK. The two groups will need to be moved next to each other on the wall so that the sticky notes belonging to both groups can also be near their original groups.
- Draw a circle around each affinity group of sticky notes, and label the circles with a category name.

- Review the groupings to make sure they are meaningful and accurate. Ask the following questions:
  - Do all the affinity groupings make sense relative to each other?
  - Do one or more groups need to be dissolved and reorganized?
- Do any of the affinity group titles need to be improved?

The end product from this exercise should be a grouping of ideas. The next step in the process would be to prioritize the ideas within each group, using tools similar to those listed in Technical Tools #25—PICK Charts. From this we can identify the top priority root causes or the best ideas by affinity grouping.

Technical Tool #24—Control Charts

Control charts are a key tool for Six Sigma (see Technical Tool #16—Six Sigma/DMAIC). Control charts are also referred to as statistical process control (SPC),[7] which is a foundational statistical analysis tool for Six Sigma (6σ). Statistical process control (SPC) and its companion statistical quality control (SQC) are tools utilized by a 6σ improvement process. The original objective of SPC is to provide productivity and quality information about a production process real-time. The focus was on process control and continuous improvement. The operators become their own inspectors and control their own processes.

Control charts visually organize time series data collected as observations of a process. The visual display of quantitative data makes it easier to observe how a process is behaving. It differentiates between variation due to "noise" (also called common cause variation) and variation that signals a significant change in the process (also called special cause variation).

Control charts are time series run or line charts. The vertical axis usually represents some quantitative measure of the process output as sampled at a fixed interval. The chart typically has three equally spaced horizontal lines running across the chart. The center line is the expected average of the measurements, the upper line is the upper control limit (UCL), and the lower line is the lower control limit (LCL). Data points that fall above or below the control limits indicate a change has occurred in the process, and an adjustment should be made to the process. As long as the data points

---

[7] Some of this material was developed by the author for an article in the Encyclopedia of Management.

fall between the UCL and LCL, the process is behaving normally and no action should be taken.

In control charts or SPC, the most critical part of the process is the validation that you are measuring the right thing and thereby motivating the correct response. Additionally, if one measure can take the place of several measures, then that one measure should be identified, thereby simplifying the measurement process. Once a measurement has been selected, then we are ready to set up the data collection process and to establish control charts that will monitor the performance of this data.

The control charts are built around a specific product parameter that requires monitoring because of its impact on the overall quality of the product. The following discussion is an extremely basic overview of the SPC process, and should not be considered to be sufficient for implementing an SPC process. Rather, this discussion is simply intended to give the reader a basic overview of the process.

The next step in the SPC process is to establish a set of control variables which includes an average (X) and a range (R). These can be established by going to the drawings and reviewing the initial part specifications using the expected value as X and the tolerance range as R, or these variables can be established using historical values and calculating the historical average (X) and range (R) for the data.

Having established an X and R value, we can calculate an upper control limit (UCL) and a lower control limit (LCL).

$$UCL = X + R$$
$$LCL = X - R$$

From these values, a pair of control charts is created. These charts are used to plot the SPC data as it occurs. They are used as a visual tool to monitor the process. Figure 6.22 is an example of the X-bar SPC chart that monitors a process. For this chart we will use X = 1.23 and R = 0.45.

From Figure 6.22 we can see how the measurement data is recorded on the chart at the time each measurement occurs. The objectives behind this data collection process are several. One is to catch outliers in the data (anything above the UCL or below the LCL). These outliers are quality failures and must immediately stop the process. Another purpose for the measures is to identify trends. For example, data points 1 through 5 indicate a strong trend to failure approaching the LCL. Corrective action should be taken immediately to avoid the possibility of producing bad parts. Another

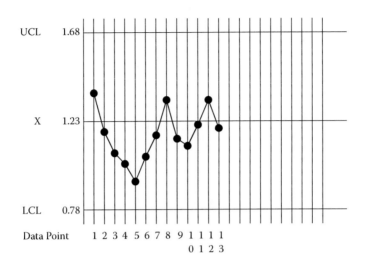

FIGURE 6.22
X-bar chart.

objective can be seen in data points 7 through 13 which indicates that perhaps our LCL and UCL are too far and need to be brought in tighter, thereby giving us a higher level of performance and a higher level of quality.

Another methodology for applying SPC processes is by collecting data, not on every event, but on a random sampling of the event. This occurs when there is a large volume of activity and the time required to measure each event is too burdensome. A statistical sample is taken, and from that sample the average of the sample data (X_1) and the range of that sample $(R_1$ = highest minus lowest measure) is calculated. For example, if our random sample size was five data points and our sample included the measures of 1.4, 1.45, 1.2, 1.3, and 1.65, then X_1=1.4 and R_1= 1.65 – 1.2 = .45. This X_1 value would then be the first data point plotted on Figure 6.22.

Using the statistical random sample, a range chart would also need to be created. Figure 6.23 is an example of a range chart, and the first data point of the chart would be the plot of the data corresponding to the example given. For this example, the lower limit is zero, which states that there is no deviation between each of the data points of that sample. The center point is R (.45), and the UCL is equal to 2 times R (.90).

In the example of the range chart (R chart), the lower the value, the better. A lot of vibration all over the chart suggests that the process may be going out of control. Also, a trend moving upward, as we see from data points 5 through 10, would indicate that a process is starting to go out of control, and corrective action should be taken immediately.

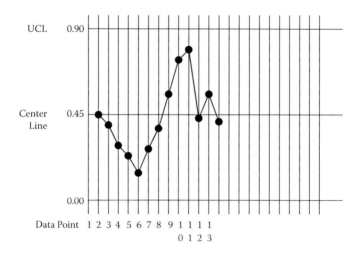

FIGURE 6.23
R chart.

With the X-bar and R charts, we can now create summarized reports, like the histograms and frequency distributions that were discussed earlier. This allows a long-term, summarized perspective of the process, rather than the chronological timeline that the X-bar and R charts offer.

Once the control chart is set up, the person closest to the work should be placed in charge of taking the samples and entering the data in the chart. UCL and LCL values can be determined mathematically based on sample size and standard deviation of the data points already collected. UCL and LCL values can also be identified as customer specifications.

Control charts and SPC are the means to measure performance. They identify normal versus abnormal variation and facilitate corrective action. Be sure to see Technical Tool #16—Six Sigma/DMAIC, which ties in with this Technical Tool.

Technical Tool #25—PICK (Possible, Implement, Challenge, Kill) Chart/Impact/Effort Matrix

Step 6 of the 9-Step A3 problem solving tool shown in Chapter 3 generates a list of improvement tasks that will need to be completed in order to solve the root causes (Step 5) of the "Problem" defined in Step 1. Generally, an organization does not have sufficient resources to execute all the improvement tasks at the same time, so a prioritization of the tasks is necessary. Numerous tools exist that facilitate prioritization, some of them extremely

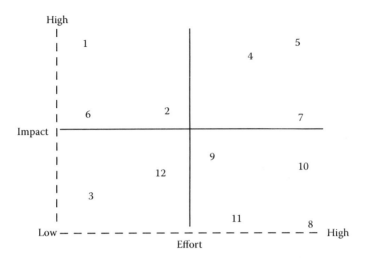

FIGURE 6.24
Impact/effort matrix.

complex. The author has found that the complex tools gain very little over the simple. The author will only present a simple tool which has worked extremely well for him. The process proceeds as follows:

1. Number the improvement task items.
2. Meet as a team and use brainstorming to classify each of the improvement tasks on a basis of impact and effort.
3. Post each of the tasks on the impact/effort matrix based on (see Figure 6.24):
   a. The impact that this task will have on the success of the improvement process
   b. The effort that will need to be extended in order to implement this task
   c. In the example of Figure 6.24 we see:
      i. Task 1 has a very high impact (large effect toward achieving the goal of the improvement opportunity) and very low effort task (low utilization of resources).
      ii. Task 8 is the opposite extreme, having a very low impact (minimal effect toward achieving the goal of the improvement opportunity) and high effort task (high utilization of resources).

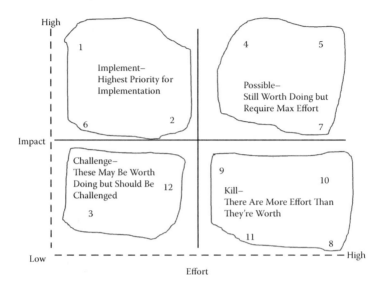

FIGURE 6.25
PICK categories.

    iii. Task 5 is a task that will need to be performed because it has
         a very high impact (large effect toward achieving the goal
         of the improvement opportunity), but unfortunately it also
         requires a high effort (high utilization of resources).
  4. Categorize each of the four quadrants by the PICK categories
     (Possible, Implement, Challenge, Kill) as in Figure 6.25.
  5. Execute the tasks starting with the "Implement" category items first.

From this example you can see how the PICK (Possible, Implement,
Challenge, Kill) Chart/Impact/Effort Matrix can facilitate the prioritization of tasks generated by Step 6 of the 9-Step A3 problem analysis exercise
(see Chapter 3).

Another variation of this tool that has been extremely useful in the
IT world is referred to as "feature–function prioritization." With this
tool, prioritize the feature or function from the customer's perspective. The chart looks the same, except that the "Impact" vertical is now
"Customer Preference." The "Effort" horizontal remains the same. This
time we plot the highest customer's feature–function priorities near
the top of the chart, and the customer's lowest priorities near the bottom. The upper left hand quadrant again has the highest priority for
implementation.

Technical Tool #26—Theory of Constraints (TOC)/Bottleneck Analysis

Similar to JIT (see Technical Tool #9), TOC is both a management philosophy and a set of operating principles. The best approach to understanding of TOC is to start by reading the book *The Goal* by Eli Goldratt. The book is an easy read, and it will leave you with a clear understanding of many of the principles. If you read this book first, then many of the principles we will now discuss will make more sense.

A basic principle of TOC is that everything is viewed as a "system." Nothing can be viewed as an isolated element without considering its integrative effect on the overall system. TOC views all systems as an interconnected link of process chains. Within this network of chains there are several links, referred to as constraints. These constraints limit the amount of work that can be processed through that step in the chain. TOC attempts to identify the system constraints, optimize the constraints, and improve the productivity of the entire workflow.

Management Philosophy

As with all process systems, TOC requires that we first define a goal around which we will then build an optimized system. The goal of all organizations is to make money. And this goal is best supported by focusing on operational efficiencies in three subareas:

- Increase throughput
- Decrease inventory
- Decrease operating expense

With goals in place, we next need to reexamine all the actions and measures that exist to make sure they properly serve to support the goal. This process begins by searching for the most limiting constraint (bottleneck) in the "system" that you are trying to improve. The strength of any chain depends on the weakest link, the bottleneck. This chain may be the internal process chain, or it may be the external supply chain.

A constraint is anything that limits us from moving toward or achieving our goal. Constraints can be:

- Resources
- Environment (external and management)

- Policies
- Control system
- Markets

Analysis of the constraints proceeds as follows:

1. ***Identify*** the constraint
2. ***Exploit*** the constraint. Analyze the constraint and determine how to maximize its throughput.
3. ***Subordinate*** everything else to the constraint. Make every operational decision focused to eliminate or reduce the constraint.
4. ***Elevate*** the constraint to where it is no longer a bottleneck.
5. Once you break the constraint, ***return*** to step 1 and identify the next constraint. There will always be another constraint to work on.

TOC is a change management philosophy which focuses on:

1. What to change
2. What to change to
3. How to cause the change

Operating Principles

A bottleneck is a process area that does not have sufficient capacity. If a bottleneck exists, then we need to optimize the flow through the bottleneck. Here are some general guidelines to follow:

1. Setup time (preparation time) on the bottleneck needs to be minimized. By minimizing setup you will maximize the amount of bottleneck time available for throughput.
2. A buffer needs to be established in front of the bottleneck so that there will always be plenty for the bottleneck to do. It would be foolish for the bottleneck to be sitting idle.
3. Priority should be given to the processes that offer the most profitability. We should focus on those processes that will give our plant the most bang for the buck.

There are two types of bottlenecks, real and wandering. An example of a wandering bottleneck is the process wave. Employees who work inefficiently will affect the ability for employees further down the process sequence to complete their jobs on time. This causes a wave effect that runs throughout the system. The result is a false bottleneck.

From a process perspective, we need to understand the impact of the bottleneck. The bottleneck controls the total throughput of the system. Failure to optimize the bottleneck results in less than optimal profitability.

TOC teaches that we focus on the beat of the system. This must be the optimum cadence, and it must be in harmony with the system environment. The system user should set the beat, and this beat is referred to as the ***Drum***. To satisfy the beat of the drum, you will need to ***Buffer*** the throughput of the bottleneck. You also need a signal to cycle the system. You need to keep the entire system synchronized, working together at the desired harmonic. Selecting what this desired harmonic is, and tying it to the other elements of the system, is referred to as the ***Rope***. This harmonic comes from the pull signals that are synchronized. The operational principles for running an efficient TOC system require the optimized use of the ***Drum-Buffer-Rope*** principles.

The result is that bottleneck analysis helps to identify the specific step(s) in a process that are holding down the throughput of the entire process. Since every process has one step that is slower than the rest, that one step controls the throughput potential of every other step in the process. Trying to improve the throughput of a process by improving any step other than the bottleneck step cannot improve the throughput, and will most likely actually make things worse. Here are some recommended steps in identifying and optimizing bottlenecks:

- Each step in the process must be identified and its throughput capacity measured.
- Value Stream Mapping (VSM) is the ideal tool for mapping out all the steps in a process (see Technical Tool #2).
- Each step must be measured for its throughput capacity under normal conditions.
- Units of measure must be normalized across the VSM.
- The steps must be compared. A bar graph is an excellent tool for this by placing common units of measure on the vertical axis and a separate bar for each step in the process. A horizontal line representing the throughput speed required to meet customer expectations is also useful. The bar graph makes it visually obvious which step is the bottleneck (the shortest bar). The bar graph also easily shows if there are any other steps that cannot meet the required processing rates.

TOC or bottlenck analysis assists in the identfcation of areas where process improvements can deliver optimal results.

Technical Tool #27—Project Charter

The project charter is a contract between a project champion, a team leader, the project team, and the dollar resources that will be needed. There are several levels where we may need a charter. In Chapter 3 we learned about the 9-Step A3 report. A charter should be generated on or before Step 3 to make sure you have a team and the appropriate leadership support to implement the task list that will be generated. Then the 9-Step A3 generates a task list in Step 7. Each of these tasks may also require a charter to make sure we get the appropriate meaningful support to complete this activity.

The project charter specifies what the project is, who is participating in the project, and the timing of the project. Information that is generally included in the charter is:

- Project/process name
- Champion—The person with the money to see this through/someone who believes in the potential benefits of this improvement process
- Process owner—whose workplace will be directly affected by this change
- What are all the areas that will be impacted by this process change?
- Product/service being impacted
- Team leader—Assigned by the champion
- Facilitators—not necessarily experienced with the project or process, but highly experienced in the Lean process
- Dates (actual and estimated)
  - Project start date
  - Measurement completed
  - Preanalysis completed
  - Improvements (tasks) completed
  - Project completion date
- Expected savings/benefits
  - What are the KPIs (key performance indicators), and what is the anticipated improvement goal for each
  - Who owns the metric
  - Benefits to the external customer
- Rapid improvement event (RIE) or project dates and time

- Linkage to the strategic roadmap—the project needs to tie directly to the organization's strategy
- One paragraph explanation of the improvement opportunity
- One paragraph description of the desired outcomes/results
- Project deliverables
- Project scope—where does the process start and end (as far as this improvement process is concerned)?
- Team members/where assigned (what office do they work in)/contact information (phone and e-mail)
- Follow-up plan
  - Executive out brief of the results of the exercise to the champion and the process owners
  - Follow-up meetings—How often will we have follow-up status meetings? Who should attend?
- Approvals
  - Champion approval signature and date
  - Process owner approval signature and date
- Executive out brief date

Filling out the charter and getting the appropriate signatures is critical in making sure that everyone is on board with what is happening. Without a signed-off charter you may find yourself spinning your wheels when it comes time to spend money on the actual improvements suggested.

SUSTAINMENT

It is not enough to run a Lean activity where we do the acceptance and technical processes outlined in this chapter, and then just brag about our successes and go away. True success in Lean is found in the sustainment of the process. What this means is that the "events" do not stop just because the facilitator leaves the scene. The culture of the organization is such that they strive for continued improvements, always looking out for more opportunities. The Lean culture remains in place, and facilitators are continuously called on to organize events around newly identified opportunities. And the Lean process continues forever.

For the facilitator, sustainment means that as many people as possible should be involved in the process and should find ownership in the Lean process. This allows a maximum number of people to be familiar with the Lean process and to want to keep it operational. Additionally, this means training for as many people as possible. The larger the number of people that understand the objectives and workings of Lean, the greater the chance of continued success.

COMPARISON OF METHODS

Some contention exists between the advocates of Lean, Six Sigma, and Theory of Constraints (TOC). Each adherent believes their tool is best and will give you all kinds of reasons why the other tool is not as good. The reality is that all three of these tools have their appropriate need and fit. Each is better at solving certain types of problems than the other. And they also cross-utilize each other's tools. For example, Lean uses Six Sigma as a statistical tool when quality process variation needs analysis. And Six Sigma uses Value Stream Mapping (VSM) when process flow problems exist (Figure 6.26). Table 6.1 attempts to give an abbreviated comparison of the tools.

SOME SUCCESS STORIES

Recently, the author was the facilitator for a Lean process which involved engineering and design, supply chain logistics, contracting, IT in a systems redesign, a major construction and remodel of the facility, and the automation of an extensive documentation process. Some of the results of this one-year activity include:

- A 75% reduction in travel time
- A reduction in queue levels from 200 jobs to 14 jobs, with a goal of moving to below 10 jobs
- A reduction in flow days from 141 days down to 81 days before the remodel and 45 days after the remodel
- A reduction in "jobs on hold" from 14 jobs down to 1 job

Additional IT-related Lean process improvements include:

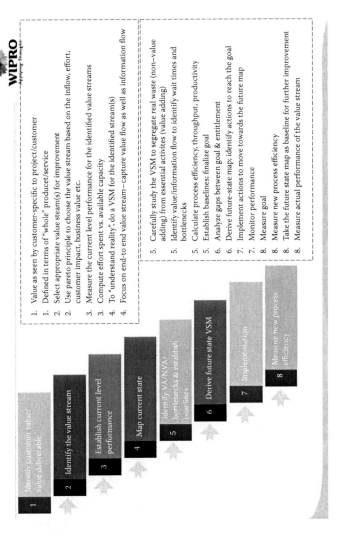

WIPRO
Applying Thought

1. Value as seen by customer-specific to project/customer
1. Defined in terms of "whole" producet/service
2. Select appropriate value steam(s) for improvement
2. Use pareto principle to choose the value stream based on the inflow, effort, customer impact, business value etc.
3. Measure the current level performance for the identified value streams
3. Compute effort spent vs. available capacity
4. To "understand reality", do a VSM for the identified stream(s)
4. Focus on end-to end value stream – capture value flow as well as information flow

5. Carefully study the VSM to segregate real waste (non–value adding) from essential activites (value adding)
5. Identify value/information flow to identify wait times and bottlenecks
5. Calculate process efficiency, throughput, productivity
5. Establish baselines; finalize goal
6. Analyze gaps between goal & entitlement
6. Derive future-state map; identify actions to reach the goal
7. Implement actions to move towards the future map
7. Monitor performance
8. Measure goal
8. Measure new process efficiency
8. Take the future state map as baseline for further improvement
8. Measure actual performance of the value stream

1 Identify customer value/ value deliverable

2 Identify the value stream

3 Establish current level performance

4 Map current state

5 Identify VA/NVA/ bottlenecks & establish baselines

6 Derive future state VSM

7 Implementation

8 Measure new process efficiency

FIGURE 6.26
Value Stream Mapping.

TABLE 6.1

Comparison of Tools

	Lean	Six Sigma	TOC
Goal	Reduce waste, increase process speed, increase customer satisfaction	Improve performance on the Customer's CTQs (critical to quality), reduce variation	Manage constraints
Tools	TPS (Toyota Production System) tools	DMAIC and TQM tools	Bottleneck analysis
Focus	Process flow or system focused	Problem focused	System constraint focused
Method	Kaizen events, Value Stream Mapping (VSM)	DMAIC and SPC (statistical process control)	Constraint/ bottleneck analysis
Metric	Speed (cycle time), waste reduction, quality, customer satisfaction	Quality, cost	Increase throughput, reduce cost
Loop	9-Step or PDCA	DMAIC	Constraint focused
Assumptions	Waste removal will improve business performance	A problem exists	Emphasis on speed and volume
Where should it be used?	In process or flow environments, especially if we have a repetitive process	In data intensive environments, for example in quality defect analysis	In process flow environments that have a bottleneck which disrupts and limits throughput

- A 40+% decrease in process cycle times
- A 64% lead-time reduction for forecast development
- A 75% lead-time reduction for kitting scheduling
- A 90% reduction in non-value-added time
- A 93% front office research time reduction
- A 93% reduction in order processing time
- A 70% reduction in lead time from the logistics carrier
- A 99% reduction in equipment maintenance flow days
- A 99% increase in medical records processing efficiencies
- A 90+% accuracy in data input quality (formerly less than 20%)
- A 98% increase in accuracy for digital orders

- A 76% decreasing in screening cycle time
- A 100% decrease in laboratory labeling errors
- A 100% improvement in patient safety from reduced labeling errors
- A 200% in operating room utilization due to improved, accurate scheduling

And the success stories go on and on in all areas of industry and specifically in IT and the front office which interacts with IT the most.

CASE STUDY: WIPRO (CONTINUED)

Continuing the Wipro story from Chapters 2, 3, 4, and 5, we now look at an example of Wipro's VSM methodology (Figure 6.26). This is an invaluable example of how VSM should be effectively adapted in IT. [8]

SUMMARY

This chapter was intended to give the reader a quick overview of what Lean is and how it works. It is not intended to certify the reader as a Lean black belt. This chapter gives the reader the tools that will allow him or her to successfully facilitate Lean IT process improvement activities. These tools, in conjunction with the 9-Step A3 process described in Chapter 3, are the foundation for successful Lean IT success stories.

Figure 6.27 offers a summary of where the different tools fit into the 9-Step A3 analysis process. This is not an absolute list, but a guideline of what tools are available for each of the steps in the process.

There is a lot more to Lean than can be discussed even if this entire book was dedicated only to the details. But most of those tools are not specifically relevant for Leaning an IT process. However, some additional information may be useful. For example, the training that a facilitator should go through could be a book all by itself. There are numerous support materials on the subject of Lean that would give the reader more depth of understanding. Some suggested books for further reading would include:

---

[8] The charts used in this case study come from a Wipro presentation on Lean implementations created by Seema Walunjkar in the Wipro Global Delivery Organization.

Team Members:	9-Step Opportunity (Problem) Analysis Tool	Approval Information/Signatures
1. Clarify & Validate the Problem TT3-SIPOC (Supplier/Input/Process/Output/Customer) TT4-SWOT (Strength/Weaknesses/Opportunities/Threats) TT5-VOC (Voice of the Customer) TT7-Gemba Walk (Go and See Analysis) **2. Perform a Purpose Expansion on the Problem** Acceptance Tool #1-Breakthrough Thinking/Concept Management/Purpose Expansion **3. Break Down the Problem/Identify Performance Gaps** TT3-SIPOC (Supplier/Input/Process/Output/Customer) TT6-Systems Flow Chart/Information Flow Diagrams TT20-Brainstorming TT21-Fishbone Charts TT22-Pareto Charts TT23-Affinity Diagrams TT24-Control Dharts TT26-Theory of Constraints (TOC)/Bottleneck Analysis **4. Set improvement Targets** TT1-7 Wastes TT2-Value Stream Mapping (Current State/Ideal State/Future State) TT8-B-SMART Targets TT22-Pareto Charts TT24-Control Charts	**5. Determine Root Cause** TT3-SIPOC (Supplier/Input/Process/Output/Customer) TT6-Systems Flow Chart/Information Flow Diagrams TT7-Gemba Walk (Go and See Analysis) TT10-Spaghetti Chart TT16-Six Sigma/DMAIC TT19-5 Whys TT20-Brainstorming TT21-Fishbone Charts TT22-Pareto Charts TT23-Affinity Diagrams TT24-Control Charts **6. Develop Improvement Task List** TT1-7 Wastes TT2-Value Stream Mapping (Current State/Ideal State/Future State) TT6-Systems Flow Chart/Information Flor Diagrams TT10-Spaghetti Chart TT20-Brainstorming	**7. Esecute Improvement Tasks** TT5-VOC (Voice of the Customer) TT8-B-SMART Targets TT9-JIT (Just-In-Time)/Kanban/Cells TT11-Lean Events/RIE (Rapid Improvement Events)/Kaizen Events TT12-Improvement Project TT13-Just-Do-It TT14-5S TT15-Poka-Yoke TT16-Six Sigma/DMAIC TT17-TPM (Total Product Maintenance) TT18-Standard Work TT23-Affinity Diagrams TT24-Control Charts TT25-Pick (Possible, Implement, Challenge, Kill) Chart/Impact/Effort Matrix TT27-Project Charter **8. Confirm Results** TT22-Pareto Charts TT23-Affinity Diagrams TT24-Control Charts **9. Standardize Successfull Process** TT18-Standard Work TT20-Brainstorming

FIGURE 6.27
What technical tool (TT) fits where?

- *Breakthrough Thinking: The Seven Principles of Creative Problem Solving* by Gerald Nadler and Shozo Hibino
- *Built to Last: Successful Habits of Visionary Companies* by Jim Collins and Jerry I. Porras
- *Good to Great: Why Some Companies Make the Leap … and Others Don't* by Jim Collins
- *Lean Thinking: Banish Waste and Create Wealth in Your Corporation* by James P. Womack and Daniel Jones
- *Making Innovation Happen: Concept Management through Integration* by Gerhard Plenert and Shozo Hibino
- *Maverick: The Success Story behind the World's Most Unusual Workplace* by Ricardo Semler
- *Reinventing Lean: Introducing Lean Management into the Supply Chain* by Gerhard Plenert
- *The eManager: Value Chain Management in an eCommerce World* by Gerhard Plenert
- *The Game of Work: How to Enjoy Work as Much as Play* by Charles A. Coonradt
- *The Goal* by Eliyahu M. Goldratt and Jeff Cox
- *The Toyota Way Fieldbook: A Practical Guide for Implementing Toyota's 4Ps* by Jeffrey K. Liker and David Meier

Then, once the reader has a more detailed understanding of this material, they will also have a clearer understanding of the overall/enterprise-wide/supply-chain-wide power of Lean.

APPENDIX 6-A

The JoHari Window Assessment Test[9]

Directions

Using a 5-point scale, you assess yourself and other coworkers on inter-personal communication styles and the use of 24 behaviors important for respectful and trust-building human relations. Read each behavior and determine how much it is like you, or if you are rating someone else, then how much this behavior is like that other person (from your perspective). Select a numerical value from the scale and enter the number in the appropriate space to the right.

> **Step 1:** Total the scores you gave yourself for the odd-numbered questions (all questions with (T) in front of them). This total represents your evaluation of your willingness to express yourself. Record the score on the **TRUST** axis in Figure 6.A1. Next, total the scores you gave yourself for the even-numbered questions (all the questions with (R) in front of them). This is your willingness to listen to others. Record this score on the **RESPECT** axis. Then find the point where the two scores intersect and shade in the enclosed area.
>
> **Step 2:** You are now ready to analyze the scores you gave your coworker. Similar to Step 1, total the scores you gave your coworker for all odd-numbered questions (all questions with (T) in front of them). Record the score on the **TRUST** axis using a chart similar to Figure 6.A1. Next, total the scores you gave your coworker for the even-numbered questions (all questions with (R) in front of them. Record this score on the **RESPECT** axis. Then find the point where the two scores intersect and shade in the enclosed area.
>
> **Step 3:** Exchange evaluations with your coworker.
>
> **Step 4:** Compare your self-evaluation and your coworker's evaluation of you with the four interpersonal self-disclosure style types in

[9] This test was taken from the MainStream Management Consultant database, and they got it from TAMCO, Training and Management Consultants, Inc., who in turn picked up the test from:

Luft, Joseph, *Group Process: An Introduction to Group Dynamics*; National Press, 1970;

Manning, G., Curtis, K., and McMillan, S., *The Human Side of Work: Building Community in the Workplace*, South-Western Publishing, 1995;

Petrick, Joseph A., and Furr, Diana S., *Total Quality in Managing Human Resources,* St. Lucie Press, 1995.

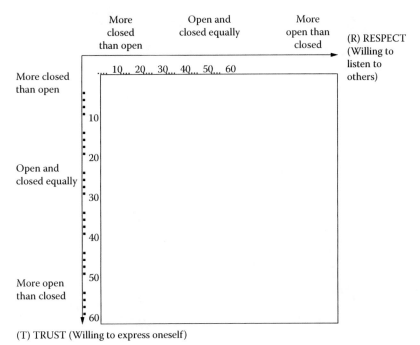

FIGURE 6.A1
JoHari test.

Figure 6.A2. Which style do you think you are most like? Which does your coworker think you are most like? Does your coworker see you as you see yourself?

Step 5: Go back to the questionnaire and ask your coworker what specific things you could do to raise your low scores. Also, give recommendations to your coworker to raise low scores.

Step 6: Discuss the importance of self-expression (showing trust) and listening (showing respect) as they relate to your relationship.

Interpretation

The scores in this instrument are designed to produce four standard profiles: the Turtle profile, the Owl profile, the Bull-in-the-China-Shop profile, and the Picture Window profile. As indicated in Figure 6.A2, each category exhibits different degrees of respect and trust. The four profiles differ in three important respects: (1) skills used in listening and expressing, (2) effects on the individual, and (3) the effects on the relationship.

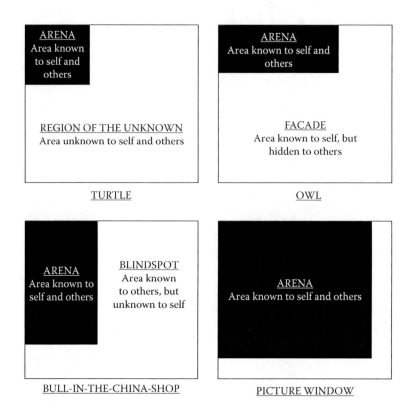

FIGURE 6.A2
JoHari test interpretation.

The optimal interpersonal self-disclosure profile is the Picture Window, because it enlarges the areas known to self and others, thereby allowing more of the performance potential of an individual to be recognized and invested in the organization.

JoHari Window Test

Scale

Value	Meaning
5	Extremely characteristic; always does this
4	Quite characteristic; usually does this
3	Somewhat characteristic; occasionally does this
2	Quite uncharacteristic; seldom does this
1	Extremely uncharacteristic; never does this

	Human Relations Behavior	**Self**	**Coworkers(s)**
(T) 1.	States opinions in an uncensored manner	____	____ ____ ____ ____
(R) 2.	Invites ideas from others; does not dominate discussion	____	____ ____ ____ ____
(T) 3.	Admits to confusion or lack of knowledge when uncertain	____	____ ____ ____ ____
(R) 4.	Shows interest in what others have to say through body posture and facial expressions	____	____ ____ ____ ____
(T) 5.	Expresses self openly and candidly	____	____ ____ ____ ____
(R) 6.	Gives support to others who are struggling to express themselves	____	____ ____ ____ ____
(T) 7.	Admits to being wrong, rather than attempting to cover up or place blame	____	____ ____ ____ ____
(R) 8.	Keeps private conversations private; does not reveal confidences	____	____ ____ ____ ____
(T) 9.	Tells others what they need to know, even if it is unpleasant	____	____ ____ ____ ____
(R) 10.	Listens to others without being defensive	____	____ ____ ____ ____
(T) 11.	Is honest with his or her feelings	____	____ ____ ____ ____
(R) 12.	Shows respect for the feelings of others	____	____ ____ ____ ____
(T) 13.	Shares concerns, hopes, and goals with others	____	____ ____ ____ ____
(R) 14.	Does not act as if others are wasting their time	____	____ ____ ____ ____
(T) 15.	Shares thoughts, no matter how "far out" they may seem	____	____ ____ ____ ____
(R) 16.	Does not fake attention or merely pretend to listen	____	____ ____ ____ ____
(T) 17.	Speaks truthfully, refuses to lie	____	____ ____ ____ ____
(R) 18.	Does not act hurt, angry, or mistreated when others disagree	____	____ ____ ____ ____
(T) 19.	Is sincere; does not pretend	____	____ ____ ____ ____
(R) 20.	Values suggestions from others	____	____ ____ ____ ____
(T) 21.	Uses language and terms others can understand	____	____ ____ ____ ____
(R) 22.	Tries to prevent interruptions, such as telephone calls and people walking in during important discussions	____	____ ____ ____ ____
(T) 23.	Tells others when they are wrong or need to change	____	____ ____ ____ ____
(R) 24.	Encourages others to express themselves	____	____ ____ ____ ____

7

Are We Working on the Correct Problem? Or Are We Creating More Problems?

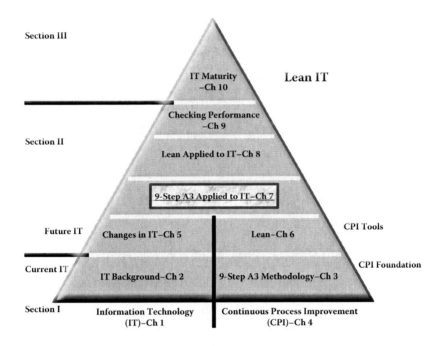

We will move faster if we hurry less.

Spencer W. Kimball (1895–1985)

Now that we have an understanding of the 9-Step A3 process, the Lean process, and the areas of IT that can be impacted by Lean, we will now go back to Chapter 3 and review the 9-Step A3 in more detail, with examples demonstrating how this tool organizes and executes an improvement initiative.

A QUICK REVIEW OF A3 PROBLEM ANALYSIS

My recommendation in Chapter 3 was:

> As soon as you are done with this chapter, do not initiate another IT project without first going through an A3 analysis to make sure the project is justified.

Then I recommended that it would probably be smart to review many of the projects that are already in process. The 9-Step A3 tool becomes critical in eliminating "waste."

THE A3 STEPS

This book recommends the 9-Step A3 for IT, which looks like the example in Figure 7.1. This same report format is used for:

- Opportunity analysis (using only the first 3 to 5 steps)
- Project presentation (a status check during various stages of the project)
- Project justification (through Step 7 when you know what the benefits [Step 4] and the costs [Step 7] are)
- Project performance review (Step 8)

When you use the same A3 format consistently for all these stages of a project, you do not need elaborate Power Point presentations. The entire team (management and users) become familiar with the format, and you do not waste time explaining each box. Everyone knows what they are looking for, and they go right to the box that interests them.

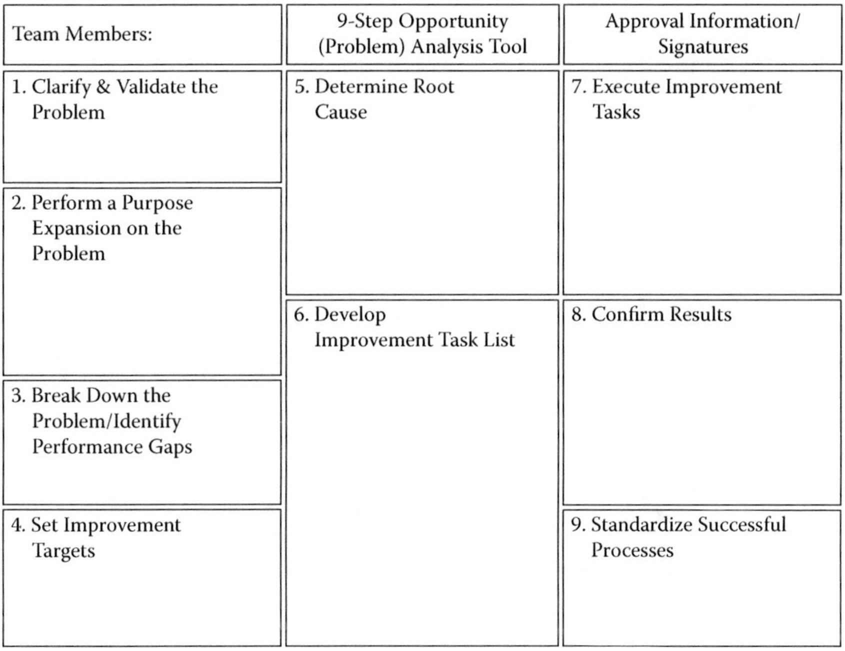

Team Members:	9-Step Opportunity (Problem) Analysis Tool	Approval Information/ Signatures
1. Clarify & Validate the Problem	5. Determine Root Cause	7. Execute Improvement Tasks
2. Perform a Purpose Expansion on the Problem		
	6. Develop Improvement Task List	8. Confirm Results
3. Break Down the Problem/Identify Performance Gaps		
4. Set Improvement Targets		9. Standardize Successful Processes

FIGURE 7.1
9-Step A3.

In this chapter we will go through each of the boxes in the A3 using a couple of examples. The book will demonstrate how each step in the 9-Step A3 was used. In this discussion you will hear about a variety of tools and techniques that were described in Chapter 6. Figure 7.2 repeats Figure 3.3, which offers a brief description of the purpose of each of the boxes, and this can be used for reference.

THE TWO CASE EXAMPLES

The two cases that we will be considering are intentionally very different in their level and in their approach. The first case is a very high-level, strategic look at the enterprise resource planning (ERP) IT environment of a multiplant enterprise. The second case is the A3 for a rapid improvement event (RIE) focused on reducing the amount of time it takes to implement patches across an enterprise with dozens of locations and hundreds of computers at each location. Both of these case examples are summarizations

Team Members: Who are the individuals that worked on this 9-step report	9-Step Opportunity (Problem) Analysis Tool	Approval Information/Signatures: Who are the Champions for (Signers of) this Project
1. Clarify & Validate the Problem State the basic overall fundamental problem that needs to be solved and validate that it is strategically aligned with the enterprise objectives. **2. Perform a Purpose Expansion on the Problem** Confirm that we are doing the right things. **3. Break Down the Problem/Identify Performance Gaps** What are the facts? List what specifically needs to change to solve the problem and what are the performance gaps to be closed to realize required performance. Prove it! **4. Set Improvement Targets** Set improvement targets. Identify annual and long term stretch targets as appropriate	**5. Determine Root Cause** Define the root-causes of the current problem and the reason for current performance gaps. What caused the need for this change? **6. Develop Improvement Task List** List the specific actions that need to be implemented to create change and close performance gaps. Validate that all the root causes listed in step 5 have been accounted for and resolved. What needs to change in order to eliminate the root cause?	**7. Execute Improvement Tasks** Prioritize the actions listed in step 6, time sequence them, identify specific completion dates, assign responsibility for the completion, and state where help is needed in order to complete the action. What are the deliverables and their due dates? **8. Confirm Results** Report progress made on the improvement targets listed in step 4. Confirm that we are doing the right things in the right way by improving the desired performance areas. Did you achieve your desired results? (At-a-glance status) **9. Standardize Successful Processes** List ways to institutionalize best practices and processes learned from implementing this change. How can we institutionalize this "best practice?"

FIGURE 7.2

9-Step A3—with definitions.

taken from actual events. First we will work our way through Case #1, and later in the chapter we will introduce and work through Case #2.

CASE #1

The intention with this case is to demonstrate how executives would approach a strategic IT problem. The chief operating officer (COO) and the chief information officer (CIO) are struggling with the rash of new acquisitions. The ERP environments of the various locations are extremely divergent from each other. In one ERP environment, the data is actually owned by the vendor, and it resides on the vendor's server, and this vendor will not share the database with any other vendor application. Month-end summary data that is sent to corporate has to be re-input into the computer. Other locations use SAP, others use Oracle, some use the SCM software of i2 as their ERP, and some locations are still on small-sized ERPs like Made-2-Manage. The COO is livid at not being able to get consolidated operating statements from these organizations. The integration of the data takes months, and the average operations reports are three months out of date. And then there is the concern about data accuracy. Do the summary numbers coming from the different systems mean the same thing? Are they calculated in the same way? By the time the COO receives operational information, it is too late to make meaningful decisions.

The CIO suggested that they need to go out and talk to each of the major ERP environments, from an operations perspective and from an IT perspective. The COO suggested that, rather than going out to visit each of these locations in isolation, they should get representatives from each of these environments together in a room and engage in an interactive exercise where the key players drive toward a consolidated and integration solution to this mess. The CIO readily agreed. The CIO needed direction from operations on how to solve this mess, and the COO needed meaningful decision making information. They decided that they would:

A. Identify a Lean facilitator to organize and drive this activity
B. Draft a charter to define the direction and objectives of this exercise
C. Use the facilitated team to work through the 9-Step A3 process
D. Come forward with recommended solutions

Step A was easy. With the facilitator in place, it became the facilitator's responsibility to drive Steps B, C, and D. The facilitator started by using the standard format for the charter (Technical Tool #27 in Chapter 6). The charter required the following information, and it was filled in as follows.

Project Charter

- Project/process name
  - Enterprise ERP data standardization/consolidation/integration
- Champion—The person with the money to see this through/someone who believes in the potential benefits of this improvement process
  - COO and CIO are cochampions.
- Process owner—Whose work place will be directly affected by this change
  - ERP managers at the various locations
- Product/service being impacted
  - Timely operations information
- Team leader—Assigned by the champion
  - The CIO selected his ERP team lead from the corporate office to be a co-team lead for this project.
  - The COO also selected someone from his office who is directly responsible for consolidating the ERP data and made him a co-team lead.
- Facilitators—Not necessarily experienced with the project or process but highly experienced in the Lean process
  - The CPI (continuous process improvement) office selected and assigned a black belt Lean facilitator who was unfamiliar with ERP, but who had facilitated numerous high-level strategic events.
- Dates (actual and estimated)
  - Project start date
    - Two weeks out.
  - Measurement completed
    - Data about how long it takes each of the ERP environments to generate consolidation data is being accumulated.
  - Preanalysis completed
    - The COO and his team have been analyzing the delays, and this analysis will be brought to the event team meeting.
  - Improvements (tasks) completed

- None defined at this point.
  - Project completion date
    - One year out.
- Expected savings/benefits
  - What are the KPIs (key performance indicators), and what is the anticipated improvement goal for each
    - Time from last day of the month until the consolidated operations summary reports are delivered to COO
  - Who owns the metric
    - COO
  - Benefits to the external customer
    - Greater responsiveness to performance issues and therefore more responsive to customer expectations in quality and delivery
- Rapid improvement event (RIE) or project dates and time
  - No RIE scheduled at this time. This will be a team brainstorming exercise which may lead to future RIEs.
- Linkage to the strategic roadmap—the project needs to tie directly to the organization's strategy
  - Customer satisfaction and cost performance efficiency are both strategic priorities and are addressed by this exercise.
- One-paragraph explanation of the improvement opportunity
  - Consolidated operations information is received around three months after the end of the month, too late to make corrective decisions.
- One-paragraph description of the desired outcomes/results
  - Operations reports need to be available at most two to three weeks after the completing of an operating cycle.
  - Operations decisions about shifting capacity and workloads between operation locations should be facilitated by readily available operating data.
- Project deliverables
  - A defined plan for integrating operations information from each of the operating units
  - A standardized method of reporting for each of the units
  - An enterprise-wide consolidated database that can be manipulated via spreadsheets
  - Revised and updated enterprise-level analytics and reporting

- Project Scope—where does the process start and end (as far as this improvement process is concerned)?
  - The project looks at the ERP environments of each unit and evaluates the transfer of ERP data up the food chain to the enterprise in some standardized format. The data gets passed to the enterprise so it can evaluate the data using analytics software.
  - The project starts at the ERP level of the business units and ends by defining the information that is passed to the COO.
- Team members/where assigned (what office they work in)/contact information (phone and e-mail)
  - The team members included operations and IT ERP representatives from each of the different types of ERP environments. The team also includes enterprise-level CIO representatives to describe the enterprise-level IT requirements. It also includes enterprise-level COO representatives who will be the voice of the customer.
- Follow-up plan
  - Executive out-brief of the results of the exercise to the champion and the process owners.
    - The workshop was scheduled for five days, and an out-brief to the champions and process owners was scheduled for the afternoon of the fifth day.
  - Follow-up meetings—How often will we have follow-up status meetings? Who should attend?
    - Monthly meetings will be held to review the implementation of the recommended changes and to do a status check to see if the objectives of the exercise have been met.
- Approvals
  - Champion approval signature and date
  - Process owner approval signature and date
  - Executive out-brief date
- The project facilitator successfully acquired the appropriate approval signatures from the CIO and COO and scheduled the out-brief for the afternoon of the last day of the workshop.

Facilitator Activities

The Lean facilitator is a critical piece of the success of this project. The lack of knowledge that the facilitator has about ERP or its functions is actually an advantage. It leaves the facilitator in the position of being able to ask the "dumb questions" that will help move the team "out of the box." During the start-up process the facilitator:

1. Develops the project charter in conjunction with the champions
2. Defines the teams in conjunction with the designated team leads and gets everyone on board with their schedules
3. Gets champion sign-off on the charter
4. Plans the logistics of the event
   a. Location
   b. Timing (start, end, breaks, etc.)
   c. Meals
   d. Whiteboards or flip charts
   e. Computer screens, computers, etc.
   f. Schedule champions to come at the start of the event for an "introduction" and again at the end of the event for an "out-brief"
   g. Etc.
5. Executes event pre-work
   a. Surveys
   b. Data collection
   c. SIPOC
6. Plans and facilitates the Lean training that occurs at the start of the event
7. Executes the event by facilitating, attending, and keeping the event on track
8. Facilitates the creation of the 9-Step A3
9. Prepares the "out-brief" presentation in conjunction with the team leads—the team leads will make the presentation, not the facilitator
10. Post-event activities
    a. Plan follow-up meetings
    b. Stay in touch with the change owners of each of the recommended tasks and makes sure the changes occur as defined and recommended
11. Finalizes the 9-Step A3 by executing Step 9, sharing the knowledge with other parts of the enterprise.

Event Pre-Work

Following the sign-off of the charter, the facilitator initiates the pre-work. This requires making contact with the team members and collecting information about them personally, about the issue under study, and about any data collection that will be needed in order to execute the event. The areas of pre-work include:

1. A team member assessment needs to be performed. The author recommends the following for this particular case example:
    a. Team Effectiveness Survey (Acceptance Tool #2—Chapter 6)— This survey will tell the facilitator how ready the team is to work together.
    b. Change Readiness Survey (Acceptance Tool #3—Chapter 6)— This survey will tell the facilitator if he/she is going to have issues with the team's openness to change.
    c. Myers–Briggs Assessment (Acceptance Tool #4—Chapter 6)— This assessment tells the facilitator who the dominant personalities are going to be on the team. Also, the facilitator is going to see if there is an imbalance in the team in favor of one type of personality over another. This could create some facilitation nightmares if not handled correctly.

    The results of these surveys and assessments are presented to the team as part of the initial half-day introduction and training that the team will go through to start the event. The facilitator will explain what the surveys mean and how this will affect the work of the event.

2. SIPOC (see Technical Tool #3)—The SIPOC collects information from each team member about the Supplier-Input-Process-Output-Customer from the perspective of each of the team members. This information is then consolidated by the facilitator and reviewed during the first part of the event. It tends to be eye-opening as team members see the divergence of perspectives.

3. Data collection—Any data, for example in this case, a history of the arrival delays of ERP information to the enterprise IT department, is useful in that it helps the team see the reality of the problem. Personal opinions and conjectures are driven away when the actual data is presented. This data needs to be available for the one week

event and, if possible, should be made available earlier to the team members to help them in their preparation.

4. Dissemination of pre-work information to the team members should include timing and location of the event, agenda, dress codes, etc. Additionally, a copy of the charter and any prepared data should be sent out to give the team a heads-up of what they will be focusing on.

Event Execution

The actual execution of the event follows this schedule:

- Day 1
  - 30 min.—Introductory comments by the champions stressing the importance of the event
  - 4 hrs—Lean training—explain the 7 Wastes (Technical Tool #1) and the 9-Step A3 tool (Chapter 3) and any other tools that may be used during this event, like in this case the Team Effectiveness Survey, the Change Readiness Survey, Myers–Briggs (Acceptance Tools #2, 3, and 4), SIPOC (Technical Tool #3), Voice of the Customer (Technical Tool #5), etc.
  - 30 min.—Review of the data.
  - 3 hrs (finishing out the day)—Start the actual Lean event by working through the SIPOC and reviewing the data that came in from the team members. A team consensus needs to be agreed upon for who the customer is, what the outputs are, what the necessary inputs are, and what the suppliers should be. Detailing out the process piece will become the focus of the next couple of days.
- Day 2
  - 4 hrs—Start working on the 9-Step A3 using the following steps:
    a. **"Team Members" Box**—Taken from the Charter.
    b. **"Approval Information/Signatures" Box**—The Champions, in this case the COO and the CIO.
    c. **"1. Clarify and Validate the Problem" Box**—Start with the information on the Charter and get the team's consensus on a one-paragraph statement of what the problem really is. Review the questions in Chapter 3 for Box 1, and make sure each of the questions is resolved in this box. Case #1—Box #1 is shown in Figure 7.3.

1. Clarify & Validate the Problem

Problem Statement: **Consolidated Operations Information is received around 3 months after the end of the month, too late to make corrective decisions.**

Strategic Alignment: **Customer Satisfaction and Cost Performance Efficiency are both strategic priorities and are addressed by this exercise.**

GembaWalk: **None Performed**

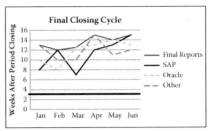

Supporting Information: **The data shows that our average reporting time for each period takes at least three months and in some cases exceeds three months**

Desired Future State: **Operations reports need to be available at most two to three weeks after the completing of an operating cycle. Operations decisions about shifting capacity and workloads between operation locations should be facilitated by readily available operating data.**

FIGURE 7.3

Case # 1—9-Step A3—Step 1 example.

d. **"2. Perform a Purpose Expansion on the Problem" Box**— The team was challenged with the question, "What is the purpose of solving this problem?" The answer: "To give the COO the information he needs in order to manage operations." Then the team was asked, "What is the purpose of giving the COO better information?" The answer: "So he can make better capacity decisions, which will improve productive and quality performance." The next question asked was, "What is the purpose for improving capacity, productivity, and quality?" The answer: "Customer satisfaction." Since customer satisfaction is a strategic priority, the decision was to move forward with the initiative. This information about the questions and the corresponding answers is placed into Box 2.

e. **"3. Break Down the Problem/Identify Performance Gaps" Box**—Again you should look carefully at the questions posed for Box 3 in Chapter 3. For Case #1, they went through a detailed review of the SIPOC and generated information flow diagrams for the data transfer process from the ERP system to the enterprise consolidation of operations data. They agreed to do a detailed Value Stream Map (See Technical Tool #2 in Chapter 6) of the entire process, incorporating

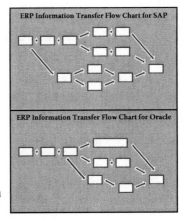

3. Break Down the Problem/Identify Performance Gaps

The data from Step 1 proves that the delays in processing operations data are real and that the consolidated information is rarely less than 3 months out of date.

The data from Step 1 demonstrates that the problem is real and that it is not be blamed on any one particular ERP system. Each ERP environment has it's own good and bad performance cycles.

The data does not point at any specific root causes—it looks like each of the ERPs are equally guilty of causing information consolidation delays.

SIPOC data has been generated and Process and Information Flows will be generated to facilitate further analysis.

ERP Information Transfer Flow Chart for SAP

ERP Information Transfer Flow Chart for Oracle

FIGURE 7.4

Case # 1—9-Step A3—Step 3 example.

all environments. The discussion resulted in the example of Figure 7.4.

 f. **"4. Set Improvement Targets" Box**—It is again important to review the questions and considerations for Box 4 that were outlined in Chapter 3. The improvement targets define whether this project is a success or failure. So they need to be set thoughtfully and carefully. Based on the goals of the COO, the team set an improvement target to have the maximum final closing cycle time be 3 weeks and to achieve this goal within 6 months. Additionally, the team felt they needed to develop a current state Value Stream Map to see if they could identify enough areas of "waste" to make this goal realistic and feasible.

- 4 hrs—The second half of the day was focused on mapping out the current state process—how do each of the "suppliers" provide their "input." They mapped out the CS-VSM (Technical Tool #2). For Case #1, each of the ERP teams built a process flowchart which shows every physical and IT step that needed to occur to transfer data from their ERP environment to the enterprise database.
- Day 3
  - 8 hrs—The day was focused on continuing to map out the Current State Process. The current state Value Stream Map (CS-VSM) charts were similar to the one shown in Figure 7.5.

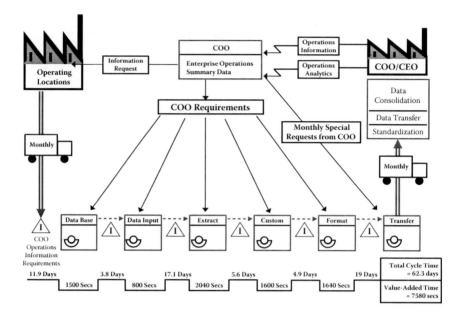

FIGURE 7.5
Case # 1—CS–VSM example.

The CS-VSM is evaluated by the team with a focus on eliminating waste. There are large wastes in Figure 7.5, especially the transition times, like 11.9 days, 3.8 days, 17.1 days, etc. The consolidations and reorganizations that the team came up with are shown in Figure 7.6. And the final FS-VSM can be seen in Figure 7.7.

The differences between the CS-VSM and the FS-VSM will intimately define the process gaps that need to be fixed. But first we will return to the 9-Step A3 and see how Step 4 looks (Figure 7.8).

- Day 4
  - 4 hrs—The first part of the day was focused on continuing to develop the 9-Step A3 report, looking next at Step 5—Determine Root Cause. Having gone through the CS and FS-VSM exercise, the team has an in-depth understanding of the process and its shortcomings. Additionally, the SIPOC exercise had taught the team about potential sources of input. Reading through the discussion in Chapter 3, we see there are numerous tools that can be used to assist in focusing on the "root cause." In this case the facilitator felt that there may be several root causes and that they may

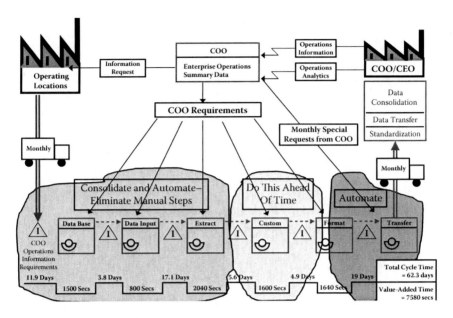

FIGURE 7.6
Case # 1—FS development—VSM example.

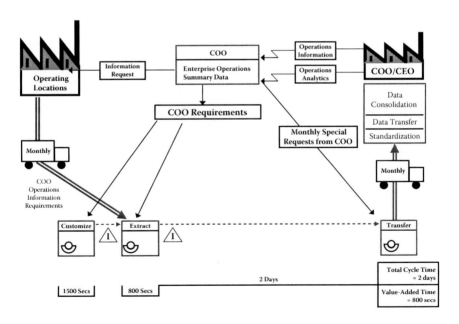

FIGURE 7.7
Case # 1—FS–VSM example.

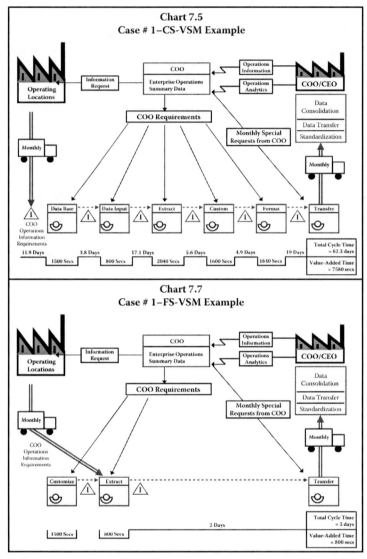

4. Set Improvement Targets

Goal Assessment:

Initially the COO set an arbitrary improvement target of 3 weeks, which seemed optimistic.

After the team developed a CS-VSM and a FS-VSM the team was able to set an improvement target 1 week, which they would strive to achieve within three months.

FIGURE 7.8

Case # 1—9-Step A3—Step 4 example.

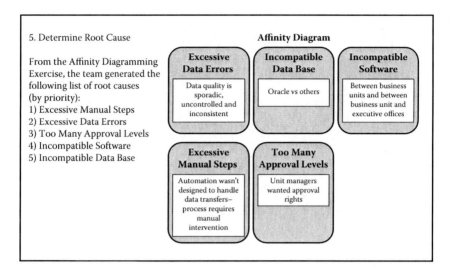

FIGURE 7.9
Case # 1—9-Step A3—Step 5 example.

not specifically be graphed out on a fishbone chart (see Technical Tool #21). He also felt that the five whys (see Technical Tool #19) may not lead the team to all the different possible root causes. So the facilitator chose to use brainstorming (see Technical Tool #20) and the affinity diagramming exercise (see Technical Tool #23) to "fish out" the root causes. The facilitator asked the team to use sticky notes and write any and all causes for the three-month delays. Each cause needed to be on a separate sticky note. The notes were all posted randomly on the wall. After everyone had run out of ideas, the facilitator asked for three or four volunteers to come up and "group" the sticky notes, realizing that there would probably be a lot of duplicates. After the grouping, the team was asked to prioritize the root causes. The results of the groupings, and associated findings were placed in Step 5 of the A3 and looked similar to Figure 7.9.

- 2 hrs—The remainder of the day was focused on Step 6 and Step 7 of the 9-Step A3 process. As we saw in Chapter 3, for Step 6 we are challenged to identify and list out all the tasks needed to accomplish the expected changes. First the team looks at the CS-VSM and compares it to the FS-VSM. Then they list all the changes necessary to get from CS to FS. Next the team looks at the root causes and makes sure that every root cause has been resolved in

6. Develop Improvement Task List

Task	Task List	Issue Resolved	Resource Demands
1	Eliminate Manual Interventions through automation	Reduce delays caused by excessive manual steps	3 persons and 1 software developer 3 weeks
2	Dig deeper into the root causes of the data errors (this may require a lean event at the user site)	More reliable data for the COO–less confusion	3 persons doing analysis and data collection for 1 month
3	Review the need for site approvals at each of the sites	Reduce delays caused by excessive reviews	1 person 1 month
4	Develop a software conversion routine that will make the site ERPs compatible with the Enterprise software	Reduce delays caused by excessive manual transfers	3 developers 1 month

FIGURE 7.10
Case # 1—9-Step A3—Step 6 example.

the newly generated task list. If the "root causes" have not been resolved, then the problem has not been solved. Generating this task list is generally pretty quick, because the team is intimately involved in the process and knows what needs to be changed. Be sure to refer to Chapter 3, which includes a list of questions that need to be responded to in order to generate a complete task list. In the example of Case #1, the list became quite large. There were similar changes that had to be accomplished for each of the existing ERP environments, and each case was unique. In the end, the task list had over 60 tasks that needed to be accomplished. An abbreviated example of the results can be seen in Figure 7.10.

- 2 hrs—With the task list in hand, the team can now focus on Step 7 of the 9-Step A3 process. As we saw in Chapter 3, Step 7 asks us to evaluate each of the tasks for priority, due date, primary responsible party, and secondary responsible party. This often involves some debating on the part of the team, but is usually a reasonably fast process. A summary of the results can be seen in Figure 7.11.
- Day 5
  - 4 hrs—The first half of the day is focused on reviewing the 9-Step A3 for completeness and accuracy and making some cosmetic improvements to make the A3 look better, realizing that in the

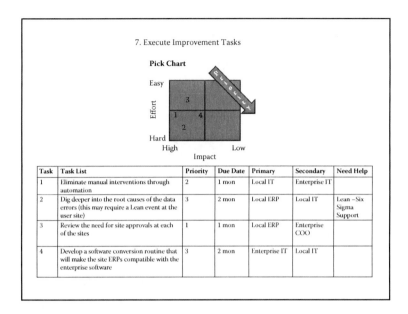

FIGURE 7.11
Case # 1—9-Step A3—Step 7 example.

afternoon the team leaders will need to present the team's findings to the champions.

• 2 hrs—The last big activity of the day is the out-brief to the champions. This usually occurs in the same room where the event was
held, so the champions can see the work, like the SIPOC, the
affinity chart, and the CS-VSM and FS-VSM. The champions are
presented the A3, and the team lead explains each of the boxes
of the A3 to the champions. The champions normally ask questions, and the team jumps in to respond to the questions, using
the information posted on the walls for explanation.

Contents of the A3

At this point, the A3 should look similar to Figure 7.12.

Steps 8 and 9 will be filled in as we validate the improvement process
and make sure that the improvements had the desired effect.

Post-Event Activities

The post-event activities are often referred to as the governance of the
process. The champions and team leader determine a regular interval

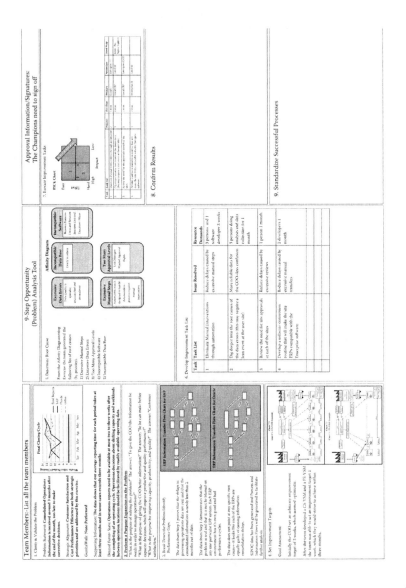

FIGURE 7.12

Case # 1—9-Step A3—post event.

for progress checks, initially monthly and later quarterly. The purpose of these checks is to make sure:

1. The tasks are getting executed on schedule
2. No new roadblocks have been encountered
3, The desired results are actually being achieved through these changes
4. We are "doing the right things"

As part of this process, we start to report back the improvement results in Box 8—Confirm Results. The team leader is responsible for scheduling regular meetings, as needed, and bringing the team together to collect data and to develop status reports. This information is summarized into Box 8 and reported to the champions on a regular basis. For Case #1, Box 8 would look similar to Figure 7.13.

At some point during these follow-up meetings the event will be declared a success. At that point several things need to happen. These include:

1. A presentation needs to be made to higher levels in the organization, in this case the CEO, demonstrating the success of the project. The team should be in attendance, and the presentation should be made by the team leader.
2. Box 9 of the 9-Step A3 needs to be filled out. This is important because the lessons learned from this event should be shared with other internal elements of the organization, so they can learn from

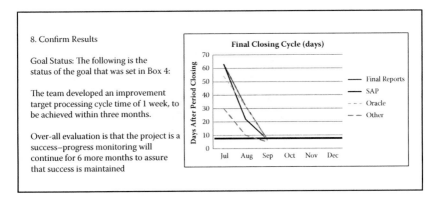

FIGURE 7.13
Case # 1—9-Step A3—Step 8 example.

9. Standardize Successful Processes

Standardization Actions Taken	Due Date	Responsible
Publish the success story in the Enterprise Newsletter	L mon	Marketing
Build a storyboard (3 foot high, 6 foot long) poster that will be display on the wall that tells the story of the improvement process	L mon	Enterprise ERP team
Give awards to the team members—public recognition for success	L mon	HR
Post the story on the enterprise website	2 mon	IT/ Marketing

FIGURE 7.14
Case # 1—9-Step A3—Step 9 example.

the success. There may also be an interest in advertising the success outside of the organization. During one of the status-check presentations to the champions, the champions are asked how they would like to share the knowledge gained. Their recommendations are then organized into a list, and the tasks on the list are assigned out to various team members, much the same as during Steps 6 and 7. The CEO may also have suggestions for additional communication. Be sure to look at the discussion of Box 9 in Chapter 3. There are several questions listed that should become part of this "communication" process. An example of what occurred in Case #1 is seen in Figure 7.14.

CASE #2

The intention with this case is to demonstrate how tasks are processed as A3s. For example, in Case #1 there were several tasks identified in Steps 6 and 7. Some of these tasks will require further assessment and possibly even an RIE. For example, in Case #1, Task #2 (see Figure 7.11), each location will need to perform a detailed assessment of their data quality. This will require an RIE and the development of a 9-Step A3 at each of these locations. Case #2 is an example of one of these "lower-level" assessments and RIEs.

Case #2 is the A3 for an RIE focused on reducing the amount of time it takes to implement patches across an enterprise with dozens of locations and hundreds of computers at each location. This is an RIE that was generated at the enterprise level because of a strategic security concern. A strategic initiative about security generated numerous tasks, one of which was to improve the implementation of security patches throughout all the systems in the enterprise. If all the locations did not maintain the same level of security, then there could be data and information leaks to competitors.

The CEO assigned the CIO to be the champion of this activity. The CIO selected a team lead and arranged for a Lean facilitator to work on this problem. The three of them decided on a team composed of IT personnel responsible for implementing patches. In this case, the champion is also the customer along with the CEO of the company. A security officer was also included on the team.

The CIO, team lead, and facilitator developed a project charter which would give the team clear direction and a goal. This team would work through the 9-Step A3 and the RIE.

It was suggested that the team needed to go out and talk to a few of the major IT organizations at the various company sites to see what their struggles and concerns may be. The result of these conversations would give the team a better understanding of the major issues, and it may also result in additional team members being added.

With the facilitator in place, it became the facilitator's responsibility to drive the charter and the RIE. The facilitator started by taking the standard format for the charter (Technical Tool #27 in Chapter 6). The charter required the following information, and it was filled in as follows:

Project Charter

- Project/process name
  - Reduce patch processing time
- Champion—The person with the money to see this through/someone who believes in the potential benefits of this improvement process
  - CIO
- Process owner—Whose workplace will be directly affected by this change
  - IT staff at the various locations
- Product/service being impacted
  - Security/IT standardization
- Team leader—Assigned by the champion
  - The enterprise IT person responsible for patch implementations

- Facilitators—Not necessarily experienced with the project or process but highly experienced in the Lean process
  - The CPI (continuous process improvement) office selected and assigned a black belt Lean facilitator
- Dates (actual and estimated)
  - Project start date
    - Two weeks out
  - Measurement completed
    - Data about how long it takes to implement patches is automatically collected by the enterprise computer and is readily available to the team.
  - Preanalysis completed
    - The CIO and his team have been analyzing the delays, and this analysis will be brought to the event team meeting.
  - Improvements (tasks) completed
    - None defined at this point
  - Project completion date
    - Six months out
- Expected savings/benefits
  - What are the KPIs (key performance indicators), and what is the anticipated improvement goal for each
    - Time from the release of a new patch until 95% of the company's systems have the patch implemented. This allows for people to be on vacation or for hardware that is being serviced.
    - A second metric of 100% patch implementation is also being collected to see how long it takes for 100% to be achieved
  - Who owns the metric
    - CIO
  - Benefits to the external customer
    - Greater responsiveness resulting from fewer systems failures
- Rapid improvement event (RIE) or project dates and time
  - An RIE is scheduled for two weeks out
- Linkage to the strategic roadmap—The project needs to tie directly to the organization's strategy.
  - Customer satisfaction and security are both strategic priorities and are addressed by this exercise.
- One-paragraph explanation of the improvement opportunity
  - Computer patches are taking too long to be implemented on the various computers throughout the enterprise. This presents a

security risk and has also caused some inconsistent standardization in documents.

- One-paragraph description of the desired outcomes/results
  - Patches need to be implemented on time based on priority. 95% of high-priority patches need to be implemented within one week, medium-priority patches within three weeks, low-priority patches within two months.
- Project deliverables
  - A defined/standardized plan for patch implementation that will be implemented enterprise-wide.
  - Documentation supporting the patch implementation plan needs to be developed.
- Project scope—where does the process start and end (as far as this improvement process is concerned)?
  - The scope of the project starts when the enterprise IT department releases a patch to the corresponding IT units for implementation and ends when it is 100% implemented.
- Team members/where assigned (what office they work in)/contact information (phone and e-mail)
  - The team members included enterprise and local IT representatives that are involved in the patch implementation process
- Follow-up plan
  - Executive out-brief of the results of the exercise to the champion and the process owners
    - The RIE was scheduled for five days, and an out-brief to the champion was scheduled for the afternoon of the fifth day.
  - Follow-up meetings—How often will we have follow-up status meetings? Who should attend?
    - Monthly meetings will be held to review the implementation of the recommended changes and to do a status check to see if the objectives of the exercise have been met.
- Approvals
  - Champion approval signature and date
  - Process owner approval signature and date
  - Executive out-brief date
- The project facilitator successfully acquired the appropriate approval signature and scheduled the out-brief for the afternoon of the last day of the workshop.

Facilitator Activities

The Lean facilitator is a critical piece of the success of this project. The lack of knowledge that the facilitator has about IT patches or their functions is actually an advantage. It leaves the facilitator in the position of being able to as the "dumb questions" that will help move the team "out of the box." During the RIE initiation process the facilitator:

1. Develops the project charter in conjunction with the champion and team leader
2. Defines the teams and gets everyone on board with their schedules
3. Gets champion sign-off on the charter
4. Plans the logistics of the event
   a. Location
   b. Timing (start, end, breaks, etc.)
   c. Meals
   d. Whiteboards or flip charts
   e. Computer screens, computers, etc.
   f. Schedule Champions to come at the start of the event for an "introduction" and again at the end of the event for an "out-brief."
   g. Etc.
5. Event pre-work
   a. Surveys
   b. Data collection
   c. SIPOC
6. Plans and facilitates the Lean training that occurs at the start of the event
7. Executes the event by attending and keeping the event on track
8. Facilitates the creation of the 9-Step A3
9. Prepares the "out-brief" presentation in conjunction with the team members
10. Post-event activities
    a. Plan follow-up meetings
    b. Stay in touch with the change owners and make sure the changes occur as defined and recommended
11. Finalize the 9-Step A3 by executing Step 9, sharing the knowledge with other parts of the enterprise

RIE Event Pre-Work

Following the sign-off of the charter, the facilitator initiates the pre-work. This requires making contact with the team members and collecting information about them, about the issue under study, and about any data collection that will be needed in order to execute the event. The areas of pre-work include:

1. A team member assessment needs to be performed. The author recommends the following for this particular activity:
   a. Team Effectiveness Survey (Acceptance Tool #2—Chapter 6)—This survey will tell the facilitator how ready the team is to work together.
   b. Change Readiness Survey (Acceptance Tool #3—Chapter 6)—This survey will tell the facilitator if he/she is going to have issues with the team's openness to change.
   c. Myers–Briggs Assessment (Acceptance Tool #4—Chapter 6)—this assessment tells the facilitator who the dominant personalities are going to be on the team. Also, the facilitator is going to see if there is an imbalance in the team in favor of one type of personality over another. This could create some facilitation nightmares if not handled correctly.

   The results of these surveys and assessments are presented to the team as part of the initial half-day introduction and training that the team will go through to start the event. The facilitator will explain what the surveys mean and how this will affect the work of the event.

2. SIPOC (see Technical Tool #3)—The SIPOC collects information from each team member about the Supplier-Input-Process-Output-Customer from the perspective of each of the team members. This information is then consolidated and reviewed during the first part of the event. It tends to be eye-opening as team members see the divergence of perspectives.

3. Data collection—Any data, for example, in this case, a history of the patch implementation times, is useful in that it helps the team see the reality of the problem. Personal opinions and conjectures are driven away when the actual data is presented. This data needs to be available for the one-week event and, if possible, should be made available earlier to the team members to help them in their preparation.

4. Dissemination of pre-work information to the team members should include timing and location of the event, agenda, dress codes, etc. Additionally, a copy of the charter and any prepared data should be sent out to give the team a heads-up of what they will be focusing on.

Event Execution

The actual execution of the RIE event follows this schedule:

- Day 1
  - 30 min.—Introductory comments by the champion stressing the importance of the RIE.
  - 4 hrs—Lean training—explain the 7 Wastes (Technical Tool #1) and the 9-Step A3 tool (Chapter 3) and any other tools that may be used during this event, like in this case the Team Effectiveness Survey, the Change Readiness Survey, Myers–Briggs (Acceptance Tools #2, 3, and 4), SIPOC (Technical Tool #3), Value Stream Mapping (VSM) (Technical Tool #2), etc.
  - 30 min.—Review of the data.
  - 3 hrs (finishing out the day)—Start the actual Lean event by working through the SIPOC and reviewing the data that came in from the team members. A team consensus needs to be agreed upon for who the customer is, what the outputs are, what the necessary inputs are, and what the suppliers should be. Detailing out the process piece will become the focus of the next couple of days.
- Day 2
  - 4 hrs—Start working on the 9-Step A3 using the following steps:
    a. **"Team Members" Box**—Taken from the charter.
    b. **"Approval Information/Signatures" Box**—The champions, in this case the CIO.
    c. **"1. Clarify and Validate the Problem" Box**—Start with the information on the charter and get the team's consensus on a one-paragraph statement of what the problem really is. Review the questions in Chapter 3 for Box 1, and make sure each of these questions is resolved in this box. Case #2—Box #1 is shown in Figure 7.15.
    d. **"2. Perform a Purpose Expansion on the Problem" Box**—The team was challenged with the question, "What is the purpose of solving this problem?" The answer: "To improve

1. Clarify & Validate the Problem

Problem Statement: **Computer patches are taking too long to be implemented on the various computers throughout the enterprise. This presents a security risk and has also caused some inconsistent standardization in documents.**

Strategic Alignment: **Customer Satisfaction and Security are both strategic priorities and are addressed by this exercise.**

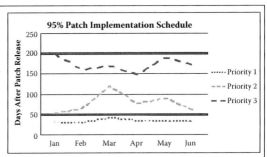

GembaWalk: **Performed as a team at several sites.**

Supporting Information: **The data shows that our average patch implementation time for achieving 95% implemented on Priority 1 patches is 3 months**

Desired Future State: **Patches need to be implemented on time based on priority. 95% of High priority patches need to be implemented within one week, Medium priority patches within three weeks, low priority patches within two months.**

FIGURE 7.15
Case # 2—9-Step A3—Step 1 example.

information security and standardization." Then the team was asked, "What is the purpose of improving security and standardization?" The answer: "So we can perform with more consistent quality for the customer and to maintain a competitive edge." The next question asked was, "What is the purpose for improving consistent quality and maintaining a competitive edge?" The answer: "Increase customer satisfaction from an enterprise perspective." Since customer satisfaction is a strategic priority, the decision was to move forward with the initiative. This information about the questions and the corresponding answers is placed into Box 2.

e. **"3. Break Down the Problem/Identify Performance Gaps" Box**—Again you should look carefully at the questions posed for Box 3 in Chapter 3. For Case #2, the team went through a review of the SIPOC. The SI and OC were readily agreed upon, but the P became more complicated and would require several Value Stream Maps (VSMs) to do a complete and thorough analysis. The team decided to do a detailed Value Stream Map (See Technical Tool #2 in Chapter 6) of the entire process incorporating all environments. The discussion resulted in the example of Figure 7.16.

3. Break Down the Problem / Identify
   Performance Gaps

> The data from Step 1 proves that
> the delays in processing patches is
> real and that 95 % of the Priority 1
> patches are rarely implemented in
> less than 3 months.

> The data does not point at any specific root causes.

> SIPOC data has been generated and
> VSMs will need to be generated to
> facilitate further analysis.

SIPOC Data
Supplier – Enterprise IT organization

Input–The patch
Process–Requires VSMs
Output–The completed Patch
Customer–The Enterprise ITCIO

FIGURE 7.16
Case # 2—9-Step A3—Step 3 Example

  f. **"4. Set Improvement Targets" Box**—It is again important
     to review the questions and considerations for Box 4 that
     were outlined in Chapter 3. The improvement targets define
     whether this project is a success or failure. Targets need to be
     set thoughtfully and carefully. For Case #2 the CIO's goals
     were detailed out in Step #1—future state. The team would
     now generate VSMs to see if these goals were feasible.
  • 4 hrs—The second half of the day was focused on mapping out
    the current state process. How do each of the locations schedule
    and implement patches that come from the enterprise IT organization? Map out the CS-VSM (Technical Tool #2). For Case #2
    several of the patch processes were mapped until the team was
    satisfied that they had covered the majority of the cases.
• Day 3
  • 8 hrs—The day was focused on continuing to map out the current
    state process. Mapping was accomplished using VSM (Technical
    Tool #2). The current state Value Stream Map (CS-VSM) charts
    were similar to the one shown in Figure 7.5.[1]
  • The CS-VSMs are evaluated by the team with a focus on eliminating waste. There are large wastes in Figure 7.5, especially
    the transition times, like 11.9 days, 3.8 days, 17.1 days, etc. The

---

[1] Showing another set of VSMs seemed redundant to the author. They all look similar to the ones
shown in Figures 7.5, 7.6, and 7.7.

consolidations and reorganizations that the team came up with are similar in Figure 7.6. And the final FS-VSM can be seen in Figure 7.7.

- The differences between the CS-VSMs and the FS-VSM define the process gaps that need to be fixed. The 9-Step A3—Step 4 looks similar to Figure 7.8.

- Day 4
  - 4 hrs—The first part of the day was focused on continuing to develop the 9-Step A3 report, looking next at Step 5—Determine Root Cause. Having gone through the CS and FS-VSM exercise, the team has an in-depth understanding of the process and its shortcomings. Reading through the discussion in Chapter 3, we see there are numerous tools that can be used to assist in focusing on the "root cause." In this case the facilitator felt that the fishbone chart (see Technical Tool #21) would be the most useful in evaluating the root causes. He also felt that the five whys (see Technical Tool #19) may lead the team to root causes.
    - The fishbone chart is explained in Chapter 6, and the results of the charting exercise can be seen in the 9-Step A3—Step 5, which is shown in Figure 7.17. Similarly, the 5 Whys are explained in Chapter 6, and these results can also be found in Box 5.

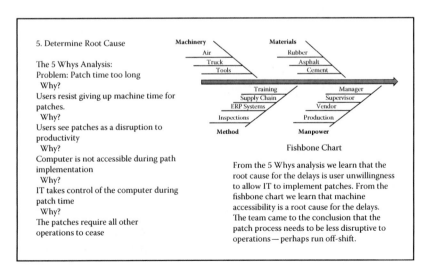

FIGURE 7.17
Case # 2—9-Step A3—Step 5 example.

- 2 hrs—The remainder of the day was focused on Step 6 and Step 7 of the 9-Step A3 Process. As we saw in Chapter 3, for Step 6 we are challenged to identify and list out all the tasks needed to accomplish the expected changes. First the team looks at the CS-VSM and compares it to the FS-VSM, and lists all the changes necessary to get from CS to FS. Then the team looks at the root causes and makes sure that every root cause has been resolved in the newly generated task list. If the "root causes" have not been resolved, then the problem has not been solved. Generating this task list is generally pretty quick, because the team is intimately involved in the process and knows what needs to be changed. Be sure to refer to Chapter 3, which includes a list of questions that need to be responded to in order to generate a complete task list. In the example of Case # 2, the list included about five items. The problems turned out to be similar at each location, and the same set of tasks had to be accomplished. An example of how Step 6 would look for Case # 2 can be seen in Figure 7.10.
- 2 hrs—With the task list in hand, the team can now focus on Step 7 of the 9-Step A3 Process. As we saw in Chapter 3, Step 7 asks us to evaluate each of the tasks for priority, due date, primary responsible party, and secondary responsible party. This often involves some debating on the part of the team, but is usually a reasonably fast process. A summary of the results can be seen in Figure 7.11.
- Day 5
  - 4 hrs—The first half of the day is focused on reviewing the 9-Step A3 for completeness and accuracy and perhaps making some cosmetic improvements to make the A3 look better, realizing that in the afternoon the team leader will need to present the team's findings to the champions.
  - 2 hrs—The last big activity of the day is the out-brief to the champions. This usually occurs in the same room where the event was held, so the champions can see the work, like the SIPOC, the fishbone chart, and the CS-VSM and FS-VSM. The champions are presented the A3, and the team lead explains each of the boxes of the A3 to the champions. The champions normally ask questions, and the team jumps in to respond to the questions, using the information posted on the walls for explanation.

- At this point, the A3 should look similar to Figure 7.12. Steps 8 and 9 will be filled in as we validate the improvement process and make sure that the improvements had the desired effect.

Post-Event Activities

The post-event activities are often referred to as the governance of the process. The champion and team leader determine a regular interval for progress checks, initially monthly and later quarterly. The purpose of these checks is to make sure:

1. The tasks are getting executed on schedule at all the locations
2. No new roadblocks have been encountered
3. The desired results are actually being achieved through these changes
4. We are "doing the right things"

As part of this process, we start to report back the improvement results in Box 8—Confirm Results. The team leader is responsible for scheduling regular meetings, as needed, and bringing the team together to collect data and to develop status reports. This information is summarized into Box 8 and reported to the champions on a regular basis. For Case # 2, Box 8 would look similar to Figure 7.18.

At some point during these follow-up meetings the event will be declared a success. At that point several things need to happen. These include:

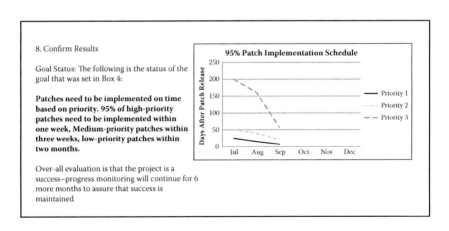

FIGURE 7.18
Case # 2—9-Step A3—Step 8 example.

1. A presentation needs to be made to higher levels in the organization demonstrating the success of the project. The team should be in attendance, and the presentation should be made by the team leader.
2. Box 9 of the 9-Step A3 needs to be filled out. This is important because the lessons learned from this event should be shared with other internal elements of the organization, so they can learn from the success. During one of the presentations to the champion, the champion is asked how they would like to share the knowledge gained. These recommendations are then organized into a list, and the tasks on the list are assigned out to various team members, much the same as during Steps 6 and 7. Be sure to look at the discussion of Box 9 in Chapter 3. There are several questions listed that should become part of this "communication" process. An example of what occurred in Case # 2 is similar to what we see of Case # 1 in Figure 7.14.

USING THE 9-STEP A3 TOOL

At this point the reader should have seen that the 9-Step A3:

a. Is a tool for organizing projects/opportunities/problem resolutions
b. Goes way beyond just the IT world, but is critical within it
c. Identifies responsible parties (champions and team members)
d. Identifies that we are working on the right problem (Boxes 1 and 2)
e. Forces us to validate that the problem needs fixing (Boxes 2 and 3)
f. Forces us to prove that by fixing the problem we will have a positive impact on enterprise performance (Boxes 2 and 4)
g. Makes sure that we are addressing the root cause of the problem and not just the symptoms (Box 5)
h. Helps us build a plan of attack for resolving the problem (Boxes 6 and 7)
i. Forces us to be accountable for the progress we predicted (Box 8)
j. Forces us to share our understanding and lessons learned with the remainder of the enterprise (Box 9)

The first five steps (boxes) are focused on "Are we doing the right thing?" (analysis of the opportunity/problem), Steps 6 and 7 are focused on "Are we doing things right?" and "How do we fix it if it's broken?" Steps 8 and 9 are focused on reporting what we have done. Step 8 gives us a quick, at-a-glance status of performance, and Step 9 shares what we have learned. What is left is for us to define when, where, and how we share this information.

SUMMARY

At this point in the book we have had an overview of the most powerful Lean change management tool that exists, and we have seen two case examples of how it can be used. With the 9-Step A3 process, anyone can analyze a change opportunity or problem and determine its viability and find the appropriate corrective action. The book will now discuss two additional pieces of the Lean IT puzzle, the RIE and Metrics. Both of these are critical to Lean IT, and the reasons will be explained in the next couple of chapters.

8

The Lean IT Event

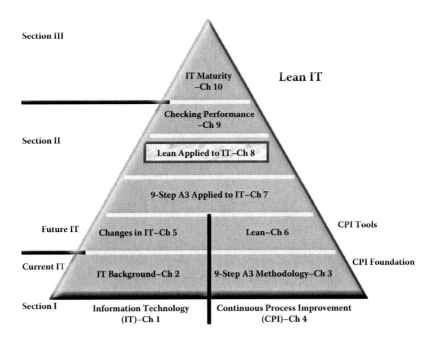

Section III

IT Maturity –Ch 10

Lean IT

Checking Performance –Ch 9

Section II

Lean Applied to IT–Ch 8

9-Step A3 Applied to IT–Ch 7

Future IT

Changes in IT–Ch 5

Lean–Ch 6

CPI Tools

Current IT

IT Background–Ch 2

9-Step A3 Methodology–Ch 3

CPI Foundation

Section I

Information Technology (IT)–Ch 1

Continuous Process Improvement (CPI)–Ch 4

I never did a day's work in my life—it was all fun.

Thomas Edison

In the last chapter we learned how the 9-Step A3 process works. It discussed how champions, team leaders, teams, and facilitators are needed for the Lean process to work. In this chapter we will dive into more detail about the RIE (rapid improvement event) process. This chapter expands on the "event" piece of the cases discussed in the last chapter.

THE RIE

The team is selected based on the recommendations of the champion and the team leaders. The team receives a cultural assessment, using the acceptance tools discussed in Chapter 6. Then, with an appropriate team structure in place, the team meets for the first time where they:

- Receive direction directly from the champion by having the champion come to the kickoff of the event (the morning of the first day) and he/she describes the goal and vision for the event
- Receive appropriate training from the facilitator of any Lean tools that will be used during the event
- Set team rules
- Identify team leaders and scribes
- Set team goals for the event
- Study the current state of the process thoroughly
- Identify a future state
- Perform a gap analysis and develop a list of action items specific to this event
- Assign team members to work each of the action items
- Monitor and measure the improvement process

The event starts off with all-day meetings running for about one week. After that, the complexity of the changes needs to be reviewed. An event can run for one week, or it may run for years, depending on the complexity of the event. If the event goes beyond the initial week, then regular weekly or biweekly meetings need to be arranged so that the team can make sure that progress continues to be made on the event action items.

On the last day of the first week, the event team reports their progress to the champion. It is important for the champion team to stay in the loop regarding the team's activities. The event team should also debrief the champion at regular intervals, for as long as the event team remains organized.

THE ROLE OF THE FACILITATOR

It is important to define the characteristics of a good facilitator. The facilitator should be someone who is highly trained and experienced in the Lean process. He/she is an agent of positive change, a results-oriented generalist, flexible, and adaptable as opposed to narrow specialist. One of the facilitator's most valuable contributions to a team's growth and development is helping the team members become aware of the team's own processes, enabling them to discuss their own communication, problem solving, decision making, and conflict resolution practices. The facilitator helps the team learn how to work more effectively to fulfill their charter, roles, and responsibilities, not doing it for them, but by helping them to do it and to take ownership in it. The facilitator must not allow the team to run from the responsibility of taking control of the change process.

Not everyone is an effective mentor and facilitator. It is an art developed and mastered through practice, not by formal education. Most important is willingness, real experience, desire, and motivation to help others learn. The criterion for the selection of a facilitator is to select individuals who have been doing this naturally all their lives. Many people have a natural tendency to help others grow. We continue to develop these characteristics and these interpersonal competencies by practicing:

- Empathy
- Acceptance
- Authenticity
- Active listening
- Artful intervention

LEAN TRAINING

The first half day of any Lean event involves a training session. The subjects that should be included in this half day include:

1. Team member introductions (name, job assignment, do they have any experience with Lean, something personal about the person)
2. Rules of engagement
   a. Break schedule/10 min breaks every hour?
   b. One person talking at a time.
   c. Everyone participates/everyone has a voice in this process.
   d. No dumb questions/no dumb observations.
   e. Respect each other/respect each other's comments.
   f. Keep sidebar comments to a minimum/save for breaks.
   g. Use a parking lot to capture ideas/great ideas will not be lost.
   h. Cell phones off.
   i. Decisions will be by consensus.
   j. No retribution or attribution.
3. The material in Chapter 1 of this book
4. Figure 3.3 in this book
5. The Acceptance Tools used for this event (show Figure 8.1 and discuss the team's acceptance scores)
6. 7 Wastes (Technical Tool #1—Chapter 6)
7. Value Stream Mapping (current state/ideal state/future state) (Technical Tool #2—Chapter 6)
8. SIPOC (Supplier/Input/Process/Output/Customer) (Technical Tool #3—Chapter 6)
9. Project charter (Technical Tool #27—Chapter 6)
10. Any other technical tools that will be used during this event

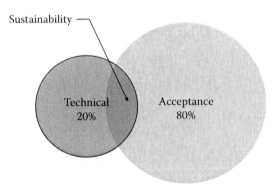

Sustainability = Technical • Acceptance

FIGURE 8.1
Lean technical and acceptance tools.

The depth and level of detail that the facilitator chooses to go into depends on the team. If they are familiar with Lean events, then the training can be abbreviated. Otherwise, it is critical that the team has a clear understanding of what Lean is and what they are trying to accomplish.

LEAN TOOLS

Lean change management is not a specific methodology. It is more about adaptation, goal fulfillment, and sustainment. Lean tools and concepts focus the organization on changing the system or the process so that it is capable of adapting to changing customer needs. But because *"change is hard,"* we find that the technical implementation of Lean alone will not create the acceptance required to sustain the change. Looking at Figure 8.1, we see that the acceptance process is 80% of the effort in a Lean implementation, and that the technical tools are only 20% of the effort. We also see that sustainability cannot be achieved with only one or the other of these two elements. Both are required.

In Chapter 6 we learned about the Lean Acceptance Tools and the Technical Tools that are applicable to IT.

HOW THE LEAN PROCESS WORKS

There are three stages to the Lean process: the acceptance stage, the technical stage, and the sustainment stage. We start with the acceptance stage, where we try to get the organization to recognize the need for change.

Acceptance Stage

The first thing we need in the Lean process is a trained facilitator who is highly experienced in the Lean process and its available tools. This facilitator will initially talk to the champion of the organization in order to get some guidance on where they want him or her to focus their efforts. Since Lean is disruptive, there has to be a compelling reason to do Lean. This compelling need must come from the organization's strategic priorities, for example its position in their respective industry and their need to be able to adapt to changes that might affect their growth and survival. The facilitator needs to come away from the meeting with the champion having a clear, measurable objective for his Lean activity.

The facilitator may next choose to perform a scan of the team members. This involves holding a short 15- to 30-minute face-to-face meeting with each of the team members to get their perspective on the upcoming event. The information from this scan is only for the eyes of the facilitator, and the purpose of the scan was to identify the key areas of concern and who the key players are in the process. The facilitator now knows all areas of the organization, all customers, all suppliers, and any other stakeholders that need to participate in the RIE.

Once the team has been identified and invited, some of the acceptance tools discussed in Chapter 6 and further explained in Chapter 7 are needed. These tools are used to evaluate the change readiness and the team dynamics of the team. All this is done before the team meets, so that the facilitator can prepare for the team dynamics that he or she will be encountering.

Now we are ready to get the team together in the same room. We start with a training session, teaching them the whys and hows of Lean. Then we show them what their role will be in the Lean process.

The facilitator is not the leader of the Lean effort. The facilitator should subordinate himself or herself to the champion and team leader and will take direction from them on what needs to be done, when it needs to be completed, and how it should be done. The process owners are the team, and they need to own the changes to the process. The facilitator needs to give the team direction in the form of training about the Lean tools. And the facilitator needs to share findings, problems, and successes with the team.

Technical Stage

The technical stage begins with the event, which almost always is some type of process-mapping activity where the team tries to thoroughly understand the process or system under study. The primary tool for this is almost always a Value Stream Mapping (VSM) exercise (see Technical Tool #2 in Chapter 6), where the current "value stream" is mapped out in detail (CS-VSM). There are also other tools, like spaghetti charting (see Technical Tool #10) which focuses on the people movement, or systems flowcharting (see Technical Tool #6) which focuses more specifically on the information flow of the organization. The objective of all these maps and charts is to study the process in as much detail as possible so that

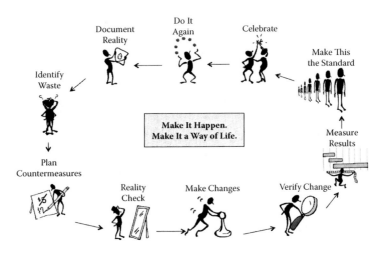

FIGURE 8.2
Lean sustainment.

waste, bottlenecks, systems holes, and other opportunities for improvement can be identified.

After the technical assessment, the findings are used to develop improvement task lists. Each event creates a task list, also referred to as an action item list or a Lean newspaper. This action item list is then moved forward until each action item is resolved.

Sustainment Stage

The sustainment stage is where the Lean effort takes on a life of its own. At this point everyone has been trained at all levels of the organization, and they now have taken ownership of their piece of the process. The Lean process no longer needs the facilitator. The champion meets regularly and requests reports from, and gives direction to, each of the event RIE team leads. RIE teams are organized as new areas for improvement are identified, and obsolete RIE teams are disbanded as they achieve their desired goals. Lean becomes a way of life for the organization as a whole (see Figure 8.2).

CASE STUDY: WIPRO (CONTINUED)

Continuing the Wipro story from Chapter 2, 3, 4, 5, and 6, we now look at one last example of Wipro's successful Lean IT implementations. Here we are looking at a global healthcare company. In this case the focus of the problem was on a large ERP integration. The IT problem included a focus on discrepancies in the ticket handling process. Different modules required multiple skill sets, and bottlenecks were occurring in getting the correct teams of talent working on a particular problem at the same time. The Lean improvement process incorporated Value Stream Mapping with a focus on non-value-added activities. They incorporated visual controls and mistake proofing checklists. The results included a 69% reduction in resolution cycle time and an average 300% increase in productivity.

For additional information about the Wipro Lean IT process, please contact the author with specific questions, and he will direct you to the appropriate Wipro personnel.

SUMMARY

This chapter was intended to give the reader a quick overview of what Lean RIEs are all about and how they work. Use this chapter in conjunction with Chapter 7, which shows how the 9-Step A3 is applied, and with Chapter 6 which describes the Lean tools. There are numerous other supportive materials on the subject of Lean that would give the reader more depth of understanding. Some suggested books for further reading would include:

- *Balanced Scorecard: Translating Strategy into Action* by Robert S. Kaplan and David P. Norton
- *Breakthrough Thinking: The Seven Principles of Creative Problem Solving* by Gerald Nadler and Shozo Hibino
- *Built to Last: Successful Habits of Visionary Companies* by Jim Collins and Jerry I. Porras
- *Good to Great: Why Some Companies Make the Leap … and Others Don't* by Jim Collins
- *Lean Thinking: Banish Waste and Create Wealth in Your Corporation* by James P. Womack and Daniel Jones
- *Making Innovation Happen: Concept Management through Integration* by Gerhard Plenert and Shozo Hibino

- *Maverick: The Success Story behind the World's Most Unusual Workplace* by Ricardo Semler
- *Real Numbers: Management Accounting in a Lean Organization* by Jean E. Cunningham, Orest Fiume, and Emily Adams
- *Scenario Planning: The Link between Future and Strategy* by Mats Lindgren and Hans Bandhold
- *The eManager: Value Chain Management in an eCommerce World* by Gerhard Plenert
- *The Fifth Discipline: The Art and Practice of a Learning Organization* by Peter M. Senge
- *The Game of Work: How to Enjoy Work as Much as Play* by Charles A. Coonradt
- *The Goal* by Eliyahu M. Goldratt and Jeff Cox
- *The Seven Habits of Highly Effective People* by Stephen R. Covey
- *The Toyota Way Fieldbook: A Practical Guide for Implementing Toyota's 4Ps* by Jeffrey K. Liker and David Meier

A second layer of books for the reader who just cannot get enough includes:

- *5S Implementation Manual: Starting Lean Manufacturing* by Catherine Parrill and Bob Rosinski
- *Kaizen for Quick Changeover: Going beyond SMED* by Keisuke Arai and Kenichi Sekine
- *Kanban* by David J. Anderson
- *Leadership and the New Science: Discovering Order in a Chaotic World* by Margaret J. Wheatley
- *Leading Change* by John P. Kotter
- *Lean Manufacturing for the Small Shop* by Gary Conner
- *Learning to See: Value Stream Mapping to Add Value and Eliminate MUDA* by Mike Rother and John Shook
- *Measure and Improve the Effectiveness of Your Employees* by Harvard Business School Press
- *Mining Group Gold: How to Cash in on the Collaborative Brain Power of a Team for Innovation and Results,* 3rd ed. by Thomas A. Kayser
- *One Piece Flow: Cell Design for Transforming the Production Process* by Kenichi Sekine
- *Organizational Culture and Leadership* by Edgar Schein
- *Organizational Dynamism: Unleashing Power in the Workforce* by Wayne R. Pace

- *Performance by Design: Computer Capacity Planning by Example* by Daniel A. Menasce, Lawrence W. Dowdy, and Virgilio A.F. Almeida
- *Process Consultation Revisited: Building the Helping Relationship* by Edgar Schein
- *Productive Workplaces* by Marvin R. Weisbord
- *Standard Work for the Shop Floor* by the Productivity Press Development Team
- *The Machine That Changed the World: The Story of Lean Production—Toyota's Secret Weapon in the Global Car Wars That Is Now Revolutionizing World Industry* by James P. Womack, Daniel T. Jones, and Daniel Roos
- *The Perfect Engine: How to Win in the New Demand Economy by Building to Order with Fewer Resources* by Patricia E. Moody and Anand Sharma
- *The Toyota Production System* by Taiichi Ohno
- *When Giants Learn to Dance* by Rosabeth Moss Kanter
- *Who's Counting? A Lean Accounting Business Novel* by Jerrold M. Solomon

Then, once the readers have a thorough understanding of this material, they will also have a clearer understanding of the power of Lean.

9

Meaningful Metrics

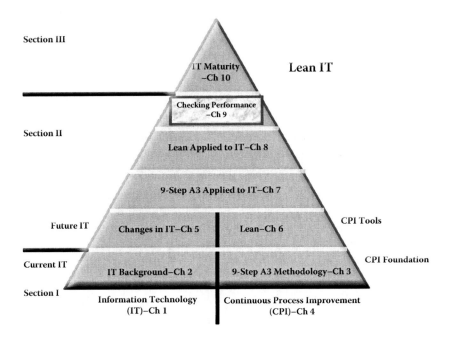

When performance is measured, performance improves. When performance is measured and reported, the rate of improvement accelerates.

Thomas S. Monson

In one of the old episodes of *The Twilight Zone* there was the story of a lady who was becoming frustrated with life. She was betrayed by her friends, lost her job, had an ever-increasing number of bills, and nothing seemed to be going right. During a very frustrating and discouraging evening, as she sat depressed, there was a knock on the door. Opening the door she saw a man with a black box, in the center of which was a button. The man handed her the box and told her that if she would press the button she would get a million dollars; however, "someone whom she did not know and who did not know her would die." Then the man left.

She thought this was the stupidest thing she had ever heard. She would never press this button have someone killed, no matter how much money it got her. She put the box high on a shelf.

As time went by her discouragement started to get the better of her. She reasoned that maybe the person that would die was really sick and was on the verge of dying anyway. Or maybe it was a convicted murderer that deserved to die anyway. She took the box down and nearly pressed the button in a moment of panic, but then regained her composure and put the box back on the shelf.

However, as time went on, she eventually lost her will to resist and in a moment of panic she took the box down and pushed the button. Immediately there was a knock on the door. There stood the man with a check for one million dollars. He handed her the check and asked her for the box. She was a little surprised by the request for the box, but she got it, and as she handed it to him she asked; "What are you going to do with the box?"

He responded, "I'm going to give it to someone you do not know and who does not know you!"

How would that change your perspective? It makes you think, doesn't it? Does it make you wish you had more data/information?

The author was in a meeting with an Air Force general who was frustrated with continuous process improvements (CPIs). He claimed that he had nearly a dozen improvement activities over the last year, but he had nothing to demonstrate that any of these improvement processes had a positive impact. He stressed that without measures, he could not really say that any of it was worthwhile.

THE ROLE AND PURPOSE OF MEASURES

There are numerous clever quotes about metrics or measures. Let us start with one:

IF IT CAN'T BE MEASURED,
THEN IT WON'T BE IMPROVED!

By way of explanation, how do you know something has improved if there is not a way of saying how or what has improved. How do you identify that improvement? This requires some form of quantification, or it is meaningless hearsay.

Measures are critical to a successfully performing IT department. Measures are not a tool for data collection. They are not implemented because the accounting department wants another piece of information. They are only implemented when they add value to the process. The only valid reason for a measurement system is motivation. No matter what you measure, the simple fact that you are measuring it will encourage employees to think that it is important to you, and they will therefore do their best to make those numbers look good. And employees can be very good at making numbers look good. So, if it is not important, or in the extreme case where the measurement detracts from the results you really want, then eliminate that measure and only implement measures that truly add value.

THE ROLE AND PURPOSE OF CONTROL SYSTEMS

In far too many organizations, the measurement system and the employee reward systems are based on units produced. Often this directly results in quality taking a less important role. These organizations generate what they measure—large volumes of output. So their solution was to add control systems, like statistical process control (SPC) (see Technical Tool # 24), which, in and of itself, is a very good system when applied as a performance enhancement tool used to measure process performance "as it happens." But as a control system, which was "after the fact," it had no effect on quality output. It identifies a varying number of areas where errors occurred. But it does little to aid in identifying solutions.

INAPPROPRIATELY APPLIED CONTROL SYSTEMS ARE THE ENEMY OF AN EFFICIENT SUPPLY CHAIN ENVIRONMENT.

Control systems:

- Add steps to the process
- Increase the opportunities for failure since there are now more steps in the process
- Increase the overall cycle time
- Misdirect employees on what is important in achieving overall goals
- Waste resources (time, floor space, etc.)
- Waste capacity
- And most importantly, they move the error to somewhere else in the process rather than fix or eliminate the error

AN INDUSTRIAL EXAMPLE—MANAGING YOUR SUPPLY CHAIN USING EVENT MANAGEMENT[1]

Toward the end of the twentieth century, large manufacturing companies began focusing on their core competencies. This meant they started doing the things they do best, and this required them to subcontract many of their fabricated parts to suppliers. The result was the creation of increasingly elaborate supply chains to support their end product. This transition introduced a new way of doing business, one that caused more sophisticated supply chain management requirements than ever before. Companies previously focused on managing only their internal processes were now forced to manage global supply chains.

A leading aerospace manufacturing company began their transformation into the supply chain world through the use of event management. They felt that they could enhance supplier connectivity through the implementation of an event management communication tool requiring

---

[1] This section is taken from a case example developed for the University of San Diego, Supply Chain Management Institute by Wink Williams and Harold Loth.

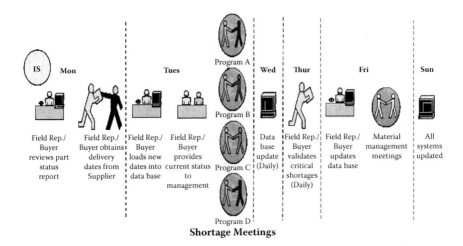

FIGURE 9.1
Before event management.

suppliers to provide status to them on major milestones in the manufacturing process. The hope was that they would gain a competitive advantage and realize lower costs.

As shown in Figure 9.1, in the old way of operating, field representatives and buyers are tasked with ensuring timely inputs from the supply chain and reporting this information to the various programs and material management. This is done verbally, through visibility reports, presentations, etc. An internal database provides a means for the collection of the data and the interfacing to shortage reports. Because of the physical requirements of the process (i.e., traveling to and from the suppliers and calling suppliers), it takes an average of 7.32 minutes per part delivery to collect the required information. This process had survived in an environment of only 10,000 to 50,000 part number deliveries per year. However, a growth in business has generated over 160,000 part number deliveries to track.

Change was required. A new concept of operations was developed to have suppliers provide milestone status through an event management tool. As shown in Figure 9.2, the new process would reduce the amount of field representative/buyer attention and would allow them to only focus on exceptions, those parts with problems or parts not supporting the need date of the assembly line. Aside from scheduled meetings during the week with management, other tasks would be completed in a continuous process and would not be subject to particular timetables.

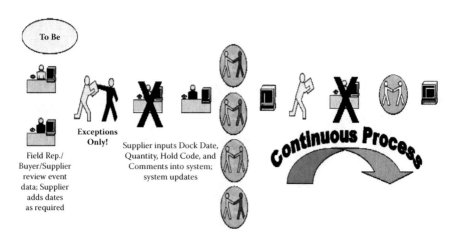

FIGURE 9.2
Using event management.

The project was created and originally dubbed "Supplier Connectivity." Since supplier connectivity has so many other connotations, the name was revised early on to "Supplier Connectivity—Event Management." To ensure completion of the project and to demonstrate top-management buy-in, the task was added to the company's annual operating plan (AOP). A team was assembled consisting of two co-project managers, a technical manager, process manager, field representatives, buyers, and software representatives. Most importantly, the team had a sponsor at the director level, whose support throughout the program was exceptional.

Two software suppliers were chosen to pilot their event management tools over a three-month period. Since the project team was located in southern California, 16 part suppliers (eight for each software tool) were chosen from the area. This was done to provide better assistance for any issues or problems that might arise during the pilot. These were local suppliers that provided machined parts to 15 different programs from the company's different manufacturing sites around the United States.

The main objectives of the pilot were identified as:

- Pilot both software tools and associated processes
- Gather supplier acceptance and performance data
- Finalize internal process and concept of operations
- Measure success
- Obtain sufficient data and knowledge to support down-select process

The team had their software, their concept of operations, and objectives. They were ready to begin their pilot.

Two separate kickoff meetings were held to start the pilot, with each software supplier conducting training that was assisted by company personnel. It was hoped the part supplier could also benefit from the use of the software, but this was not considered a major factor to the success of the project.

The suppliers were asked to communicate the status of their parts through the event management tool by providing planned and actual dates for the following events on all part numbers on which they had open purchase orders with the company:

- P.O. receipt
- Raw material ordered
- Tooling available
- Raw material available
- Fabrication start
- Postprocessing start
- Inspection start
- On-dock date

The suppliers received their first set of data the following Monday after the kickoff sessions.

Communication is always important, and while the team and suppliers were communicating well, the event management communication was failing miserably. Early on in the pilot, it was evident there were two problems:

1. Neither software tool was user friendly. This resulted in major revisions to both.
2. Including all parts and all events would not be feasible in production. The pilot needed to ask for less data elements if any success was to be gained.

The issues were catastrophic enough to halt the pilot so that these problems could be addressed. The corrections to the software were significant and took weeks before being rolled back out to the part suppliers. The software suppliers were extremely supportive.

The pilot resumed with the revised software and continued for four to eight weeks. The team dubbed this the "Lite" version, because it entailed the following events and data:

- Fabrication start (critical shortages and first time make parts only)
- Postprocessing start (critical shortages and first time make parts only)
- Inspection start (critical shortages and first time make parts only)
- On-dock date (all parts)
- Ship quantity (all parts)
- Internal/external comments (as required)
- Hold codes (as required—a number of hold codes were determined to help with the communication of supplier holding factors)

Amy Azzam notes, "Event management gets away from screaming on the phone at your supplier and gets down to managing by exception and trying to minimize the number of exceptions."[2]

After the pilot's end, it took about 30 days to gather sufficient data from the pilot to reach meaningful conclusions. This information would aid the transition of the event management process into production. As shown in Figure 9.3, the pilot time studies proved that it takes

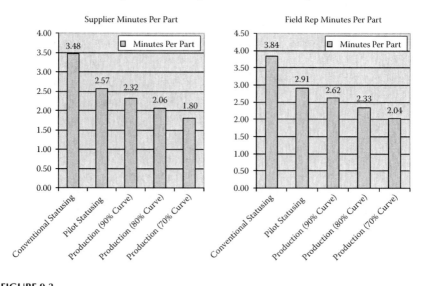

FIGURE 9.3
Pilot time study results.

[2] Azzam, Amy M., "Looking Down the Road," *APICS—The Performance Advantage*, March 2003.

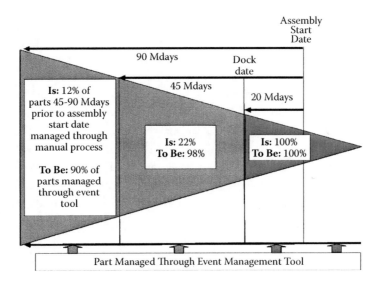

FIGURE 9.4
Parts managed using events management.

less time to obtain and communicate the status of parts in the supply chain using an event management tool. It proved we could conservatively save over 25% of the time field representatives were spending on statusing parts and allow them to focus more on relieving the holding factors and working technical issues. If they were tracking 160,000 part deliveries during the year, this would equate to a savings of almost 5000 man-hours in a year. After a learning curve in production, the savings would be even greater.

The pilot also validated that more parts could be used because of the increased visibility and communication with the supply chain (see Figure 9.4). For instance, in today's environment they would only be able to gather the status of 22% of the parts that were within 45 manufacturing days (Mdays) of the assembly need date. Through the use of the event management process they will be able to gather status of 98% of the parts in that window.

Many lessons were learned from the pilot, including:

- The system must be simple, quick to use, and error-proof to ensure part supplier support.
- The connectivity system is only as good as the effort a supplier puts into it.

- Programming the process is much more complicated than previously thought.
- An ideal system is Web-based to avoid software issues on supplier computers.
- The system must be easily adaptable to constantly changing demands.
- Event management is also adaptable to major subcontract parts.

Peter Stiles tells us, "The most frequent issue we have observed with commercial software is that software designers tend to develop fixed-event models. They do this by defining the commonly observed milestones and events in the supply chain and assume that these satisfy the majority of the monitoring requirements."[3]

Their biggest challenge in implementing event management during the pilot was taking inflexible tools and trying to make them adaptable to a dynamic supply chain. But once that hurdle is overcome, the benefits and applications of event management are limitless.

DEFINING THE MEASUREMENT SYSTEM

Measuring Too Much Is No More Valuable Than Measuring Nothing Because It Confuses the Motivational Signals.

So how do we select a measurement system? There are some process simplifications that can be applied. For example, the selection of a production planning system should be directly reflective of the enterprise goals and priorities. If we are trying to motivate labor efficiency, then job sheets that report job starts, stops, and volumes are very appropriate. However, if we are interested in materials efficiency, then we should eliminate the time reporting on the job sheets and instead measure inventory levels, cycle time, and scrap rates. If we are interested in quality, we should measure defect performance rates, on-time delivery performance, employee change recommendations, and employee turnover. An excellent collection for world-class areas of performance measurement is found in the Baldrige criteria. This changes from time to time, so an updated version should be accessed; search the Web for Baldrige Award, but the basic award criteria are built around:

---

[3] Stiles, Peter, "Demystifying Supply Chain Management," www.ascet.com.

- Quality of products and services
- Comparison of quality results
- Business process and operational and support-service quality improvement
- Supplier quality improvement

Often false measures are introduced that claim to be something that they are not. For example, ISO 9000 certification or QS certification claims to be a measure of quality performance. However, these systems are not quality, they are a structure upon which a quality system can be built. They are not, in themselves, a measure of quality. Statistical process control (SPC) claims to be a quality system. However, the author received a call from a company who said that a consultant had come in and installed SPC about one year ago, and they have been collecting data ever since. They were wondering what they should do with all the data. My answer was that they should "throw it out," because SPC is a tool for identifying areas that need continuous, real-time, improvement "during the run" rather than just a data collection system. Other companies have found that SPC is an excellent tool for motivation. They set up an SPC system to measure an area that they are trying to motivate better performance in, and then never really do anything with the data. The measurement process by itself motivates employee interest in the area and the employees make corrections to the process so that the numbers look good. We need to give employees credit for the fact that they can make any number look good; we just have to find the right numbers that we want to see improved. This brings us back to the discussion that motivating performance in a non-critical resource area can actually decrease, rather than increase, profitability.

In the area of performance of the worker and performance of the process, we need to focus on the critical resource for measurement. This also suggests that measuring a process performance indicator like cycle time affects many areas, like customer on-time delivery performance, quality, and inventory levels, and is therefore more meaningful than "quality units produced by employee."

A measurement system should be used to motivate, not as a data collection device.

WHAT IS THE BEST MEASURE FOR YOUR ORGANIZATION?

Lean focuses on the "long-term health of your organization." This is translated to mean that your Lean enterprise should focus on performance. And improving performance means improving quality, cost, and delivery. To facilitate this, there are numerous effective measures of Lean performance. The most commonly used operational metrics are focused on:

1. Cycle time, which incorporates inventory reductions and capacity increases
2. On-time performance to customer expectations
3. Quality, which is the foundational building block of a satisfied customer base
4. Lead time, which causes buffers of materials and capacity
5. Total cost of operations

But the most important criteria for effective measurement systems in any IT environment are that they focus on motivating the correct response from the employee base. The measure that will fit your organization the best depends on:

- The goals of the organization
- The expectations of the customer
- The response that employees or suppliers will have to the measure
- The accessibility and reliability of the measure

You start by looking at these criteria for a measurement system, and then you attempt to identify as few measures as possible that will drive everyone's response toward optimizing that measure. You should never base your measurement system on tradition. An appropriate and effective measure may be challenging to identify, but it will be surprising how directly it can affect overall organization performance.

Unfortunately, operational measures are not the only measures that drive an IT organization. Financial performance measures have become an IT performance driver. For example, IT can no longer be considered a "necessary evil"/cost center of an organization. The IT department needs to look at themselves as a profit center which generates an ROI (return on investment). This introduces performance metrics like:

- Throughput—the increased rate of cash generated by the IT department and its solutions/deliverables
- Inventory—the investment in IT solutions that are still "in process" and are not generating cash
- Operating expense—cash paid out for the day-to-day operations of the IT department including personnel, equipment, facilities, maintenance, etc.
- Assets—funds invested on a long-term basis including buildings, servers, etc.

The throughput generated minus the operating expenses is the net profit. The inventory plus the assets equals the investment. The ROI equals the net profit divided by the investment. And this ROI value is a critical success measure for all profit centers, including the IT department.

MEASUREMENT REPORTING TOOLS

There are two dominant measurement reporting tools that have also demonstrated themselves as being effective in measuring IT performance. These are:

a. Dashboard
b. Balanced scorecard

The dashboard is a tool which looks at operational measures of performance. For example, if we are measuring IT quality, the dashboard would be a matrix table that highlights successes and failures. Looking at Table 9.1, we see an example of a quality IT dashboard.

Additionally, the dashboard would have highlights; for example the box labeled Business Implementations with Priority Issues Taking More Than 2 Days is highlighted because its value is higher than the allowable range defined by the CIO.

The balanced scorecard is a high-level, organization-wide tool balancing both financial and operational metrics and aligning them with the enterprise vision/strategy. For IT the focus would be on strategic issues and implementation strategies. To utilize the balanced scorecard, we evaluate

TABLE 9.1

Quality IT Dashboard Example

Functional Area	Internal Failures	Customer Complaint First Calls	Customer Complaint Second Calls	Priority 1 Issues Taking More Than 2 Days	Priority 2 Issues Taking More Than 2 Weeks	Complex On-Going Issues Not Resolved
Physical implementation	12	3	1	2	3	2
Technical implementation	7	2	2	3	2	2
Business implementation	5	4	2	4	1	3
Ongoing sustainment	9	3	1	3	1	2

performance in four dimensions, each time defining the IT department's strategic alignment. The four dimensions are:

- Financial perspective—Corporate and IT ROI (defined earlier in this chapter)
- Customer perspective—Partnering with your customer to provide IT services that will enable their success
- Internal process perspective—Develop and maintain an information systems environment which meets strategic needs
- Innovation and learning perspective—Foster an environment that attracts and retains employees and encourages creativity

Identifying the four dimensions is the easy part. Defining the strategic metrics that will support each of these dimensions is the challenge. However, once defined, the dashboard becomes a quick and consistent tool to evaluate organizational performance.

SUMMARY

In an attempt to use information technology (IT) to enable the global supply chain management of a micro-motor manufacturing company headquartered in Hong Kong, the KE Group was commended by financial analysts as one of the few local companies that was unaffected by the Asian economic crisis. The reported, measurable results of this implementation included a 43.3% growth in net profit with only an 8% increase in sales.[4]

Without meaningful measures, you will achieve your goal: NO MEANINGFUL RESULTS. And with incorrect measures, you will receive incorrect results. The selection and proper implementation of a measurement system is critical to successful IT process improvements.

People respond to what is INSPECTED not what is EXPECTED.

---

[4] Taken from a 2005 IRMA presentation in San Diego titled "IT Enabled Global Supply Chain Management: A Case Study" by Narasimhaiah Gorla, Administrative Staff College of India, Harish Verma, Wayne State University, and Tam Wai Chou, Hong Kong Polytechnic Institute, Hong Kong.

Section III

Lean Information Technology (IT) on into the Future

10

IT Maturity

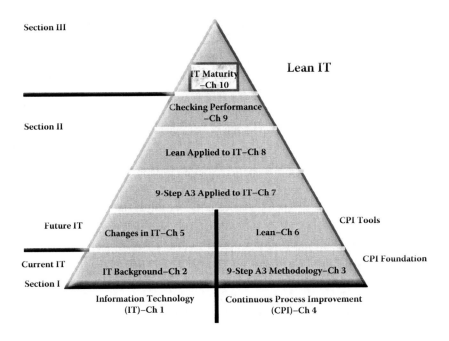

Information technology has been wonderfully successful in many ways. But those successes have extended its ambition without necessarily broadening its outlook.

John Seely Brown and Paul Duguid
The Social Life of Information, *HBS Press, 2000, p. 14.*

The author was working on a project for a multinational corporation that had just acquired factories in several locations and in the United States and China. All the plants had a similar product line, but their production planning and scheduling processes were extremely different. They had everything from spreadsheet-based ERP systems, to SAP and Oracle. The questions that the author was faced with included:

- Is there one ERP that would work well for all locations, or should they each maintain their individual ERP environments?
- If they maintain their current environments, what will it take to integrate these environments for reporting purposes?
- If ERP standardization is best, which ERP system would be best to manage all these environments?
- How long will it take to integrate these environments and how much will it cost?

Problems of this nature are not new or unique for IT in that they:

- Involve a process that is unfamiliar to the IT staff (ERP)
- Require user involvement in the decision process (which ERP is best is not an IT decision)
- Contain a high-pressure timeline
- Involve a high degree of IT involvement in whatever decision is made

The future of IT requires that the IT department is ready for these types of challenges and does not view them as disruptions and frustrations to their normally comfortable, isolated world. As the last chapter indicated, the IT world is shifting its role to that of a profit center. They need to be ready to compete for enterprise resources, as does any other department, and they need to be ready to demonstrate that, through their efforts, they are profitable.

Being profitable is just one indicator of an organization's level of IT maturity. This chapter will explore numerous other indicators.

EVALUATING YOUR WORLD-CLASS STATUS

One excellent tool for evaluating an organization's level of maturity is the step chart. The step chart contains four levels of organizational development, which are:

- Clerical—basic capabilities
- Mechanical—able to perform routine functions
- Proactive—searching for improvement opportunities
- World class—actively engaged in improvement opportunities and has realized a large degree of success

There is no perfect step chart specifically right for you. Additionally, what is world class changes over time. This book will present you with an example step chart, which you can use as a foundation for the development of your own organizational step chart. Start by developing a list of best practices for your type of organization. Once you have created a list of best practices, these are now categorized into the four classifications of a step chart. Each of the categories identifies a different type of organization. They are:

- Clerical—The clerical organization is one that operates in a foundational mode. It is dictatorial, top-down directed, and has a militaristic style. It generally contains some type of dominant authority figure. This organization is generally a manual operation that is nonreceptive to leading-edge concepts and opposes change.
- Mechanical—The mechanical organization has recognized the need to introduce some minimal level of technology. This organization is still missing integration and organization-wide direction. The focus of the organization is departmentalized, and the focus is on the performance of the individual department. Communication beyond the organization to the customer or the vendor is minimal.
- Proactive—The proactive organization is one that feels the need for integration within the organization. Company goals are established, and the various departments attempt to align themselves with these goals. There is some recognition of the need to interface with vendors and customers, but these relationships are still arms-length. Some teaming exists. Quality optimization and some levels of automation are being introduced.
- World class—This is the ideal, perfect world for your industry. It contains a high level of integration both within the organization and external to the organization with customers and vendors. It contains automation and leading-edge, sophisticated management, planning, and scheduling systems. Appropriate, goal-based metrics and the

supportive data collection systems exist. And change is a goal and has become a natural part of the organization.

Figure 10.1 is an example of an enterprise step chart. It is not intended to be all-inclusive, nor will it fit your specific industry. But it is a starting point.

Looking at Figure 10.1 we are now ready to rank the current state of our organization. The hard part is being honest with ourselves. The tendency is to over-rank ourselves. Simply because one of our 10 facilities has ERP does not mean that we are proactive. We need to look at our organization as an outsider would, and realistically evaluate our performance. If, for example, we have some, but less than half of the characteristics of a mechanical environment generally applied throughout our organization, then we should not be ranked more than a 4. If we have about half, we would probably rate about a 4.5. And we would use similar rankings for all categories of organizations. This gives us our "current state ranking."

Again, looking at Figure 10.1, we should now look at where our organization is heading. Again, we must be careful to be meaningful. We do not want to know where you personally think the organization is heading. We want to know where the rhetoric and the actions of the leadership of the organization seem to be guiding us. And again, we want to carefully and realistically rank the future state of the organization on the scale of 1 to 10. This assessment will give us the "future state" ranking.

Often it is helpful to assess the current state and future state graphically. As can be seen in Figure 10.2, the current state is the darker background (a ranking of 3.9), and the future state is the lighter background and bold (a ranking of 7.1). This ranking process is a clear delineator of where we are now and where we project ourselves to be in the future. The gap between the two becomes opportunities for improvement. And, as you have learned from this book, the first thing you need to do is to perform a 9-Step A3 analysis for each of the items in this gap to see how best to proceed with their implementation. We are now ready to develop an improvement strategy for the future, which includes the task listed generated by the 9-Step A3.

Here is a detailed look at the components of each classification of each of the four enterprise proficiency categories. This is the detail behind some of the categories found in the step chart of Figure 10.1. It will help you in identifying your true ranking. They are:

- Clerical
  1. Goal: Bottom-line impact: overhead

Clerical

Goal: Bottom-line impact
Focus: Inward
Data: Historical and Minimal
Metrics: Minimal and Transactional
Systems/Technology: No Automated ERP System
Staffing: Minimal training/No cross-training/no teaming/no reward system
Management: Top Down, Reactive
Process: Manual paperwork based process, redundant, highly transactional
Change: Lack of foresight/no linkage to continuous improvement/strong resistance
Work Environment: Silos
Inventory: Poorly planned—too much in some areas and too little in others

Mechanical

Goal: Bottom-line impact – Revenue
Focus: Inward, putting out fires, react to complaints
Emphasis: Purchase price, cost and budget conscious
Data: Minimal data interface, on request, batch reporting
Reporting: Low level
Metrics: Focused on function and transaction activity
Systems/Technology: Computers process paperwork
Relationships: Transactional/Adversarial
Staffing: Cross-training minimal, employee recognition systems
Management: Top down with less layers
Vendor/Customer Relationships: Minimal and sporadic
Quality: Measure and address problems as they arise
Change: No continuous process improvement program in place
Work Environment: Silos
Supply Chain Management: Reactionary
Inventory: Overhauling of material, minimal inventory management

Proactive

Goal: Bottom-line impact
Focus: Fulfill social responsibility, customer focus
Strategy: Reduce non-value added
Emphasis: Cost, Quality, timeliness; bottom line, revenue driven
Data: Central repository
Reporting: Reduce forecasting errors, high-level reporting
Metrics: Focused on company goals, but not integrated or cross-functional, departmental focus
Systems/Technology: ERP systems
Relationships: Transactional and collaborative
Staffing: Development of cross-functional teams
Management: Participative Management considered
Vendor/Customer Relationships: Focus on improving customer satisfaction
Process: Integrated to pull materials and minimize transactions
Quality: Focus on defect free materials
Change: Internal continuous process improvement program in place
Work Environment: Automation, e-Commerce
Supply Chain Management: Perceived as adding value; involved in strategy development
Inventory: Point of use supermarkets

World Class

Goal: Company-wide goals and initiatives
Focus: Total cost of ownership (TCO)
Strategy: Strategic planning
Emphasis: Performance to customer & shareholders expectations
Data: Utilized for strategic planning
Reporting: Regular reporting to the executives, customers, and vendors
Metrics: Extensive Lean and change focused metrics
Systems/Technology: Lean and Cycle-Time Reduction Initiatives
Relationships: Collaborative cross-functional teams involving both customers and suppliers
Staffing: Extensive training programs
Management: Participative / Empowered teams
Vendor/Customer Relationships: Strategic Sourcing; Customer Focus
Process: Integrated to pull material, minimize transactions,
Quality: Near Zero defects internal and external
Change: Lean, TQM, Change Management Systems
Work Environment: Pull Based Lean/TOC/JIT/Kanbans
Supply Chain Management: Integrated Supply Chain and Logistics systems
Inventory: Inventory levels minimized

1   2   3   4   5   6   7   8   9   10

FIGURE 10.1
Foundational step chart.

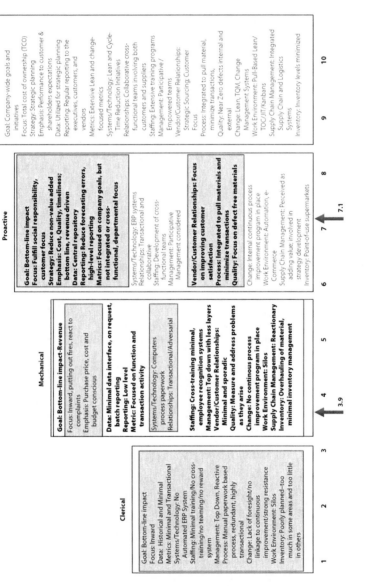

FIGURE 10.2
Ranking using the step chart.

2. Focus: Inward
3. Strategy: None, reactive, focused on immediate need
4. Emphasis: Convenience and expediency, focus on paycheck
5. Data: historical and minimal
   - Back pocket lists/no sharing
6. Reporting: Very low level, no empowerment
   - Minimal with routine follow-up
7. Metrics: Minimal and transactional
   - Focused on sales/profits
8. Systems/technology: No automated production planning system
   - Informal and not integrated, primarily manual
   - Planning performed at the department level
9. Relationships: Personal/self centered
10. Staffing: Minimal training/no cross training/no teaming/no reward system
11. Management: Top down, reactive
12. Vendor/customer relationships: No collaboration between SCM members
    - Often adversarial/do not see need for partnerships
13. Process: Manual paperwork-based process, redundant, highly transactional
14. Quality: Not emphasized/minimum measurements
15. Change: Lack of foresight/no linkage to continuous improvement/strong resistance
16. Work environment: Inbound and outbound work in silos
    - Control system focus—Confirm the actions of others
    - Departmental relationships
    - Pull environment
17. Supply chain management (SCM): Viewed as little or non-value add, "order placers"
    - Paper/phone communication with supply chain
18. Inventory: Poorly planned—too much in some areas and too little in others
    - Manual shortage lists/buying cards used
- Mechanical
  1. Goal: Bottom-line impact—revenue
     - Not defined clearly
  2. Focus: Inward, putting out fires, react to complaints
  3. Strategy: Reduce transactions, share supply base

      – Minimal, react to requisition release, last-buy basis
4. Emphasis: Purchase price, cost and budget conscious
5. Data: Minimal data interface, on request, batch reporting
      – Limited availability, based on history
      – Manual data used to measure performance
6. Reporting: Low level
      – Report to logistics/warehouse/transportation manager
      – Available for completed transactions
7. Metrics: focused on function and transaction activity
      – Minimal and inconsistently monitored
      – Group metrics by department
      – No metrics to measure success of IT policies
      – No benchmarking
8. Systems/technology: Computers process paperwork
      – Multiple ERP systems
      – Allows for exception reporting, not integrated, shortage lists
      – Stand-alone procurement system
      – Technology deployed too late without looking at the process
9. Relationships: Transactional/adversarial
10. Staffing: Cross training minimal, employee recognition systems
      – Reward system based on internal performance
      – Employee selection and training informal
      – Departmental teams to implement IT solutions
11. Management: Top-down with less layers
12. Vendor/customer relationships: Minimal and sporadic collaboration
      – Recurring interaction between buyers and suppliers
      – Emphasis on unit price
      – Limited supply base/single sources/proliferation of sources
      – No strategic sourcing teams in place
      – Minimal customer involvement
13. Process: Transactional focus, less transactions and approvals
      – Expediting is high
      – Push with some simple pull processes
14. Quality: Measure and address problems as they arise
15. Change: No continuous process improvement program in place
      – Done only when necessary
16. Work environment: Work as individual silos
      – Local and national operations

17. Supply chain management: React to requisitions
    - Not involved in the front end of the business/key source selections
    - React to requisitions
    - Common logistics provider
    - Organization is investigating larger processes
    - Engineering data communicated to suppliers through mail or hand delivered
18. Inventory: Overhauling of material, minimal inventory management
    - Replenishment decisions based on historical demand

- Proactive
    1. Goal: Bottom line impact—profit contributor
    2. Focus: Fulfill social responsibility, customer focus
    3. Strategy: Reduce non-value-added supplier relationships, focus on value-add activities, best-value analysis, identify issues early
    4. Emphasis: Cost, quality, timeliness; bottom line, revenue driven
    5. Data: Central repository
        - Bar coding
        - Real-time data available internally within functional unit
        - Large degree of data interface
        - Information flow laterally
        - Self-generated, standard reports with some customization
        - Information and engineering data communicated to suppliers through traditional methods, electronic data exchanges such as EDI (electronic data interface) and PDM are being considered
    6. Reporting: Reduce forecasting errors
        - High-level reporting
    7. Metrics: Focused on company goals, but not integrated or cross-functional, departmental focus
        - Measures focused on quality and timeliness
        - Benchmarking utilized on a limited basis
    8. Systems/technology: Requirements planning systems
        - Initial ERP integration
        - Interface with tier 1 suppliers only
    9. Relationships: Transactional and collaborative
    10. Staffing: Development of cross-functional teams
        - Cross-training programs

- Employee empowerment
- Employee selection and training criteria and expectations defined, focused on functional development
- Reward program in place to promote better performance
11. Management: Participative management considered
12. Vendor/customer relationships: Focus on improving customer satisfaction
    - Long-term contracts/vendor relationships/supplier development
    - Customer involvement, active source selection
    - Competitive bidding/active source selection
    - Strategic sourcing teams
    - Supplier relationship management system considered
    - Customer focus—slogans and posters
    - Competitive bidding, supplier partnerships and agreements, supply base reduction; primarily domestic; international sources considered
13. Process: Process and systems integrated to pull materials and minimize transactions
    - Pull Systems and Just in Time considered, some Kanban exists with vendors
    - Documented operating procedures
14. Quality: Focus on defect free materials
    - Considered to be an order winner, improvement ongoing
15. Change: Internal continuous process improvement program in place
16. Work environment: Automation, e-commerce
17. Supply chain management: Perceived as adding value; periodically involved in strategy development
    - Inbound and outbound logistics
    - Plan for recurring requirements
    - Accurate SCM measurement systems
    - Supplier selection, classification, commodity management, and planning are integrated but not fully aligned to the SCM strategy
    - Minimal internal goals are aligned with the objectives of the supply chain
    - Cost drivers affecting the entire SCM process begun to be identified and monitored
    - Logistics managed and tracked through manual methods

18. Inventory: Point of use supermarkets
    - Managed and some reduction realized
- World class
  1. Goal: Company wide goals and initiatives
     - Internal goals are aligned with the objectives of IT
     - Shingo Award winner
  2. Focus: Total cost of ownership (TCO)
     - Outward toward the extended enterprise and beyond. Functional to process
     - Minimal cash-to-cash cycle time integrated across the whole supply chain
     - Environmentally conscious
  3. Strategy: Strategic planning
     - Supplier partnerships, focus on value-added activities, total cost analysis, risk management, and time to market
  4. Emphasis: Performance to customer and shareholder expectations
  5. Data: Utilized for strategic planning
     - Self-managed for customization, integrated into supply chain
     - Minimal paperwork
     - Data and paperwork are moved using the pull system
     - Information and engineering data communicated to suppliers through electronic data exchanges such as EDI and PDM
     - Real-time data utilized and shared with suppliers and customers alike. Information is shared frequently, freely, formally, and informally
  6. Reporting: Regular reporting to the executives, customers, and vendors
  7. Metrics: Extensive lean and change-focused metrics
     - Integrated with cross-functional goals and value-add activities with stakeholder accountability
     - Minimal number, high-level business focus
     - Reward and measurement system in place supporting IT
  8. Systems/technology: Lean and cycle time reduction initiatives
     - RFID and UID
     - Bar coding fully implemented
     - Integrated ERP (enterprise resource planning) with vendor and customer interfaces
     - Advanced planning and scheduling (APS) systems

9. Relationships: Collaborative cross-functional teams involving both customers and suppliers
10. Staffing: Extensive training programs
    - Employee mentoring, employee empowerment
    - Employee selection and training supports best-in-class philosophies
    - Skilled in applying world-class IT tools
    - JIT (Just in time)
    - TOC (Theory of Constraints)
    - Self-motivated. Employees are empowered and decision makers
11. Management: Participative/empowered teams
    - Integrated risk management
12. Vendor/customer relationships: Strategic sourcing
    - Supplier partnership alliances
    - Collaborative planning and scheduling
    - International interfaces in place
    - Leverage supplier technology
    - Early involvement in product designs
    - Commodity teams/commodity strategies
    - Suppliers ISO certified
    - Customer focus: mission, values, and goals embody voice of customer; developed by employees and management
    - Total integration from R&D (research and development) to customer. Suppliers supplier through customers customer; we look at all elements of the process starting with the suppliers to our suppliers and ending with the customers to our customers
13. Process: Process and systems integrated to pull material, minimize transactions, and support NPI cross-functionally
    - Standardized best practices
14. Quality: SPC (statistical process control) or TQM (total quality management) used to manage all quality processes
    - Near zero defects internal and external
15. Change: Lean, TQM, change management systems
    - Done proactively as part of business. Realized as part of continuous improvement
    - Continuous improvement systems
    - Agile, Six Sigma initiatives

16. Work environment: Pull-based Lean/TOC/JIT/Kanbans/QFD (Quality Functional Deployment)
    - Extensive e-integration throughout the supply chain
    - Extensive use of event management
17. Supply chain management: Integrated supply chain and logistics systems
    - Reports at the executive level, fully integrated in strategic planning and operations, cross-functional integration, minimal management layers, practice participative management
18. Inventory: Real-time traceability of materials
    - Supplier-managed inventory (SMI)
    - Inventory levels minimized
    - Buffers used strategically only
    - Matches demand. Right parts, right quantities. Real-time traceability
    - Managed centrally

At this point you have a fairly detailed example of what an enterprise step chart should look like. What you still need to do is to customize the step chart for your organization.

IT BEST PRACTICES

This is not a book on IT best practices, but there are some IT tools and techniques that play well into Lean process improvements. A few of these will be listed, and they should be incorporated into your IT step chart as appropriate.

As a foundation for a discussion of best practices, the author will use the IT Infrastructure Library (ITIL) which utilizes a list of best practices for a CMMI (Capability Maturity Model Integration) framework. This framework was designed to help organizations achieve their business objective through world-class IT processes. This framework has become the worldwide standard in service management. The ITIL map of best practices includes:*

---

* A good discussion of this material can be found in *Lean, Agile and Six Sigma Information Technology Management: New Stratagems to Achieve Perfection,* by Peter Ghavami at pghavami@u. washington.edu.

1. Delivering IT Service—What services are expected from IT for optimal business performance?
   a. Service level management—Set service targets that meet customer's expectations for availability, support, troubleshooting, and performance.
   b. Capacity management—Capacity planning, forecasting, and provisioning of network bandwidth, server capacity, storage and transaction volume planning—balancing demand against availability.
   c. IT service continuity management—Plans for service during downtimes.
   d. Availability management—Facilitate high availability while reducing down time and system failures.
   e. Financial management—Contract management, purchasing, and procurement.
2. Application management—Software development lifecycle
   a. Application portfolio management
   b. Project portfolio management
   c. Resource portfolio management
3. Service support—Assures users have IT access
   a. Help desk—Service desk
      - Incident control
      - Communication
   b. Incident management—Handling incidents in a way that provides service continuity
   c. Software asset management
   d. Problem management—Identify the root cause (using 9-Step A3s) and make appropriate changes
      - Error control process
      - Problem control process
   e. Configuration management—Procedures for proper systems configuration
      - Planning
      - Identification
      - Control
      - Status accounting
      - Verification and audit
   f. Change management—Lean and the 9-Step A3
      - Request for change

     – Forward schedule of changes
   g. Release management—Managing approved changes to the IT environment
     – Major software releases
     – Minor software releases
     – Emergency software releases
4. Infrastructure management
   a. ICT (information and communication technology) designing and planning
   b. ICT deployment
   c. ICT operations management—Guidelines for the operations of systems
   d. ICT technical support
   e. Security management
   f. Network service management—Like WiFi infrastructure and components
   g. Management of local processors—For example, a common protocol for backups
   h. Computer installation and acceptance—Like server placement, cooling, networking requirements, etc.
   i. Systems management—Documents and systems integration, security, data integrity, etc.
5. Business perspective—Meeting business requirements
   a. Business continuity management—Like disaster recovery
   b. Business change management—Change control and configuration management/documentation
   c. Transformation of business practices
   d. Partnership and outsourcing—Vendor management/outsourcing

The ITIL list is a generalized list of categories of best practices, and it is a useful validation list to make sure your organization is identifying improvements in each of these areas. Some specific tools and processes that the author has found cited in numerous IT publications and journals, and which should be part of a best practices IT list include:

1. Change management/Lean (the topic of this book)
2. A3 structured thinking (see Chapter 3)
3. The IT factory—Identifying the repetitive processes within your IT environment and making them standard work (see Technical Tool #18)

4. Six Sigma (see Technical Tool #16)
5. TOC (Theory of Constraints) (see Technical Tool #26)
6. Resource Mapping (see Technical Tool #6—Information Flow Diagrams)
7. IT Workcells—developing work-groups with standard work functions and roles (see Technical Tool #18)
8. 5S (see Technical Tool #14)
9. Joint Application Development—An IBM technique of involving the user in all aspects of the development process (see Technical Tool #5)
10. Flat World Thinking—The Thomas L. Friedman concept that international software development with local implementations is the future of IT from his book *The World Is Flat: A Brief History of the Twenty-First Century*
11. Feature/Function Prioritization (see Technical Tool #25)
12. Simulation—The testing of the feasibility of concepts and ideas before doing a full development including the testing of full business systems like ERP or Inventory Management

SUMMARY

IT maturity can be evaluated using tools like the step chart. The purpose for this evaluation is to see where your organization currently stands, and where it would like to be. From this we generate a list of gaps that need to be filled in order to bring the organization to its desired state. This list of tasks is prioritized using the effort/impact matrix (see Technical Tool #25), and then we start working on the highest-priority task first. We use the first four steps of the 9-Step A3 to evaluate the task. After that, if it is still something the champion wants to do, we move forward with the project. If it is a project, the champion identifies a project manager. If it is a "just do it" the champion identifies someone to do it. And if it is an RIE, we use the principles listed in Chapters 7 and 8 to execute an improvement process. That's it! Now you know how to bring your IT environment to world-class status. Let the work begin.

11

Wrap-Up

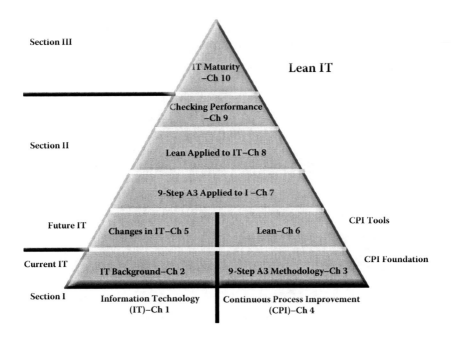

There is no worse death than the end of hope.

Pelagius

If NASA wanted to go to the Moon today, they could not do it. All the brainpower and experience that got them to the moon no longer exists. They would have to relearn all the lessons they learned before. They would have to develop an understanding of the concepts that got us to the moon, and they would have to reexperience all the lessons that were learned the first time around. What does that teach us here on Earth? Does it teach us about standard work? Does it teach us that people (acceptance tools) are more important than processes? It teaches us a large number of lessons about "waste" and how lost experiences will need to be relearned. How about a trip to Mars? Wouldn't it have been useful to take the lessons learned from the Moon trips and apply them to a Mars trip that NASA keeps discussing?

One last story, this time about a company that the author worked for. PPI, Inc. is a California-based hi-tech plastics manufacturer. They produce printed plastic that lights up. For example, signage and automotive dashboards have traditionally been clear plastic with backlighting behind it. PPI produces a product where the lighting is built right into the plastic, it is actually part of the printed plastic, and it requires a minimal amount of low-voltage electricity. Their vision is to be able to put battery-powered signage in locations, like in various locations throughout large department stores, or on grocery store shelves, where "plug ins" are inconvenient.

PPI's supply chain starts with its sourcing of colored inks and plastics and ends with the end customer that uses the product. The sourcing side of the supply chain has problems with product and schedule consistency. The arrival times of the product are often intermittent, the plastics quality is not often consistent, and the colors are not always precisely the same from batch to batch.

Internally, PPI also has struggles which affect its supply chain. The product defect rate is over 14%, customer on-time delivery is poor, and finished goods inventory is quite high. Often, PPI will produce product that has not yet been sold. They do this because it allows them to have larger batch runs of a product which they feel will probably be sold in the future. The result is that they have a lot of money tied up in finished goods inventory, a large part of which will become obsolete.

Disruptions to supply chain can occur via any of the suppliers, via the shipper, or internal to PPI's operations. But it is the poor quality and poor on-time delivery performance that has PPI worried. They fear the loss of several key customers if these issues cannot be resolved soon. What would you suggest? What options are available? Now it is your turn to get creative and search for ideas.

For PPI we see a need for a quality improvement process to occur. However, PPI needs to see a cultural change before it is ready to experience a quality transformation. As we have already seen, the measurement system is a major roadblock in achieving a focus on the importance of quality. Initially, the process required the training of managers so that they would recognize the opportunities and the need for changes in the process. This occurred over a period of several months. Then, as management became convinced of the need for change, the rest of the workforce was also brought into the process. The transformation was immediate and stunning. And the capacity gained by not having as many reruns on parts, quickly made up for the lost production time. The results can be seen in Figure 11.1, which shows the dramatic reduction in errors (15% to 2%) and also in finished goods inventory (50% reduction).

Where does IT fit into the PPI transformation? This looks like an operations and management problem, not an IT problem. The answer is "everywhere." The old adage fits:

If IT is not part of the solution,
Then it is part of the problem!

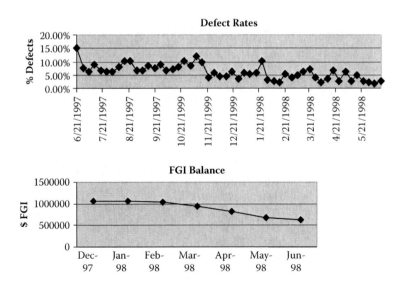

FIGURE 11.1
PPI transformation.

IT should not wait to be asked to help. IT knows there is a problem and should become the change agent that helps solve the problem. The PPI problems are systems problems, not operational problems. In the spirit of IT becoming a profit center, they could help with the supply chain problem by facilitating data access or vendor interfaces. They helped with the production planning and scheduling problem by facilitating the introduction of a manufacturing ERP system. They helped with the quality problems by facilitating data collection statistics (SPC) on the defects and their causes. IT needs to be integrally involved in everything that happens throughout the organization.

As a change agent, IT takes on the role of asking the dumb questions. For example, if someone expresses a concern about a process, we would ask questions like:

- Why is this a problem?
- What do you do when you have a problem?
- How does the process normally work? What percent of the time is it normal?
- How do you know the outcome is defect free?
- How do you know you are doing this work correctly?
- How do you do this work?
- Why do you do it this way?
- Where is it done this way, and where is it done differently?
- How is the data used?
- What has been done to improve the process?
- How do you measure this process?
- Etc., etc., etc. . . .

The author was involved in a meeting with some Toyota people who were reviewing part of their production processes. The manager was asked, "Do you have any problems?" The American manager, trying to be politically correct, answered: "No." The Japanese manager responded in broken English: "Then I do not need you. Your role is to identify problems and solve them, each time making the system better." Then, with emphasis, he said, "No problem is problem!" Remember, if you are not part of the solution, you are part of the problem.

Bibliography

Anderson, David J. *Kanban*. Sequim, WA: Blue Hole Press, 2010.

Antony, Dr. Jiju, and Mukkarram Bhaiji. "Key Ingredients for a Successful Six Sigma Program." onesixsigma.com. http://www.improvementandinnovation.com/features/articles/key-ingredients-successful-six-sigma-program.

Arai, Keisuke, and Kenichi Sekine. *Kaizen for Quick Changeover: Going beyond SMED*. Portland, OR: Productivity Press, 2000.

Berne, E. *The Games People Play*. New York: Grove Press, 1964.

Bothe, Keki R. *World Class Quality*. New York: AMACOM, 1991.

Collins, Jim. *Good to Great: Why Some Companies Make the Leap ... and Others Don't*. New York: Harper Collins, 2001.

Collins, Jim, and Jerry I. Porras. *Built to Last: Successful Habits of Visionary Companies*. New York: Harper Business, 2002.

Conner, Gary. *Lean Manufacturing for the Small Shop*. Dearborn, MI: SME, 2001.

Coonradt, Charles A. *The Game of Work: How to Enjoy Work as Much as Play*. Layton, UT: Gibbs Smith, 2001.

Covey, Stephen R. *The Seven Habits of Highly Effective People*. New York: Free Press, 2004.

Cunningham, Jean E., Orest Fiume, and Emily Adams. *Real Numbers: Management Accounting in a Lean Organization*. Durham, NC: Managing Times Press, 2003.

Drucker, Peter. "The Emerging Theory of Manufacturing." *Harvard Business Review*, May/June 1990, 94–102.

Friedman, Thomas L. *The World Is Flat: A Brief History of the Twenty-First Century*. 3rd ed. New York: Picador, 2007.

Ghavami, Peter. *Lean, Agile, and Six Sigma Information Technology Management: New Stratagems to Achieve Perfection*. Seattle: CreateSpace, 2008.

Goffman I. *The Presentation of Self in Everyday Life*. New York: Knopf Doubleday Publishing Group, 1959.

Goldratt, Eliyahu M. *The Haystack Syndrome*. Croton-on-Hudson, NY: North River Press Inc., 1990.

Goldratt, Eliyahu M., and Jeff Cox. *The Goal*. Croton-on-Hudson, NY: North River Press Inc., 1986.

Goldratt, Eliyahu M., and Robert E. Fox. *The Race*. Croton-on-Hudson, NY: North River Press Inc., 1986.

Harvard Business School Press. *Performance Management: Measure and Improve the Effectiveness of Your Employees*. Boston, MA: Harvard Business Press, 2006.

Kanter, Rosabeth Moss. *When Giants Learn to Dance*. New York: Simon and Schuster, 1989.

Kaplan, Robert S., and David P. Norton. *Balanced Scorecard: Translating Strategy into Action*. Boston, MA: Harvard Business Press, 1996.

Kayser, Thomas A. *Mining Group Gold: How to Cash in on the Collaborative Brain Power of a Team for Innovation and Results*. 3rd ed. El Segundo, CA: McGraw-Hill, 2011.

Kotter, John P. *Leading Change*. Boston, MA: Harvard Business Press, 1996.

Kullmann, John, "An Introduction to Six Sigma," onesixsigma.com. http://www.enotes.com/management-encyclopedia/statistical-process-control-six-sigma.

Liker, Jeffrey K., and David Meier. *The Toyota Way Fieldbook: A Practical Guide for Implementing Toyota's 4Ps.* New York: McGraw-Hill, 2006.

Lindgren, Mats and Hans Bandhold. *Scenario Planning: The Link between Future and Strategy.* Rev. ed. Houndmills, Basingstoke, Hampshire, UK: Palgrave Macmillan, 2009.

Luft, J., and H. Ingham. "The JoHari Window: A Graphic Model for Interpersonal Relations." 12manage.com. http://www.12manage.com/methods_luft_ingham_johari_window.html.

Luft, Joseph. *Group Process: An Introduction to Group Dynamics.* 3rd ed. New York: McGraw-Hill Higher Education, 1984.

Manning, G., K. Curtis, and S. McMillan. *The Human Side of Work: Building Community in the Workplace.* Denver: South-Western Publishing, 1995.

Menasce, Daniel A., Lawrence W. Dowdy, and Virgilio A.F. Almeida. *Performance by Design: Computer Capacity Planning by Example.* Upper Saddle River, NJ: Prentice Hall, 2004.

Moody, Patricia E., and Anand Sharma. *The Perfect Engine: How to Win in the New Demand Economy by Building to Order with Fewer Resources.* New York: Free Press, 2001.

Nadler, Gerald, and Shozo Hibino. *Breakthrough Thinking: The Seven Principles of Creative Problem Solving.* Rocklin, CA: Prima Publishing & Communications, 1990.

Nadler, Gerald, Shozo Hibino, and John Farrell. *Creative Solution Finding.* Rocklin, CA: Prima Publishing & Communications, 1995.

Ohno, Taiichi, and Norman Bodek. *Toyota Production System: Beyond Large-Scale Production.* Portland, OR: Productivity Inc., 1988.

Pace, Wayne R. *Organizational Dynamism: Unleashing Power in the Workforce.* Westport, CT: Quorum Books, 2002.

Parrill, Catherine, and Bob Rosinski, *5S Implementation Manual: Starting Lean Manufacturing.* W Publications, 2007.

Petrick, Joseph A., and Diana S. Furr. *Total Quality in Managing Human Resources.* Delray Beach, FL: St. Lucie Press, 1995.

Plenert, Gerhard. *The eManager: Value Chain Management in an eCommerce World.* Dublin: Blackhall Publishing, 2001.

Plenert, Gerhard. *International Operations Management.* Copenhagen: Copenhagen Business School Press, 2002.

Plenert, Gerhard. *Reinventing Lean: Introducing Lean Management into the Supply Chain.* New York: Elsevier, 2007.

Plenert, Gerhard, and Shozo Hibino. *Making Innovation Happen: Concept Management Through Integration.* Delray Beach, FL: St. Lucie Press, 1997.

Plenert, Gerhard J., and Terry Lee. "Optimizing Theory of Constraints When New Product Alternatives Exist." *Production and Inventory Management Journal* 34, no. 3 (1993): 51–57.

Productivity Press Development Team. *Standard Work for the Shop Floor.* Portland, OR: Productivity Press, 2002.

Pyzdek, Thomas. "Cargo Cult Six Sigma." Quality Digest. http://www.enotes.com/management-encyclopedia/statistical-process-control-six-sigma.

Robustelli, Peter, and John Kullmann. "Implementing Six Sigma to Affect Lasting Change." onesixsigma.com. http://www.referenceforbusiness.com/management/Sc-Str/Statistical-Process-Control-and-Six-Sigma.html.

Ross, Joel E. *Total Quality Management.* Delray Beach, FL: St. Lucie Press, 1995.

Rother, Mike, and John Shook. *Learning to See: Value Stream Mapping to Add Value and Eliminate MUDA.* Cambridge, MA: Lean Enterprise Institute, 2003.

Schein, Edgar. *Organizational Culture and Leadership.* San Francisco: Jossey Bass, 1989.

Schein, Edgar. *Process Consultation Revisited: Building the Helping Relationship.* Reading, MA: Prentice Hall, 1998.

Sekine, Kenichi. *One Piece Flow: Cell Design for Transforming the Production Process.* Cambridge, MA: Productivity Press, 1991.

Semler, Ricardo. *Maverick: The Success Story behind the World's Most Unusual Workplace,* New York: Grand Central Publishing, 1995.

Senge, Peter M. *The Fifth Discipline: The Art & Practice of a Learning Organization.* New York: Currency Doubleday, 2006.

Shannon, C., and W. Weaver. *The Mathematical Theory of Communication.* DeKalb, IL: Illinois University Press, 1968.

Solomon, Jerrold M. *Who's Counting? A Lean Accounting Business Novel.* Fort Wayne, IN: WCM Associates, 2003.

Taiichi Ohno. *The Toyota Production System.* Boca Raton, FL: Taylor & Francis Group, 1988.

Von Oech, Roger, George Willett, and Nolan Bushnell. *A Whack on the Side of the Head.* Menlo Park, CA: Creative Think, 1983.

Weisbord, Marvin R. *Productive Workplaces.* San Francisco: Jossey Bass, 1987.

Wheatley, Margaret J. *Leadership and the New Science: Discovering Order in a Chaotic World.* San Francisco: Barrett-Koehler, 2006.

Womack, James P., and Daniel Jones. *Lean Thinking: Banish Waste and Create Wealth in Your Corporation.* London: Simon and Shuster, 2003.

Womack, James P., Daniel T. Jones, and Daniel Roos. *The Machine That Changed the World: The Story of Lean Production—Toyota's Secret Weapon in the Global Car Wars That Is Now Revolutionizing World Industry.* New York: Free Press, 2007.

Index

About the Author

Dr. Gerhard Plenert has over 25 years of professional experience in IT quality and productivity consulting and in working on manufacturing planning and scheduling methods. He also has 13 years of academic experience. He has over 150 published articles, and he has published the following nine books:

EManager: Value Chain Management in an eCommerce World—2001
Finite Capacity Scheduling (an APICS/ Oliver White Series Book)—2000
International Management and Production: Survival Techniques for Corporate America—1990
International Operations Management (an MBA textbook)—2004
Making Innovation Happen: Concept Management through Integration
Operations Management (A United Nations Training Manual for Developing Country Factories)—2005
The Plant Operations Deskbook (an APICS series book)—1992
Reinventing Lean: Introducing Lean Management into the Supply Chain—2007
World Class Manager—1995

Dr. Plenert has extensive industry experience:

Private sector
- Kraft Foods, Smart and Final, Davis Lay, Ritz-Carlton, Hewlett-Packard, Seagate, Motorola, PPI, Clark Equipment, NCR Corporation, and AT&T
- Consulting companies—Infosys, Mainstream, AMS, IBM, SCI, SAS
- Corporate "guru" on supply chain management for AMS and Infosys

344 • *About the Author*

Government sector
- California—DCSS, DHS
- Federal—DSS, US Air Force, Air Guard
- International—United Nations
- Texas—OAG
- New York—City of New York warehousing system

Dr. Plenert has extensive academic experience:

- PhD in mineral economics at the Colorado School of Mines, which is their operations and business management degree (under Gene Woolsey)
- Eleven years as a full-time faculty member (BYU and CSUC)
- Currently teaching SCM at the University of San Diego
- Teaching operations, manufacturing, and supply chain management as far away as Malaysia and England

Dr. Plenert has:

- Worked in senior management
- Generated up to triple the office productivity with the same staffing
- Worked as an industry consultant implementing SCM, ERP, and eBusiness systems and designing a next-generation enterprise model
- Literally "written the book" on leading-edge supply chain management concepts like Finite Capacity Scheduling (FCS), Advanced Planning and Scheduling (APS), and World Class Management
- Taken a 14+% defect rate down to 2%
- Brought setup times from 20 minutes to as low as 6 minutes
- Reduced facility-wide inventories by 40%

Dr. Plenert's ideas and publications have been endorsed by people like Steven Covey and companies like Motorola, AT&T, Black & Decker, and FedEx.